The Wilder Way

The Power Game of *The Plane Makers*

Harry Dobermann – after an early career in the toy industry and psychic research, Harry moved into the fledgling world of computers and managed to be one of the few people not to make any money out of it.

Interested in film, TV and comics, he runs The Patrick Wymark Boardroom website, dedicated to the star of The Plane Makers and The Power Game.

The Wilder Way is believed to be the very first detailed examination of the business techniques of Sir John Wilder.

Also by Harry Dobermann from Scatola Publishing:

Beyond The Borders of Fear

The Wilder Way

The Power Game of *The Plane Makers*

First published in Great Britain by Scatola Publishing

ISBN SBN 978-0-9570845-1-3

Harry Dobermann

The Wilder Way

THE WILDER WAY

The Power Game of *The Plane Makers*

By Harry Dobermann

An Unofficial and Unauthorised Expose of the Business Techniques of Sir John Wilder

As played by Patrick Wymark

Cover Design by Andrew-Mark Thompson (Andydrewz64.blogspot.com)

Cartoons by Richard Farrell (Twitter @CartoonsFarrell)

Scatola Publishing

Table of Contents

PREFACE

This is a book about the career of Sir John Wilder, as portrayed in the television series *The Plane Makers* and *The Power Game.*

It is also a book about how those two series were made and how they found success. Any lessons learned will be purely academic. If the secret of success is identified, it would be difficult to apply today as the world of television is now very different to that of the 1960's.

The episode guide has its basis in the reviews on *The Patrick Wymark Boardroom* website (www.wymark.org.uk). However, a good 75% of the text has been revised and updated for this book, while another 25% has been cut for space. It is only right that the paid content should be the most up-to-date.

At the end of the book, the world of Sir John Wilder is analysed and distilled into ten steps that you can take to emulate him. It is unlikely that this section will find many admirers in modern business schools. You will search in vain for concepts such as "ethics", "diversity", "inclusiveness", "employee-centredness", "sustainability" or "public service".

As Sir John Wilder would say, the secrets of success are all there, but they are not for the faint hearted.

Harry Dobermann   2022

INTRODUCTION

I started the website, *The Patrick Wymark Boardroom* (www.wymark.org.uk), very late in the day, after several years waiting for someone else to do it. I also thought that since Patrick Wymark had been one of the biggest TV stars of the 1960's, there would be a biography out there. But no, nothing.

Sadly, his tragic early death seems to have been at the wrong time for the technology. In November 1970, a viewer suggested that *The Plane Makers* and *The Power Game* should be repeated as a tribute to Patrick Wymark. ATV replied that most of the tapes had already been wiped. Even if they had existed, British TV was on a push towards colour television. Programmes made in black and white were increasingly unwelcome. It was only in the late 1980's that either enough tapes were recovered or TV became diverse enough for Channel 4 to repeat *The Power Game*. And it was only in 2005, killing a rainy evening in the Virgin store in London's Trocadero Centre, that I came across the *Network* DVD's of *The Power Game*.

Having started late. I've always made it clear that the *Patrick Wymark Boardroom* is unofficial and unsanctioned. All the information used here is in the public domain, and I've had no time or desire to speculate beyond the public domain. In recent years, viewers too young for even the Channel 4 repeats, have rediscovered Patrick Wymark, *The Plane Makers* and *The Power Game*. I'm sure some of them will take this work forward.

JOHN WILDER - THE MAN BEHIND THE LEGEND

John Wilder was born in Birmingham in 1917, the only child of a general practitioner. Sent to a preparatory school in Wales aged 8 and a minor public school at 13, John didn't mix easily and had only one or two close friends. An average scholar, he enjoyed playing Rugby and squash. After graduating from a redbrick university, Wilder joined a small engineering firm as an apprentice, intending to work towards a senior executive post.

Wilder had joined the Territorial Army as a junior officer in 1938 and when the Second World War broke out, his unit was posted to France. Evacuated from Dunkirk in June 1940, Wilder transferred to the Royal Army Service Corps, responsible for supplying provisions to the army. Wilder's firm application of logistics impressed senior officers. Appointed to a military mission in Washington, he was excited by American mass production techniques and their emphasis on salesmanship. He resolved to become *"a damn good salesman."*

Before this, however, Wilder was posted to occupied Germany in August 1945 to assist the British Army War Crimes Investigation Teams.

After demobilisation, Wilder joined Scott Furlong as Deputy Managing Director in charge of Sales. In 1949 he was entranced by a girl he came across collecting in the street for a flag day charity. Offering her a five-pound note for her time, he invited Pamela Brown for a cup of coffee and quickly won her over. The Wilders have been happily married since 1950, with one son Nigel now away at public school. Once a month, Pamela Wilder organises a cocktail party at which Wilder can network.

On leaving Scott Furlong to join the board of Elbertson's Merchant Bank, Sir John Wilder was knighted for his services to the airline industry. Sir John subsequently served as joint Managing Director of Bligh Construction for 18 months while also joining the National Export Board. In 1966, Sir John was given a six-month appointment as Special Plenipotentiary to the European Community and in 1969, after two years as a trade consultant, Sir John was appointed Ambassador for Special Situations and Trade. Sir John then negotiated the merger of National Electric and Norton Electronics, emerging as managing director of the new company.

At heart, Sir John still considers himself a salesman, saying, *"salesmanship should be approached with the same thorough professionalism of the law, engineering or medicine."*

Grateful acknowledgement is made to research into Sir John Wilder's career by Frank Dewer Anthony Davis and Wilfred Greatorex, first published in the *TV Times*.

A Note on Audience Measurement

References to audience viewing figures for *The Plane Makers* and *The Power Game* are based on viewing figures published in *The Stage* and *Television Today*.

Until 1968 the data was provided by Television Audience Measurement Ltd, which fitted meters to a small statistical sample of sets capable of receiving both ITV and BBC signals (a small percentage of homes could still only receive BBC TV). The meters measured the percentage of homes actually tuned into BBC and ITV programmes on a minute-by-minute basis. From 1968, responsibility was passed to Audits of Great Britain Ltd for JICTAR (Joint Industry Committee for television Advertising Research).

Tapes from the back of the set were mailed back by the householder, together with a diary recording who was actually watching and what they had watched. The diary was used to cross-check the automated readings. The information was transferred to punched cards fed into a computer which plotted the weekly data.

In the published TAM ratings, the position in the Top 20 was stated as the number of sets which had been tuned into a show for its duration. The number of viewers watching could be estimated from a standard conversion of 2.2 viewers per set. So, the first episode of *The Plane Makers* was watched by an estimated 5,706,000 homes or an even more estimated 12, 553,200 viewers. This put it at number 19 in the Tam Ratings. For context, a number 1 show like *Coronation Street* could be watched by 17 to 20 million viewers.

In the 1960's there were – at most – only three available TV channels. 40 million viewers had access to ITV and BBC in 1963. This had risen to 51 million by 1971.

Case Study One: Launching The Plane Makers

How do you launch a legend? How do you give an audience what it wants, when the audience doesn't know what it wants? For Rex Firkin, the answer seems to have been "trial and error".

Rex Firkin was originally employed as a TV director by Associated TeleVision (ATV), one of the UK's first commercial TV stations. In 1957 he was drafted in to direct and eventually produce *Emergency Ward Ten* – a medical series which was only supposed to last 13 episodes, but which was successful enough for ATV to continue until 1967.

ATV initially used old theatres as TV studios, but in the early 1960's bought the old British National Film Studios in Borehamwood and upgraded it to state-of-the-art transistorised studios (The studios are still in use in the 21st Century, though now owned and operated by the BBC).

Firkin's boss was Bill Ward, Production Controller of ATV. A former BBC TV producer, he had been induced to join Associated Television for its opening night broadcast.

Firkin notes that Ward was, *"a man of exceptional ability"* but also frightening. *"His temper was violent and explosive and he used it constantly."* (1)

To Ward a drama series was *"basically an administrative problem."* A producer/director was told to produce 13 episodes of series on a given subject, sticking to a budget given to them by a budget manager. After each episode was broadcast, Firkin recalls being summoned to a post-mortem by Ward, *"shouting, thumping tables and generally terrifying whoever was in front of him."*

Firkin produced the second series of newspaper series *Deadline Midnight* (1961) before moving onto *Harpers West One* (1962 – 1963) an hour-long drama series set in a Mayfair department store. Although initially popular, it reputedly did not achieve the ratings Lew Grade, managing director of ATV expected. Grade supposedly said that the West End setting was "too toffee-nosed" and Firkin proposed to Ward that they set a replacement "*in a factory on the end of the M1...where Elstree was conveniently situated...*"

The Independent Television authority ruled that the factory couldn't make any product that could be advertised on TV, leaving ATV with a choice of either shipbuilding or planes. John Whitney and Geoffrey Bellman, the script editors of *Harpers West One*, were sent to the Handley Page aircraft company in St Albans to research a background document for the new series.

An industrial setting for one-off plays was not unique. ABC's *Armchair Theatre*, for instance, broadcast John O'Toole's *The Big Ride* on 25 November 1962. Set in an aero engine factory, it starred Andre Morell as Elmer Trask, a brusque works manager who is forced to call in his son, Simon (Brian Wilde), 15 years after sacking him. The managers want to remove Gaffney Stewart (Barry Keegan), a union convener who manipulated the rules to drive out a good worker. Simon is now an efficiency expert and suggests the first step is to promote Stewart to foreman. It sounds remarkably like some of the early *Plane Makers* episodes, and O'Toole was unsurprisingly hired for the second series.

Work began on the show seven months before its launch. The setting was established as the St Albans factory of Scott Furlong, based on the research done by Whitney and Bellman at the Handley Page company. Even at the pre-planning stage, it was noted that the chief designer of Handley Page had supplied blueprints and technical data on a fictional short-range aircraft the SF-200. "*As its production moves from the drawing board to the day of its first test flight, it will be featured in many of the stories.*" (2)

Firkin was able to cut his location budget when he learned that ATV's outside broadcast units did most of their work at the weekend on sports, church services and *Sunday Night at the London Palladium*. The rest of the week was spent on maintenance because they had no work. As ATV drama had no film unit its location filming was done by union approved freelancers. *"This made filming extremely expensive – it was all above the line."*

When Firkin checked with the accounts department, they confirmed that if he used the outside broadcast crews this would all be 'below the line' because their time and equipment was already paid for. *"As far as you're concerned you can have them for free."* While this was a cost saving, Bill Ward later rationalised that the method had artistic value. *"Even a layman can spot a filmed insert because it provides a different quality – not poorer, but different. Whereas when everything is on tape, you get ...the same atmosphere from start to finish." (3)*

In pre-publicity, Rex Firkin said the format allowed them to hire top flight writers such as Richard Harris and Geoffrey Holles by offering them one or two shows where they wouldn't be interested in a whole series. However, the opening episode, *Don't Worry About Me*, was written by a relative newcomer. Edmund Ward. A novelist with experience in construction industry journalism, his first TV play *The Casualties* (Rediffusion) had only been broadcast on August 21st 1962.

Although not an established name, Ward obviously impressed Firkin enough to be trusted with the lead episode (and, as time would show, all subsequent lead episodes).

In the factory-system of live television, every script would benefit from the input of Firkin's production secretary Joan Thorn, in charge of controlling the paperwork and phone calls that brought each episode together. The director would work in tandem with production assistant Jacky Stoller (who would later go on to produce *Hadleigh*). Stoller would draw up the timed camera scripts for each episode and then sit with the director in the gallery, calling out the sequence of shots so that the cameramen on the floor would know when they were about to 'live'.

On 31 January 1963 Firkin told The Stage," *It could be a gigantic flop or a big success. Anyway, we haven't set a limit to the number of episodes yet."*

"Firkin says there will be no regular cast in the early instalments but as time goes on a hard core of regulars – like the managing director – will emerge and will of course be played by the same actor. ATV says the series has been created to give as much scope to the writing team as possible. The fact that the company has not put an end-date to the production indicates that they think it has quite a lot of potential."

This laissez faire attitude to the production may seem quite risky to 21st Century eyes, but it had already worked for *Emergency Ward 10*. And a 1960's ATV staff member later ruefully commented that Lew Grade regarded the domestic TV budgets as *"turnover money"* – production cash paid out in return for advertising revenue and fees from the other ITV broadcasters coming in. Grade's main interest was in the ITC film shows like *The Saint* that he could sell to America.

At Elstree the studio had been laid out with machines by designer Vic Symonds (*The Long Good Friday*) to look like a large aircraft factory. Sound effects of the workshop had been recorded at Handley Page.

Starting February 4th 1963, the first series of *The Plane Makers* was broadcast live at 8pm on Monday evenings. Once the series had got underway, the production team would juggle three episodes: one starting, one on its second week of rehearsal and one being transmitted that week.

According to Firkin, the choice of directors was down to Bill Ward, who would look at his list and tell Firkin who was available. Three weeks before each episode was transmitted, ATV's casting department in London would give Firkin and the director a list of actors. A fortnight before, the actors would meet for the first read through. The actors had a full week of rehearsals, during which costume fittings took place. At the same time the lead cameraman and lighting director would discuss camera angles and lighting with the director who also had to plan out the movements of each camera. The TV cameras in this period were heavy equipment powered by trailing cables. The director had to ensure that any camera moves he asked for did not interfere with the cables. Any outside broadcast shots would be taped at the start of the third week. Camera rehearsals would start at 8.30am, the day before transmission. The sets would go up and electricians begin rigging the lights. By 4.30 pm everything was ready for rehearsal which could go on until late in the evening. On transmission day rehearsals started in the morning and ran straight into the afternoon dress rehearsals. At 7.30 pm technical checks were made and at 8pm the show went out live.

In the *Liverpool Echo* James Green speculated on the 24th January. *"It could well become the best quality series they have. There is no resident cast, but some characters such as the works manager played by James McLoughlin, will be fairly regular."*

James McLoughlin had appeared in a 1961 episode of *Harpers West One.* More recently he'd played Bradford Maddigan in the 20 Feb 1962 *Z Cars* episode *Family Feud* and Martin in Tim Aspinall's play *The Face They See* on Friday 9 November 1962.

Sadly, on 7 February 1963, the St Pancras Deputy Coroner recorded an open verdict on 39-year-old James McLoughlin, who had been found dead from a barbiturates overdose. His flat mate Brian Higgins had said earlier in the day, James was lying in bed reading his script for *The Plane Makers.* He'd asked how James was getting on learning his part as the works manager. *"He said he wasn't. Nothing would reassure him that he could learn it."*. Mr Higgins said when McLoughlin started sharing the flat in October he was *"in very good form."* Then he started worrying about his work and his doctor gave him some tablets. Dr Francis Camps said the dose of barbiturates could have been a high medicinal one. (4)

The role of Mr Anstrell, the works manager, was taken on by Harry Webster, a veteran of Dublin's Abbey Theatre. (Although Webster's episodes of *The Plane Makers* are lost, you can see him in the penultimate episode of *The Sandbaggers* (1980) as the MI6 doctor who says Burnside is burning out). The character of Anstrell appeared in eight episodes of the first series, but while planning the second series in May 1963, Rex Firkin removed the character, noting that Anstrell would resign after not making the short list for the new position of General Works Manager.

The first episode of *The Plane Makers*, Edmund Ward's *Don't Worry About Me,* entered the TAM ratings (see *A Note On Ratings* at the start of this section) at number 19, watched by an estimated 5,706,000 homes or 12, 553,200 viewers. The second episode actually increased its audience to number 18 with 13, 147,200 viewers. But by March, it had slipped out of the Top 20.

The last episode to appear in the Top 20 had been Richard Harris', *The Silent and the Damned*, in which a deaf maintenance worker played by Gordon Gostelow is scapegoated by his workmates and commits suicide. It's impossible to say that this downbeat ending actively drove viewers away, but it may have summed up the general perception of the series.

With each episode being a one-off play, and the basis of drama being conflict, Firkin admitted that the overall impression was that the factory was full of people who hated each other. And with no continuing characters, there was no-one who the audience could take to their heart. No reason to keep switching on every week.

Remarkably, Lew Grade and Bill Ward confirmed that *The Plane Makers* would go to a second series, anticipating the Lean Start-Up methodology by 40 years *("launch early, fail fast")* and accepting that he needed to learn from what went wrong in the first series. As Charles Handy observed, *"To do one's best is all that can be expected, even though some people's best may be better than others. Fruitful competition will encourage risk-taking and accept failure if it is the outcome of honest endeavour."* Charles Handy, Understanding Organisations (1985), page 247.

(Admittedly a *Plane Makers* made in 2022 would probably receive feedback from numerous marketing executives and viewer 'focus groups' before the first episode was even made)

Unhappy with Whitney and Bellman as script editors, Firkin wanted someone who could also work with other writers to shape their work. Someone suggested Wilfred Greatorex (see *Appendix 3*). An assistant editor for *John Bull* magazine, used to nurturing writers. Greatorex' first TV play had been a dramatised documentary about the Ministry of Aviation's Accident Investigation Branch and he had also written for ATV's *Probation Officer*. In Greatorex, Firkin found the 'X factor' that the first series had been missing.

The Plane Makers   Series One:

Broadcast live at 8pm, Monday evenings.

Producer Rex Firkin. Script Editors John Whitney, Geoffrey Bellman.

Feb. 4, 1963 *Don't Worry About Me*

Writer Edmund Ward. Director Quentin Lawrence.

Jack Clement (Colin Blakely) is one of the best craftsmen and *"the biggest chancers"* on the Scott Furlong shop floor. Apprentice, Sammy Metcalfe (Ronald Lacey) is in awe of him. Can training manager Frederick Parsons (Gordon Rollings) steer Sammy towards a career as a draughtsman or will the quick rewards earned by Clements turn his head? With Christopher Beeny as Maurice

Frame, Eric Woodburn as Mr James, Frederick Farley as Ken Gilbert, Victor Platt as Alf Howell, Christopher Wray as Ernest MacDonald, Neil Wilson as Bill Payne, Dickie Owen as Joe Carter.

(n.b. As of 2022 this is the only surviving episode of the first series – available as an extra feature on the Network DVD of series two)

Feb 11 1963 *Always Another Saturday.*

Writer Richard Harris. Director James Ferman.

Factory worker Tony Hastings (Frank Jarvis) develops an interest in religion, generating conflicts with his Soccer team, his work colleagues and his girlfriend Betty (Gwendolyn Watts). With Paul Dawkins as Ernie, Christopher Beeny as Maurice Frame, Johnny Briggs as Den, Alan Foss as Lipton, Christopher Wray as Ernest MacDonald.

Feb. 18, 1963 *Them: Or Us?*

Writer Robert Holles. Director Peter Sasdy.

Militant union branch secretary Davey Rankin (John Meillon) is used to fighting other people's battles but when he is offered a white-collar job resolving disputes, his personal integrity is challenged. With Annette Crosbie as Brenda, Meredith Edwards as Bert Griffin, Jerome Willis as Alf Winter. Harry Webster as works manager Mr Anstrell.

Feb. 25, 1963 *You Can't Beat the System*

Writer Leon Griffiths. Director John Nelson-Burton.

John Millett's (John Barrie) ambition to send his son Bob (Frazer Hines) to a better school antagonises fellow workers in the sheet metal shop. With Stephen Hancock as Mr Kershaw, John Junkin as shop steward Dusty Miller (who would return in season 2), Frederick Farley as Ken Gilbert, Margery Mason as May Millett

Mar. 4, 1963 *The Silent and the Damned*

Writer Richard Harris. Director James Ferman. Maintenance worker Walter Bannister (Gordon Gostelow) has a reputation for good work despite his deafness. His mates tolerate his disability until the day a scapegoat has to be found, driving him to suicide. With Michael Coles as Johnny, Dudley Foster as Harry, Judy Child as Mrs Matthews, Harry Webster as Mr Anstrell.

Mar. 11, 1963 *The Dividing Line.*

Writer Robert Holles. Director Cecil Petty.

Robert Haig-Allen (Michael Bangeter) puts on a staff dance to prove management and operatives can mix socially. But at the dance he meets Brenda (Annette Crosbie), ex-fiancée of Davey Rankin (John Meillon) and faces the real dividing line. With Anton Rogers as Adrian Fielding, Christopher Wray as Ernest MacDonald, Arthur White as Norman, Sheila Raynor as Doris, Ann Way as Violet, Royston Tickner as Nobby.

Mar. 18, 1963 *The Short Run.*

Writers Geoffrey Bellman & John Whitney. Director Geoffrey Nethercott.

For Don Cotter (Gary Watson) working in the drawing office, an unexpected vacancy could provide a final chance to plan his life. With Richard Vernon as Leonard Boaze. Robert Cartland as Wolfgang Katz. Harry Webster as Mr Anstrell. Vivienne Bennett as Mrs Cotter. Victor Brooks as Mr Webb. Gerald Harper as Laurie Bamber. Hugh Futcher as Brian Tickle.

Mar. 25, 1963 *Has Anybody Seen Costigan?*

Writer Edmund Ward. Director John Nelson-Burton.

Harry Costigan , Scott Furlong's Mr Fix-it (Gerald James) comes to the attention of works manager Mr Anstrell (Harry Webster). Some of Costigan's activities stretch his ingenuity to the limit. Gerald C. Lawson as Night Watchman. Juliet Cooke as Maureen Costigan.

Apr. 1, 1963 *Lover Come Back*

Writer Richard Harris. Director James Ferman

Anthony Booth plays Frankie Baxter, a singing star who has to return to his old trade at the aircraft factory when his popularity fades. There he meets a man who bears a grudge he never bargained for. With Kenneth J Warren as Eddie Peters, Renny Lister as Kay Peters, Gwendolyn Watts as Betty, Fred Ferris as Mr Roberts and Reginald Marsh playing a character called Wally.

Apr. 8, 1963 *Point of Contact.*

Writer Ken Taylor, Director Cecil Petty. Assembly worker, Tom Barnsley (Brian Murray) quarrels with his brother, Reg (Michael Robbins) over secretary Sue Collins (Jane Merrow). Sue asks him to come away with her for the weekend, and he thinks it's the start of something big. But Sue has other plans. With Norman Scace (Mr Harding). Meurig Wyn-Jones aka David Barry(George). Henry Soskin (Ginger). Royston Tickner (Nobby). Frances Cohen (Janet Holder).

Apr. 15, 1963 *The Testing Time.*

Writer Bill Craig, Director Geoffrey Nethercott.

As the Easter break approaches, Works Manager Mr Anstrell (Harry Webster) hands over control to his deputy, Geoffrey Berger (Leonard Sachs) but does not foresee the crisis that develops. With Vincent Ball as Nelson, Anne Pichon and Tom Macaulay as Cunliffe (the character of Cunliffe would return in the second series as a member of the Scott Furlong board).

Apr. 22, 1963 *The Veteran*

Writer Robert Holles. Director Herbert Wise.

"Give these old codger's half a chance and they hang on til they drop down dead." Only a few weeks after leaving the BBC's *Z Cars*, Jeremy Kemp was starring as Bill Casby, a worker who seizes his chance to settle his grievance with the 67 year-old storesman, when the wrong part is issued. J.G.Devlin as Arthur Cooper. Jeremy Kemp as Bill Casby, Martin Boddey as Cyril Bridges.

Apr. 29, 1963 *One of Us.*

Writers Geoffrey Bellman, John Whitney. Director Rex Firkin.

Why is Len Gower (Alfred Burke) so secretive about his reason for starting work at the aircraft machine shop? With Bryan Pringle as Ron Barby. Peter Welch as Frank Hawes. Jerome Willis as Alf Winter. Bert Palmer as Pop. Harry Webster as Mr Anstrell. Arthur White as Norman. Edward Kelsey as Dr Foley. Tom Watson as Sauchie.

May 6, 1963 *Who Goes First?*

Writer Richard Harris. Director James Ferman.

Two in five men face unemployment as the threat of job cuts hits Scott Furlong, but for capstan operator Den Heath (Johnny Briggs) redundancy could be key to his own crisis. With Harry Webster as Mr Anstrell, Tom McCauley as Mr Cunliffe, Frank Jarvis as Tony Frame, Julia Foster as Sue Barnes, Ivor Salter as Ted Barnes and John Junkin as union convenor Dusty Miller.

May 13, 1963 *The Blunt Approach.*

Writer Neil Kingsley. Director Geoffrey Nethercott.

Moving South with his family to find employment, Harry Thorpe (Jack Smethurst) finds his marriage in jeopardy. With Patricia Healey as Joan Thorpe. Judy Parfitt as Amy Skinner. Derek Newark as Alf Skinner. Kenneth Colley as Jack Moss. Edward Kelsey as Dr Foley.

May 20, 1963 *One of Those Days.*

Writer Edmund Ward. Director Quentin Lawrence.

Hidden resentments come to the surface between workers and management when a series of events upset a usually placid machinist. With William Hartnell as Wally Griggs, Michael Williams as Stephen Allsop, Anne Cunningham as Marian Allsop. Alan Foss as Mr Lipton. Harry Webster as Mr Anstrell. *(Michael Williams appears by permission of the Governors of the Royal Shakespeare Company).*

May 27, 1963 *A Good Night's Work.*

Writer Peter Draper. Director James Ferman.

Junior executive John Rodway (Alec McCowen) finds himself on an unexpected night out with a South American woman. His future depends on the success of the evening. With Erica Rogers as Anna, Ronald Radd as Mr Samaranga, Susan Clark as Janet, Tom McCauley as Reginald Cunliffe and Wendy Gifford as Sue Rodway.

Notes:

1 *Rex Firkin recalls the creation of The Plane Makers in his memoir High Drama: My Life in Television (ed Richard Marson) Kaleidoscope Publishing 2002. ISBN 978-1-900203-46-3*

2 Press release.

3 Marjorie Bilbow *The Stage* 11 July 1963

4 *Liverpool Echo* 8 February 1963 *The Daily Mirror* 9 February 1964

Case Study Two: The Plane Makers   Series Two

Producer Rex Firkin. Script Editor Wilfred Greatorex

Reginald Marsh as Sugden   Patrick Wymark as Wilder

The Plane Makers series two introduces a number of continuing characters at boardroom level. However, some early episodes seem like holdovers from the first series, being more like single plays, tenuously linked to the main characters (who sometimes only appear in a couple of scenes).

The script conference for the second series was held on 24 May 1963 when one episode of the first series was still to be transmitted. Rex Firkin and Wilfred Greatorex told prospective writers that, *"the series will start with a completed aircraft. By the end of episode one it will be in the air."* This was the springboard to move stories away from the factory floor, *"out into the fields of management, sales, test flying etc, whilst keeping the highest possible standard of characterisation."*

In order to win and hold and audience of men *and* women, continuing characters would be needed. *But not run-of-the-mill series kind. They will be capable of continual development."*

Two of the characters – John Wilder and Arthur Sugden – would be constant, *"having been chosen for their character strength and focal positions within the company. Each will be in conflict with those above and below him – and with each other. "*

The brief continued with the background to the series: *"Scott Furlong is the major company within a group of three companies. It operates two factories. The one seen in the previous series and located near St Albans. The other, a few miles away at Radley Heath, on the side of their private airfield. The other two companies in the group are some distance away and do not directly concern this series. "*

Writers were then given their first glimpse of group managing director John Wilder, who: *"before the amalgamation, was chairman of Scott Furlong. He is a driving professional who has spent his career in the industry. He was not appointed chairman of the group upon amalgamation because he was personally unacceptable to the other companies, who were financially strong enough to appoint their own nominee – a long-standing non-executive director of Scott Furlong whose background is primarily banking. "*

The appointment of Arthur Sugden, works manager of Radley Heath as General Works Manager was originally intended to have taken place before the series started. This would have triggered Mr Anstrell's resignation, and the appointment of a deputy works manager from the Heath as Mr Anstrell's successor at the main works would have inflamed old rivalries. Firkin later said, *"It's the thinking beforehand that makes (a series). This is purely abstract thinking. You inevitably make certain assumptions that may be sending you in the wrong direction. You must spot as quickly as possible which may it should go. "* The appointment of Arthur Sugden and the opposition of Wilder became the heart of the series.

Greatorex and Firkin envisaged some Scott Furlong people from the first series returning. Davey Rankin (John Meillon) in conflict with the union convenor was mentioned as one possibility, although this didn't happen in the end. A *"Costigan (Gerald James) story"* was pencilled in (which became *Costigan's Rocket*), as was "Sales Flight Lark" (which became *Anyone for The Skylark*). Greatorex would combine the ideas of *"Press stories about SF200 failure"* and *"Security Officer – individual liberties"* as *A Question of Sources*. Greatorex and Firkin also knew that they wanted a *"Woman Lead Story"*. They were also curiously adamant that there should be no stories about the Personnel Director!

At this stage, there were three possible projects to build stories around. The first was the SF 200 Medium Range Passenger Transport, which would fly in the first episode with others being launched at monthly intervals. *"By the end of the series, four will be flying."*

The other two projects were the Red Major Missile *("still under possible cancellation by the Air Ministry")* and the design stage of a Super Sonic Transport (SST).

It's clear that this briefing was very much a long-range plan. As Firkin later said, the scriptwriters, *"add all sort of touches that speed the development of the characters.* The Red Major Missile only featured in one story (*One Out – All Out)* while the SST was superseded by the VTOL in series three.

Wilfred Greatorex later told the *TV Times* that script conferences were held at his Harley Street flat. *"My conferences start at 10 am and often last til 5pm. We start with a bare piece of paper, an idea across the desk and at the end of the day the story will be pretty well planned."*

Putting Wilder Together

Rex Firkin has said that Wilder had three inspirations. One: Sir John Davies, the austere and autocratic head of the Rank Organisation resented for cutting film production at Pinewood, but also a risk-taker who went into partnership to create Rank Xerox in 1956 before a working photocopying machine even existed. Two: Basil Smallpeice, the managing director of British Overseas Airways

Corporation, who had fought to rescue the organisation from the costs and delays resulting from a government-inspired 'Buy British' policy. After a disagreement in 1963 with Air Minister Julian Amery over financial support for BOAC, Smallpeice had been forced to resign. Three: A.D. Peters, a literary agent who reputedly spent the week with his wife, and the weekends with his mistress, a relationship both women knew about. It is tempting to add a fourth, Bill Ward, whose attention to detail and legendary roastings seem like a template for John Wilder.

To play Wilder, Firkin cast Patrick Wymark a member of the Royal Shakespeare Company who had recently starred as Daniel De Bosola in *The Duchess of Malfi*. On TV, he had played press baron Sir Charles Worgan in a 1959 BBC production of Arnold Bennett's *What The Public Wants*, poisoner William Palmer in *They Hanged My Saintly Billy* (1962), Oliver Cromwell in *The Cruel Necessity* (1962) and Barabbas in *The Night Before The Execution* (1963). While it is true that Wymark's most recent stage appearance was as Bottom in the Regent's Park Open Air Theatre production *of A Midsummer Night's Dream* (1963) it's fair to say that Wymark was already known for a wide range of performances. However, Firkin said in 1965 that, *"we originally thought of John Wilder as being a very big man. But one night I saw Pat Wymark involved in an argument and I knew at once he was the actor we wanted."*

To play Wilder's adversary, Arthur Sugden, Firkin cast Reginald Marsh. Despite growing up in Worthing, Marsh mustered a convincing Yorkshire actor. Having started in repertory as a 16-year-old, Marsh had been appearing regularly on TV, including the BBC's attempted soap *Compact*.

As Pamela Wilder, Firkin cast Barbara Murray. An established film actress (*Passport to Pimlico* (1949) *Campbells Kingdom* (1957) Barbara had recently starred as a reporter in the February 1963 ITV *Play of the Week, The Cruel Deadline*. As noted above, Greatorex and Firkin had told writers they wanted *a "Woman Lead Story"*, and offered to write Pamela into two more scripts if she would agree to do the first episode. However, Barbara did her best to influence the scripts, saying they were written *"By men, for men, and the women weren't real. Weren't complete."*

With series two being an unofficial relaunch, a new title sequence was filmed backed by Trevor Duncan's stately *Citizens of the World March.* The big selling point for the TV show was a full-sized mock-up of the Sovereign, designed for ATV by aircraft makers Handley Page. The opening sequence shows technicians guiding the airliner as a tug pulls it off the tarmac, into a hangar. The mock-up couldn't fly, of course, but tricky camera work gives the impression that it taxi's under its own steam.

Rex Firkin recalled that after the run-through of *Too Much to Lose*, he went up to see Bill Ward, who had been watching the production via closed circuit TV in his office. When Firkin entered the office, Ward was writing, ignoring his presence. Firkin dreaded his generally volatile reaction. *"Then he stopped, gently put down his pen and said, 'That'll do. I reckon that'll do.'"*

The TAM Ratings showed that the revamped series was a hit with viewers. *Too Much To Lose* was number 6 in that week's Top 20 with 6, 311,000 homes (an estimated 13,884,200 viewers), with *No Man's Land* at number 10 with 6, 188, 000 homes. Ratings continued at 6, 345,000 into December before settling at around, 5, 700,000 homes or 12,540,000 viewers into the New Year.

Once again, Lew Grade and Bill Ward demonstrated flexibility now that *The Plane Makers* was a success. Where most British TV series ran for 13 episodes, the second series of *The Plane Makers* was extended to 27. With no break to plan for the next set of scripts, David Weir was drafted in as "Series Story Consultant" to bring together continuity, characters and background themes from the most successful earlier episodes. Weir's first episode, *How Do You Vote*, introduced Norman Tyrrell as Sir Gordon Revidge, the new Chairman of Scott Furlong and antagonist for Wilder.

16 September 1963. *Too Much to Lose*

Writer Edmund Ward. Director Quentin Lawrence.

Cast: Patrick Wymark (John Wilder). Reginald Marsh (Arthur Sugden). Barbara Murray (Pamela Wilder). Robert Urquhart (test pilot Henry Forbes). John Arnatt (sales manager Peter Humphreys) Bernard Brown (co-pilot Simon Wanleigh). Dennis Ramsden (Lt. Cmdr. Cooke). Martin Wyldeck (William Keeble). Tom Macaulay (Reginald Cunliffe). Fred Ferris (Sam Adams) John Ringham (Ken Swanson) Arthur White (Harry Jenkin) . Lloyd Pearson (Sir Charles Elbertson). Kathleen St. John (Mary). Aimée Delamain (Mrs. Milne) Denis Cowles (Lord Teddington). Linda Marlowe (Dorothy Minton). Brian Badcoe (Nigel Johnson). Robert Sansom (Minister of Aviation*).

The Minister of Aviation at the time was Julian Amery MP.

"We all know that you sell aircraft on politics and skulduggery. After that you sell them on glamour and ballyhoo. And then you trot out the performance figures. So, let's get the ballyhoo over and done with."

At a Scott Furlong board meeting, managing director John Wilder pushes through the christening of the new SF 200 airliner as the "Scott-Furlong Sovereign". French competitors are due to test fly their new plane and Wilder tells the board they've got to launch the Sovereign first.

Works manager Arthur Sugden (Reginald Marsh) is confident about the structure of the plane, but test pilot Henry Forbes (Robert Urquhart) - nicknamed 'Auntie' because of his cautiousness, is still running ground trials. When Wilder suggests he's being over-cautious, Forbes retorts that *"(over-cautious) is another word for attention to detail"*. Wilder over-rules Forbes, demanding that the Sovereign flies within two days.

Forbes asks if Wilder will join the test flight but Wilder replies evasively that he will be of more use on the ground. Forbes says there is a good reason behind the custom. It keeps the minds of the managers focused on safety. Later on, Wilder's wife Pamela (Barbara Murray) warns him people will say he's afraid - as they did when he arranged to be in America during a previous test-flight.

On the day of the test flight, all goes well until the Sovereign comes in to land. A wheel buckles and Forbes just manages to keep the plane under control. In the control tower, Wilder breaks the tension, saying, *"If it had been anyone else that brought that plane in, it'd have been a complete write-off. And that's the man they call Auntie."*

Edmund Ward's script deftly sets up the situation, introducing multiple characters while carrying through a complete storyline with a dynamic climax. There's a lot of dialogue explaining the power relationships but it never seems un-natural.

The climax echoes the real-life maiden flight of the Hawker Siddeley Trident in 9 January 1962, when a valve failure caused a wheel leg to jam in the undercarriage door. In reality, the Trident was shadowed by two other planes. The pilots reported the problem to the Trident's flight engineer who improvised a solution. Possibly because Wilder had pushed the test flight forward, there are no support craft for the Sovereign and the drama is heightened.

Ward sets out the industry background to the series – in which Defence Minister Duncan Sandys had forced aviation companies to merge into groups – during a meeting between disgruntled members of the Scott Furlong board.

Chairman, Sir Charles Elbertson (Lloyd Pearson) meets with Lt. Commander Cooke (Dennis Ramsden), William Keeble (Martin Wyldeck) and Reginald Cunliffe (Tom Macauley), a Scott Furlong executive who had appeared in two episodes of the first series. Cunliffe in particular thinks Wilder is *"an ambitious bully"*. He and Keeble complain about Wilder's *"steam-roller tactics"*. Sir Charles, who represents Elbertson's merchant bank tells them that, *"Before this merger went through, Scott-Furlong had orders, a good brain, no money. You two companies had plenty of investment money and no orders. The merger was automatic. A shotgun marriage had been called with me as parson. That's why I'm chairman in charge of the money. But I'm a financier. I know nothing about airplanes. Wilder does."*

When Cunliffe objects that he also knows about planes, Sir Charles replies; *"I know you do. But Wilder was appointed Managing Director."* Sir Charles later warns Wilder that his tactics have put him in a difficult position. *"If a Board meeting had been called, this test flight would have been a joint decision. As it is, it's entirely your decision."* Lloyd Pearson, who had played a bank manager in *Passport to Pimlico* (1949), plays Elbertson in a very 'Pickwickian' manner, slightly reminiscent of Arthur Lowe in delivery.

Wilder is praised by the Aviation Minister (Robert Sansom) who tells Elbertson he's *"A very capable man...solid fellow. Not like one of your Flash Harry's. Here today and gone tomorrow with a profit. He's done a lot of good for the industry."* However, it's sales manager Humphreys who gives an insight into Wilder's motivation, telling Dorothy Minton, *"He's been climbing all his life and now he's balanced at the top of the tree. One more shuffle, one more hop and he's perched for good. He'll earn himself a knighthood. Then he can write his own ticket. Politics, industry, anything."*

The imagery recurs after the near disaster of the test flight when Wilder tells Pamela why he didn't go on the test flight. *"I've got too much to lose. Romantic gestures went out with the Crusades. I'm at the top of the tree."*

"And you're afraid of falling, no matter how," Pamela chides. *"I've never fallen yet,"* Wilder reminds her. But as Pamela leaves the room, we see his mask fall as he stares into his drink and realises how close he has come to the edge. For all his pushing, his fate in the end has relied on Henry Forbes' skill and courage.

John Arnatt makes his only appearance as Sales Manager Peter Humphreys in this episode. Jack Watling, as Don Henderson would not appear until the fifth episode (by which time Arnatt had been cast as Dr Fitzgerald in ATV's *Emergency Ward 10)*. Arnatt does not have the light delivery of Watling, but is also noticeably taller than Wymark in the boardroom scenes. In 1969 he would play former detective Sidney Bulmer in Edmund *Ward's The Main Chance*.

Ullapool-born Robert Urquhart plays test pilot Henry Forbes. As a third mate in the Merchant Navy, he was torpedoed three times during the war. In peacetime he performed at the Park Theatre, Glasgow before winning an ex-Serviceman's scholarship to RADA. In 1948 he was offered a season at the Shakespeare Memorial Theatre, which he followed with repertory work at the Glasgow Citizen's Theatre. In 1952 he made his first film appearance in *You're Only Young* Twice and in 1953 he played Bassanio in the Old Vic production of *The Merchant of Venice* where Patrick Wymark made one of his early stage appearances (as Salerio). In 1956 Urquhart starred opposite Peter Cushing in *The Curse of Frankenstein* In 1961 he wrote and starred in the Rediffusion detective series *Jango*.

23 September 1963. *No Man's Land.*

Writer Leslie Sands. Director James Ferman.

Patrick Wymark   (John Wilder) Reginald Marsh (Arthur Sugden). Lloyd Pearson (Sir Charles Elbertson) Dennis Ramsden (Lt. Cmdr. Cooke). Tom Macaulay (Reginald Cunliffe). Geoffrey Alexander (Robert Ferguson). Elizabeth Begley (Margie Thomas). Frank Crawshaw (Ernie Lucas). Sheila Raynor (Mary Sugden). Jerome Willis (Frank Sugden). Norma Ronald (Kay Lingard). Joby Blanshard (Skinner). Honora Burke (Ursula). Royston Tickner (Reg Hicks). Walter Sparrow (Mack).

"Good Fellow, Wilder. Done a lot for the industry. But that sort of fellow needs a little opposition now and then." Sir Charles (Lloyd Pearson)

Arthur Sugden is on the short list for the new role of General Works Manager. But the search for the cause of the Sovereign's near fatal crash points to someone under his management at the Radley Heath assembly plant. Wilder makes it clear that the Board is looking for a scapegoat.

Wilder has created the role of General Works Manager to strengthen his control over the Scott-Furlong factories. The three contenders on the shortlist are all insiders – Ralph Bentley (nominated by the associate companies), Sugden (manager of the Radley Heath Works), and Ferguson (manager at Scott Furlong's main plant). The other two men are graduate engineers, whereas Sugden has worked his way up from being an apprentice and has a degree equivalent Diploma in Technology *("Dip. Tech.")*. Sugden has a craftsman's pride in the work of Radley Heath; *"At the main factory they make parts. We make aircraft. We create!"*

Wilder is in favour of Ferguson *("we work awfully well together")* and is against Sugden *("His technical experience is beyond question. But every man has his personal ceiling. ")*. Although the Chairman (Lloyd Pearson) tells Wilder that, *"We'd better leave personal opinions till after the interviews,"* Wilder continues to lobby on Ferguson's behalf (*"It's a question of upbringing. Background. I think he'll go far. ")*. When asked about Sugden, Wilder concedes that, *"He's an excellent technician...but it's a question of over identification with the men. We need someone who can see things from our point of view."*

We learn that Sugden's father lost his job in Yorkshire during the depression and marched for jobs with his union. He was given shelter during the march by Ernie Lucas (Frank Crawshaw), before bringing his family South (Scott Furlong is based somewhere near St Albans). Arthur was an apprentice at Radley Heath, spent ten years as a union convenor, but also progressed to the position of works manager. In contrast to the Wilders' luxurious home life with servants and cocktail parties, Arthur has a long scene with his wife Mary (Sheila Raynor) discussing how they could get central heating if he gets the job. While Arthur's younger brother (Jerome Willis*) is a fierce union man, the 1960's prospect of social mobility is shown by Arthur's son qualifying as a dentist.

*Jerome Willis trained at the Old Vic Theatre School with Patrick Wymark. Together with Prunella Scales, they performed in Vanbrugh's comedy, *A Journey to London* for the 1951 graduation show.

The episode title comes from a warning to Arthur by old friend Ernie Lucas, *"If you get the job, nobody'll cheer you, up or down. No-Man's Land, that's what you'll feel like. Just waiting to be shot down."*

The spine of the story is Wilder's quest to give the Board someone's head for the undercarriage failure in the previous episode. Wilder is not so much concerned with the truth as with demonstrating that someone has been punished. Examination of the aircraft's hydraulics points to sabotage. Wilder tells Sugden that if he can't identify the man responsible, *"Penalise those you're unsure of and put the others on less vital work.",* but Sugden is unwilling to make many suffer for one man's action.

Sugden's chain-smoking secretary Margie (Elizabeth Begley) checks the worksheets and determines that the supervisor who missed the sabotage was Sugden's friend Ernie Lucas. The man who filed through the hydraulics has already been laid off and Sugden concludes that he vandalised the undercarriage as revenge for being given notice. This leaves Lucas next in line to be Wilder's sacrificial lamb to the Board. However, Sugden still can't explain why Forbes got a signal to say the undercarriage was safely down. He keeps checking the plane and discovers that the electronics were tampered with to give a false safety signal.

At the board meeting, Sugden demonstrates that the sabotage was more complex than Wilders' immediate assumption. He tells the Board that he doesn't think the saboteur wanted to harm anyone. Just delay the work. Under normal circumstances the undercarriage would have failed on the ground during taxi-ing tests. This reminds the Chairman that Wilder decided to bring the test-flight forward although Sugden says, *"I'm blaming no-one, sir. Except the person who did it."*

The Board agrees to take the incident no further in order to avoid bad publicity. The episode ends with Sugden being told the Board was split down the middle, meaning that *"there is no particular confidence in you or your ability."* However, they offer him the post of General Works Manager for a trial period of six months.

Leeds-born playwright Leslie Sands was obviously considered an appropriate choice to flesh out the first episode to focus on the Yorkshire-born Sugden. As an actor, Sands would guest star in the 5th December 1963 episode of *The Saint* , taking the title-role of *The Well Meaning Mayor* (Coincidentally, the coroner in that episode was played by Robert Sansom, who had appeared in *Too Much To Lose* as the aviation minister). In an early scene, Sugden is shown reading a crime thriller (*'The Flesh and the Forelock'*) and he ultimately wins out by acting as a detective, refusing to rest until he'd got to the bottom of the mystery. Perhaps not surprising since both Leslie Sands and Reginald Marsh wrote stage thrillers; Marsh *The Death Is Announced,* Sands *Deadlock* (filmed in 1951 as *Another Man's Poison* starring Bette Davis and Barbara Murray).

30 September 1963 *A Question of Sources.*

Writer Wilfred Greatorex. Director John Cooper.

Patrick Wymark (John Wilder) Barbara Murray (Pamela Wilder) Robert Urquhart (Henry Forbes) Aubrey Richards (Gareth Edwards) Ewan Roberts (Todd) Douglas Muir (Tom Bancroft) . Geoffrey

Chater (Simon Stride) Geoffrey Whitehead (Jeremy Coles) James Kerry (Jimmy Shaw). Julia Jones (Mrs Edwards).

The Sovereign's engines aren't delivering full power. Technicians theorise that the position of the wings are starving the engines of air. There are two possible solutions – either redesign the wing or install a special baffle which Gareth Edwards has suggested.

A dedicated design technician, Edwards has been working on the solution at home over the weekend. To management, Edwards is showing dedication and flexibility. But to security officer Todd, he's a risk. He has been alerted by *"the usual sources"* that Edwards' 19-year-old son has joined the Communist party and this makes Edwards a potential security risk. Set during the 'Cold War', *The Plane Makers* existed against a background where the aviation industry depended on Government contracts and their technology was at risk from commercial competitors and 'unfriendly powers'.

Edwards suspects he is under suspicion for a newspaper leak about the Sovereign's problems and walks out as the deadline for his baffle design approaches. Wilder initially supports Todd, with whom he worked in Germany in 1945. *"He did quite a job there. Needling out war criminals wasn't child's play."*

Greatorex compares Todd's thoroughness with the attitude of the manual workers who are at best laid back and at worst out for themselves. Most of the workers had either served in the war or done national service and were keen to aggravate militaristic types like Todd. Greatorex also examines the double-standards of commercial life.

While Edwards eventually saves the day, Wilder instructs Technical Director Tom Bancroft (Douglas Muir – Steed's boss One-Ten in the early *Avengers* episodes) to *"get his job covered"* realising that there is a risk in one man being indispensable. As Bancroft tells Edwards, *"You've done yourself no good today."*

7 October 1963 *All Part of the Job.*

Writer Richard Harris. Director James Ferman.

"Everywhere I look, I find men working to their own advantage."
Arthur Sugden.

Reginald Marsh (Arthur Sugden). Stanley Meadows (John
Hamilton). Patricia Haines (Janet Pearce). Noel Johnson (Norman
Reynolds). Elizabeth Begley (Margie Thomas). Howard Goorney
(Mr. Brander). Campbell Singer (Jack Sefton).

Stanley Meadows (*The Ipcress File*) plays Hamilton, an ambitious
junior in the purchasing department. While his senior is on leave, an
order for tropical modifications to the Sovereign has to be pushed
forward. Hamilton visits a sub-contractor to try and cut the delivery
schedule for parts and begins to suspect that Chief Buyer, Norman
Reynolds, may have awarded the contract for personal reasons.

Reynolds is a man of outward rectitude, appropriately played by
Noel Johnson, the radio voice of four-square heroes *Dick Barton*
and *Dan Dare*. When Reynolds returns from holiday, he quickly
realises that Hamilton has suspicions about the contract. Patricia
Haines, who would appear with Meadows in *The Night Caller*
(1965), here plays disapproving Secretary Mrs Pearce. Haines,
Meadows and Johnson all convey the sweaty paranoia and tensions
of office life through expressions that say more than the dialogue.

The theme of *"men working to their own advantage"* is reflected in
supporting scenes as a tin of domestic paint bought through the firm
is exchanged for theatre tickets and an executive has the machine
shop tooling a discontinued part for his vintage Lagonda. When
Reynolds explains to Sugden that he accepted a holiday from the
sub-contractor only after the contract had been awarded, we never
know if it is true. Even if it is, the effect on Reynolds' self-image is
plain to see. The fact that his wife has had a nervous breakdown and
benefited from the holiday may be seen as special pleading, but
underlines that every man has his bending point.

A prolific contributor to crime dramas ranging from *Public Eye* to *A Touch Of Frost* , scriptwriter Richard Harris was one of the two writers Rex Firkin had named to the press as the standard of quality he was looking for. American born director James Ferman came to England with the USAF before studying at Kings College, Cambridge. In 1975 he became the Secretary of the British Board of Film Classification, where he had a controversial 24 years supervising cuts to and bans of movies.

14 October 1963 *Don't Stick Your Head Out.*

Writer Peter Draper.   Director Quentin Lawrence.

"In big business, if you stick your head out too far, there's always someone taking aim at it – with an axe! "John Wilder.

Patrick Wymark (John Wilder). Barbara Murray (Pamela Wilder). Jack Watling (Don Henderson). Ingrid Hafner (Kate Barber). Newton Blick (Emilio Copparo). Sheila Raynor (Mary Sugden). Maria Corvin (Melina Copparo). Fred Ferris (Sam Adams). Richard Bebb (Louis Benedello). Norma Ronald (Kay Lingard).

Jack Watling joins the cast as sales director Don Henderson. Since his 1942 West End performance as bomber pilot Teddy Graham in Terence Rattigan's *Flare Path*, Watling had starred in many British films such as *The Demi-Paradise* (1943), *The Birthday Present* (1957) and *Chain of Events* (1958) as laid-back or deceptive young men. His most recent TV appearance had been on 19 August 1963 opposite Sylvia Sims in Julian Symon's thriller *Miranda and a Salesman* (BBC 1). But the hook of this story is why Wilder choses to take Sugden rather than Henderson on a sales trip.

The bigger bombshell, certainly for 1963, is that Wilder takes his mistress on the sales trip. Wilder's secretary Kay Lingard (Norma Ronald) has arranged three air tickets for the trip, and Sugden assumes the third ticket is for Lingard, until Wilder brazenly arrives at the airport with Kate Barber (Ingrid Hafner) telling Sugden that *"Miss Barber will be acting as my Secretary."*

Hafner, who played Ian Hendry's receptionist Carol in the first series of *The Avengers*, portrays Kate Barber as similar in many ways to Pamela Wilder. Earlier in the episode, Wilder has arranged events so that Pamela can't accompany him on the trip. Pamela (Barbara Murray) makes it plain she can sense his guilt and says, *"You only have to tell me. You don't have to go through this elaborate pantomime so I won't go with you."*

Kate is equally resigned, telling Sugden that she had a daughter to support after her husband left her for a 17-year-old girl. *"I can do shorthand, but not very well. Parents should bring up children to assume no-one will take care of them. Mine didn't."* She describes the relationship with Wilder as being, *"Very like marriage. Marriage becomes a series of habits. So does this, except the habits are further apart. Once a year we go to the South of France. Theatre four or five times a year. Nightclubs – never anywhere too fashionable…I suppose some wives don't get that."*

Wilder himself has a sense that things are cooling off. *"When a woman has had a long, continuous relationship with a man, his more romantic image is bound to diminish. Just as no man is a hero to his valet – or his mistress."*

The episode sets the standard for Draper's later scripts with entertaining interplay between the three characters. In an early scene, Wilder joins Kate and Sugden at the hotel bar. *"I've been telling Mr Sugden that if he's in Milan long enough he ought to try and see the paintings in the Museo Poldi Pezzoli."* Wilder smiles with mild sarcasm. *"I expect you'll be dashing off first thing in the morning, Arthur!"* "You never know," Sugden grunts, *"I might have hidden depths."*

The root of the story is the mystery as to why Wilder has taken Sugden on the sales trip. The answer may have seemed a bit of a head-scratcher at the time since Wilder and Sugden debate some financial detail which is hard to take in. Caparo, the paternalistic owner of the Italian company is dying, and that makes the company too risky as a customer. Wilder puts it in poetic terms, *"You and I have been officiating at the death of an Empire. We came out specifically not to sell an aeroplane. It's very difficult to stop a salesman selling, so it's best not to put it in their hands."*

In the end, the scrupulous Sugden finds himself compromising, both on moral and business grounds. Wilder comforts him with the words, *"Everybody's soul is just a bit smaller than the mortgage on his house."*

Caparo, head of the Italian airline, is played by Newton Blick, a long-established stage performer variously described as *"a clever and subtle character actor,"* and *"looking like a squashed orange".* Blick had played Old Gobbo with Urquhart and Wymark in the 1953 Old Vic production of *The Merchant of Venice*. Both Blick and Wymark had appeared in the 1960 BBC adaptation of *Colombe* starring Sean Connery and Blick and Wymark were contemporaries in Peter Hall's first season at the Royal Shakespeare Company. At the time this episode was made, Blick was also appearing as Snout in Peter Hall's A *Midsummer Night's Dream* at the Aldwych. After his death on 13 October 1965, Olwen Wymark later organised an acting prize to be set up in his memory at the Bristol Old Vic Theatre School.

21 October 1963 *The Old Boy Network.*

Writer Edwin Ranch. Director Quentin Lawrence.

"It hasn't changed. You don't have the Means Test, but it hasn't changed. The Old Boy Network." Stan Wallace (Anthony Sagar).

Patrick Wymark   (John Wilder). Patrick Magee (William Breen). Jeremy Burnham (Nigel Carr). Bert Palmer (Ernie Wainwright) Justine Lord   (Phoebe). Anthony Sagar (Stan Wallace). Norma Ronald (Kay Lingard). Gordon Rollings (Ronnie Forster). Richard Shaw (Eddie Taylor).

Edwin Ranch's script uses humour to explore the inequality of power within an industrial setting. 63-year-old Ernie Wainwright (Bert Palmer) leaves a crate containing a cloud warning radar in the path of a reversing van. With the radar smashed, and a week before a replacement can be made, Wilder sends out an urgent memo for all managers to delay the test flight of the Sovereign modification for African Airways. Assistant works manager Joseph Breen (Patrick Magee) gives Wainwright a weeks' notice, to which Wilder comments: *"He's cost this company more than he'll ever make in his life and all we can do is sack him."*

Unfortunately, Nigel Carr (Jeremy Burnham) has come in late with a hangover, ignored his mail (including Wilder's "urgent and personal" memo) and left for a lunch date with Ronnie Forster (Gordon Rollings) of African Airways. Nigel tells Ronnie that he's written to the Chairman, confirming the test flight date. *("I'm a great believer in astonishing Chairmen by knowing things ahead of them")*. The following morning, Nigel reads his mail and confesses to Wilder that, *"I think I've made the most appalling boob."*

When he hears what has happened, Wilder tells Nigel, *"You were one of the young men I've been watching. You're intelligent and you have the right background. I want executives the men can believe in – be afraid of!! And if anything happens like this again, you'll be in trouble. Real trouble"*

Wilder covers for Nigel, but Carr's secretary (Justine Lord) tells a friend what really happened. When word gets round the factory about the unequal treatment of Carr and Wainwright the technicians working on the radar job threaten to refuse to work on the African Airlines job. Wilder reinstates Wainwright saying that, *"Mr Sugden feels very strongly that in view of this chap's age he should be given a second chance."*

Instead of being a simple management v union conflict, the balance of power is held by skilled workers. The union representative's plea on behalf of Wainwright is brushed off by management. It's the unofficial action of the skilled men who installing the radar turns matters round. Eddie Taylor (Richard Shaw) tells Wainwright, *"When was the last time the union was any good to you? I'm a skilled man. They can't just phone the labour exchange and get someone as can do my job. No, if me and a dozen of my mates down tools, the whole factory stops work. I don't rely on a union."*

28 October 1963 *Any More for The Skylark.*

Writer Peter Draper. Director James Ferman.

"You can almost feel their breath on the back of your neck already." John Wilder.

Patrick Wymark (John Wilder). Jack Watling (Don Henderson). Victor Maddern (Hammy Hoskins). Rodney Bewes (Tim Ormiston). Isobel Black (Rosalind Perry). Barbara Windsor (Marlene). John Woodvine (James Nett).Fred Ferris (Sam Adams). Malcolm Webster (Tony Maccabee).

It's a tradition that factory staff serve as passengers to provide ballast for a plane's first long haul flight and the *Sovereign* is destined for the South of France. As Don Henderson (Jack Watling) says, whoever gets the job of allocating the seats is , *"extremely popular one minute and loathed by everyone the next."*

Henderson delegates the job to Fletley in Public Relations who in turn dumps the job on Ormiston (Rodney Bewes), who sets up a lottery and talent contest are to allocate the tickets.

While a range of workers vie for the free flight the heart of the episode is Bewes' tentative romance with secretary Isobel Black. Bewes tells her, *"All I've got is a television set and a copy of the Kama Sutra. I can't promise to love you as long as I live, but I'll love you very much as long as I can."* The romance is threatened by slimy manager John Woodvine, who intends to ensure both he and Black will be sharing the flight to France.

Like Henderson, John Wilder has very little screen time in this episode. When he does appear in the story it serves to create some final act conflict. Wilder decides to use the flight as a publicity exercise and fill it with journalists. Bewes is told to cancel the lottery, but screws up his courage and confronts Wilder in his office. Bewes says cancelling the traditional workers flight is a bad decision. *"It may not be bad for the economics of the firm, but I think it may very well be bad for the morale of the firm. And that in the end has a bearing on management"* (Jack Watling in the background chokes on his drink at the coming storm).

Wilder says *"It's a ridiculous tradition"* and Bewes persists *"But it's a tradition."*

Wilder promises to think about it and when they're alone asks Henderson how old the PR man is. Henderson tells him he's 22. *"You can almost feel their breath on the back of your neck already."* Wilder says, with the benign rider, *"Keep an eye on him."*

Rodney Bewes was a year away from his defining role in the BBC comedy *The Likely Lads* but brings the same earnestness to the role of Tim Ormiston. Isobel Black (Tania in 1963's *Kiss of the Vampire*) displays a matching sensitivity. She would go on to appear as public relations assistant Eileen O'Rourke in the 1967/68 series of the BBC's answer to Wilder - *The Troubleshooters*. Old Vic actor John Woodvine (*An American Werewolf in London*) makes a nicely despicable threat to their relationship.

Getting special billing as paint-shop sprayer, Marlene, Barbara Windsor was well-known as seamstress Gloria in the BBC comedy *The Rag Trade* and would go on to star in *Carry On Spying* the following year. Marlene performs her exotic dance as part of a talent contest to win tickets on the flight, doing it to the off-key singing of the Manchester Children's Choir classic *Nymphs and Shepherds*. Victor Maddern as electrician Hammy jokes to Marlene about *Fings Aint What They Used T'Be* in one scene. Barbara Windsor had appeared in the West End production of this show in 1960.

5 November 1963 *A Matter of Self Respect.*

NB: This episode saw The Plane Makers move from Monday nights to Tuesday nights (although not every ITV region showed the series on ATV's broadcast day).

Writer Leslie Sands. Director John Cooper.

"You didn't want a job when you came here. You wanted an anaesthetic. You didn't want to think or feel. Just operate." Arthur Sugden.

Reginald Marsh (Arthur Sugden). Leslie Sands (Tim Carter). Garfield Morgan (Fred Collins). Sheila Raynor(Mary Sugden). John Horsley (Walter Strickland). Joan Peart (Susan Strickland).Joy Measures (Jennifer). Michael Segal (Sammy). David Cook (Ginger Baines).

Tim Carter, formerly a key man in design, returns to Scott Furlong after a year and a half in Brixton jail and chooses to work in the machine shop. Carter had been driving home drunk from a party and crashed into a lorry, killing his wife and the other driver. After recovering from his injuries, Carter got two years for manslaughter. Carter is in a bail hostel until the end of the week and had to sell his house to cover legal costs. Arthur Sugden gets the staff welfare section to find him lodgings with Angie Morris (June Ellis).

After three months, Carter has the respect of most of his colleagues in the workshop but when Sugden offers him a job with responsibility in the design department, Carter refuses saying he prefers to go home exhausted so there is less chance for him to fall off the wagon. *"I'm an alcoholic. There's no cure for me. Only what the doctors call recovery. But no cure."*

Sugden persists saying Carter wanted to work in the machine shop because he didn't want to think or feel, but he won't be right in the head until he can handle all his responsibilities. *"You can't destroy responsibility by ignoring it."*

Actor Leslie Sands wrote *No Man's Land*, the second episode of the series and the first to focus on Arthur Sugden. Here, the question for Sugden is how much responsibility a manager has for resolving the personal problems of employees. When the personal life affects the work performance where do you draw the line?

Staff Welfare officer Elliott is mentioned in this episode and appears (played by Tenniel Evans) in next week's episode *Costigan's Rocket*.

2 November 1963 *Costigan's Rocket*.

Writer Edmund Ward. Director John Nelson Burton.

"I ought to have a red light on this ladder, the speed I've been moving." Costigan.

Patrick Wymark (John Wilder). Jack Watling (Don Henderson). Gerald James (Harry Costigan). Sean Lynch (Charlie Barnes). Tenniel Evans (James Elliott). Brian Murphy (Sorbo). Jo Rowbottom (Maureen Costigan). Larry Dann (Dennis). Brian Haynes (Billy Bennett). Gerald C Lawson (Pop Prendergast, Night Watchman). Dickie Owen (Hiram Thomas).

Returning from the first season episode, *Has Anyone Seen Costigan?* elusive maintenance man Costigan (Gerald James) needs to pay for his daughter's forthcoming wedding and becomes a human dynamo (*"overtime Costigan, that's what we call him"*). When his friend, Pop Prendergast (Gerald C. Lawson) wins a greyhound in a raffle, Costigan establishes a syndicate to train and run the dog using the firms social club facilities.

When Costigan is quoted in the local paper saying that the dog, *"is twice as fast as the Sovereign."* When he sees the story, Wilder tells Don Henderson to find a good taxidermist, *"If the dog wins – fine! But if the dog loses, I want one stuffed greyhound and one stuffed welfare officer on that wall!"*

The episode has an impressive cast. Gerald James had a lengthy career and was memorable as the ghost hunter Tully in the second *Sapphire and Steel* story (1979). His daughter Maureen is played by Jo Rowbottom, who would go on to star opposite James Beck in *Romany Jones* (1973), while her fiancé was played by Larry Dann, later to star in Stephen Weeks' *Ghost Story* (1974) and as Sgt Alec Peters in *The Bill* (1984-1992). Dann had appeared in several productions at Joan Littlewood's Theatre Workshop, at the Theatre Royal Stratford East, as did Brian Murphy (later of *George and Mildred* fame) who plays one of the syndicate. Hiram Thomas, a gambler trying muscle in on the action is played by Dickie Owen (dubbed *Ickie Dickie Owen* by Forrest J Ackerman for his role as the Mummy in Hammer's *Curse of The Mummy's Tomb*). This episode has what must be the longest number of contractual plugs of the series. Apart from Patrick Wymark's usual nod to the Governors of the Royal Shakespeare Company, the end-titles also cite Gerald James (now appearing in the Harry Secombe Musical "*Pickwick*" at the Saville Theatre), Brian Murphy (now appearing in "*Oh What A Lovely War*" at the Wyndham's Theatre*), Tenniel Evans (now appearing in "*Portrait of Murder*" at the Savoy Theatre), Larry Dann (now appearing in "*Oh, What A Lovely War*" at the Wyndham's Theatre). * *Oh, What A Lovely War* opened at the Theatre Royal Stratford in March 1963, and transferred to Wyndham's Theatre in the West End in June 1963.

19 November 1963 *The Thing About Auntie.*

Writer Raymond Bowers. Director Geoffrey Nethercott.

"Such is the way of the righteous. They're never secret. They never even move secretly. Instead, they publicly suspect, apparently confirm, and if you don't watch the bastards, they prove whatever they want, whenever they want, right or wrong." John Wilder

Patrick Wymark   (John Wilder). Barbara Murray (Pamela Wilder). Robert Urquhart (Henry Forbes). Jack Watling (Don Henderson)

William Devlin(Sir Gerald Merle) Tom Criddle (Montgomery Roberts)

The episode introduces William Devlin as Sir Gerald Merle, a Labour MP and director of several companies including Scott Furlong's bankers. Wilder describes the MP to Henderson as *"warden of his parish church and a self-appointed keeper of the nation's conscience."*

Merle's long-term plan is exposed when the Chairman of Scott Furlong dies. With a general election looming, Merle cannot stand for Chairman. If *"the socialists"* won, he would be ruled out as Minister of Aviation if he was Chairman of a plane manufacturer. But if they didn't win, Merle would have nothing, unless he had the new Chairman of Scott Furlong in his pocket. The key to this is proving (or insinuating) that Pamela Wilder is having an affair with Henry "Auntie" Forbes.

Raymond Bowers depicts Merle as glib and pious, approving Wilder's decision not to close the factory on Sir Charles' death. *"Sir Charles would have deplored that. The sound of the man is in those engines you hear. That is His voice."*

But Merle is also calculating. In a series of cross-cutting scenes Merle interrogates Henry Forbes and Wilder explains Merles' thought processes to Henderson; *"Problem of conscience for a man of integrity. Is it deceitful to ask a question when you already know the answer? Solution? Mention both."*

1963 was, of course the year that "sex began" (as Philip Larkin put it) but it's still surprising to hear the veiled speculation about whether Forbes is homosexual (although *"The thing"* about Auntie is never named outright) and whether Wilder should be forced to dismiss him because of its then-illegality. *"What if it were true,"* Pamela Wilder asks, *"You might as well be expected to sack half the country."* Wilder responds that *"I thought it was a minority deviation,"* and Pamela says there is gossip about lots of people, *"I even ran into hints about you before I married you."*

The episode is equally frank in discussing Wilder's infidelity. *"I transgress within accepted rules,"* he tells Pamela, *"I've chosen a person outside my married life, who can't possibly embarrass my professional life…and I'm never seen with her at places or on occasions when I should only be seen with my wife."*

Foreshadowing, *The Power Game*, Pamela asks if the same rules would apply if she were to transgress. *"They're the only ones that work"* Wilder replies.

Bowers' script has more twists and turns than an episode of *Mission Impossible.* As well as trying to unravel the true intent behind Merle's insinuations (it suits Merle's purposes more for a heterosexual Forbes to be having an affair with Pamela), Wilder must also devise a counter-strategy. Much of this is delivered by Geoffrey Nethercott in technically complicated scenes where Wilder bathes and dresses (a cufflink flying off into the air at one point). The strain seems to show in the surviving export prints (on DVD). During part 3, Merle's name is overdubbed on Wymark's lips during a shaving sequence. In the next scene, a line of Henderson's dialogue is overdubbed (presumably because Jack Watling said *"India and Istanbul"* in the wrong order). A few minutes later, Merle corrects Pamela over "Pakistan" and "India", although since Pamela is being flippant it's difficult to tell if this is a scripted moment or a deft recovery by the two actors.

Whatever it originally sounded like, it was picked up in a newspaper review the next day which remarked that, *"It isn't often that you hear prompting in TV drama these days, but unless some other technical fault was responsible the prompter's services were required on more than one occasion."* Saying the cast delivered an otherwise above-average episode, the reviewer admitted that, *"towards the end I began to feel that the workings of the mind of the scheming Sir Gerald were far too complicated to be explained in a mere 50 minutes."*

The offscreen death of Sir Charles Elbertson is revealed in an amusingly unsentimental manner. Wilder arrives an hour late for the Chairman's birthday party, satisfied that Merle will be even later. Don Henderson meets him at the door to say that Sir Charles has died. *"Just Merle's luck,"* says Wilder, *"The one time he's late and his host is in no position to know anything about it."*

Born in Aberdeen in 1911, 22-year-old William Devlin had stunned audiences in 1934, as one of the youngest actors to play King Lear. Critic James Agate wrote that, *"His understanding of the text and his sense of beauty are everywhere apparent."* (Devlin would return to *Lear* at least five times). At 25, Devlin played French statesman Georges Clemenceau aged 30 to 80 in *The Tiger* by Reginald Berkeley. When wartime bomb damage closed the Old Vic, Devlin led the company performing at the Bristol Old Vic. Paul Hopkins recalls Devlin playing Dogberry in *Much Ado About Nothing "greeted with gleeful recognition,"* wearing a Civil Defence uniform and arriving on a bicycle.

In 1946 Devlin invited the then-unknown Kenneth Connor to join the company. Connor would later play Launcelot Gobbo, opposite Newton Blick in the 1953 production of *The Merchant of Venice* where Wymark made one of his earliest appearances. When the London Old Vic was finally rebuilt, Devlin opened with Peggy Ashcroft and Roger Livesey on November 14, 1950, in *"Twelfth Night"*. In the same year, Devlin appeared in Disney's *Treasure Island*.

In 1957, Devlin was re-united with stage director Henry Cass, playing Kurt Urach in *Blood of the Vampire* and in May 1958, William Devlin starred as Mr Herrick, headmaster of the Richard Pater Secondary Modern School in the BBC TV series *The Common Room*. Dealing with the problems of the staff and pupils of a comprehensive school rather than a grammar school or public school was as progressive, in its own way, as ATV later setting a series in a factory.

26 November 1963. *The Cat's Away.*

Writer John Finch. Director Hugh Rennie.

Reginald Marsh   (Arthur Sugden). Jack Watling (Don Henderson).
John Junkin (Dusty Miller). Elizabeth Begley (Margie Thomas).
Sheila Raynor (Mary Sugden). Norma Ronald (Kay Lingard).
Anthea Wyndham (Pat Henderson) Ray Mort (Jack Brough). Simon
Oates (Tim Driver)

Broadcast on the Tuesday following the assassination of John F.
Kennedy, this episode may have provided some relief from the grim
international events, although the sombre tone of the conclusion
may also have caught the mood of the times.

Wilder is in Australia negotiating a licensing agreement and in a
deliberate snub to Sugden, puts floundering Sales Manager Don
Henderson in charge. Wilder has also brought in efficiency
consultants. Sugden must deal with the consequent labour unrest
while trying to get away to see his dying sister.

Writer John Finch (*Sam, A Family at War*) had been marketing
manager for a heavy engineering firm and illustrates the panic which
would spread through the shopfloor when 'time-and-motion'
consultants were brought in, creating the fear of redundancies.
Although Sugden thinks the consultants may have some good ideas,
he can't spare the time to work with them after Henderson brings
forward the delivery date for an order. The ticking clock of a dying
sister tempts Sugden to let Henderson deal with the looming
problems. As his secretary Margie says when he puts off leaving the
office, "*They wouldn't do it for you.*"

John Junkin as Dusty Rhodes (from the first series) shows the union
convenor being a vital part of industrial relations, warning
management that the rumours on the shopfloor could spark
unofficial strike action. Ernie Lucas from *No Man's Land* provides a
contrasting view, as someone who knew Sugden as an apprentice
with the younger workers who just see Sugden as management.

Consultant Tim Driver (Simon Oates, later of *Doomwatch*) views Sugden as a familiar *"type"*; someone with a vested interest in keeping things as they are.

Pat Henderson (Anthea Wyndham) reminds us of the Board-level view of Sugden. She recalls him as, *"That cute little man with the accent...frightfully out of place at the Wilders"*. When Henderson says some people think Sugden should have been deputising for Wilder (*"He's a pretty gen bloke y'know"*) she protests, *"Oh, but Darling. The background!"*.

On a nostalgic note, Sugden first learns his sister has been hospitalised by letter. His brother-in-law only telephones when the situation becomes urgent. In 1963, 50% of households did not have a telephone, but you could post a letter on a Sunday evening in the expectation that it would be delivered by first post the next morning (the Post Office had only stopped Christmas Day deliveries three years earlier!).

On the page it may seem that events are stopping Sugden from seeing his dying sister, but Reginald Marsh gives an understated reaction when he first learns she's been hospitalised (*"Even though you're expecting it, it still comes as a shock"*) and his low-key response to her death could be interpreted another way. Sugden has used events in the factory to avoid a final parting.

3 December 1963 *Strings in Whitehall.*

Writer Wilfred Greatorex. Director Quentin Lawrence.

"Always keep in with politicians. It's a hateful job, but unfortunately, very necessary." John Wilder.

Patrick Wymark   (John Wilder). Jack Watling (Don Henderson). Donald Morley (Steve Miller). Richard Vernon (Keith Saville MP). George Woodbridge (Geoffrey Drake MP). Norma Ronald (Kay Lingard). Malcolm Webster (Tony Maccabee). Bruce Boa (Vega).

Wilder is aiming for a knighthood, *"pulling every string in Whitehall"* according to Keith Saville MP (Richard Vernon). Public Relations Officer Steve Miller (Donald Morley) is writing magazine profiles of Wilder and has arranged a TV interview, while Wilder himself is excitedly showing minister Geoffrey Drake (George Woodbridge) around the factory.

Saville (Richard Vernon) claims he can make an introduction to South American airline owner Vega, even though Scott Furlong's South American agent says Vega is anti-British. Saville says Vega respects Calvo, a contact of Saville's with route-licensing influence over in Vega's country. Calvo is definitely not anti-British and both he and Vega are over in Paris. Against Wilder's orders, Don Henderson authorises a flight to Paris for Saville. To Wilder's surprise, Saville is successful although at the cost of bringing Vega and his entire family to Britain.

Vega (Bruce Boa) offers to buy three Sovereign's but needs help with finance, claiming Scott Furlong's French rival, Aviation Chasse, has offered him ten year's credit. Forrest (Julian Somers) of the British Export Credit Guarantee Department says that Vega already owes on the planes he's currently flying. They will give Vega seven year's credit on condition that his own Government backs him. Wilder asks the aviation minister to put pressure on the Department to give more support, threatening to change his speech in the scheduled TV interview to one critical of the Government.

"The Disillusionment of Don Henderson" might have been an alternate title for this episode. Following the previous week's episode, The Cat's Away where Henderson was left in charge of the factory, the hero-worshiping Henderson sees a less congenial side of Wilder. Obsessed with his pursuit of a knighthood, Wilder berates Henderson for not being able to make a decision without consulting Wilder, but when he learns that Henderson has sent salesman Tony Maccabee to meet Saville says, *"I thought I made it perfectly clear that I was to be consulted before you sales geniuses went swanning off with professional politicians!"*

Wilder then tries to over-rule his decision to send Saville to Paris. When Henderson protests that Wilder had complained no-one in the factory could make a decision, Wilder replies, *"You made two! Both of them wrong!"*

In fact, it's too late to recall Saville and Henderson's instinct proves right (or lucky). Vega wants to buy three Sovereign's. Wilder swiftly deconstructs events; *"First we get all this intelligence about how well-suited his lines are to the Sovereign. Then this spiel about how he's anti-British. Then this 'secret' trip to Paris revealed in every aviation magazine in Europe. Then this story about how he'll only come (to England) if we bring his family. All objections meant to imply his lack of interest in the Sovereign, but such minor ones...do you know I think we might have a customer after all!"* Concluding that Vega was playing hard-to-get, Wilder takes over negotiations.

Scott Furlong's representative in South America is swiftly dropped so that Wilder can offer Vega the lucrative agency (back-dated to before he signs the agreement) and the only final obstacle to the sale of three planes is whether the British Government will extend enough credit to Vega.

When the Export Credit Guarantee Department (which exists to promote UK exports) fails to meet Vega's terms, Wilder must decide whether to risk his personal ambitions. Wilder has been lobbying for a knighthood, and is scheduled to appear on a TV show where he will praise Government policy on the Aviation industry.

Wilders' TV speech refers obliquely to the 1957 decision to end defence spending on fighter aircraft and the subsequent consolidation following the appointment in 1959 of Duncan Sandys as Aviation Minister. *"The Government's idea to rationalise the industry - to have fewer, but bigger firms - was first mooted about two years ago."* In the first draft of his speech, Wilder had said that despite initial doubts he now believes the Government was right to force the airline companies to merge. *"It was the only way to make us competitive with the rest of the world."* When Public Relations

Officer Steve Miller (Donald Morley) called it a surprising view, Wilder replied, *"There's no point in stating the obvious."*

However, on the eve of the TV show, Wilder redrafts his speech in an attempt to force the Minister to ensure the ECG gives extra credit to Vega. He now says the Government has shown insufficient support for the industry. It is this speech that leads to Henderson's final disillusionment. *"We're about to see a great man throw away something he's worked for all his life!"* Henderson tell Saville. With the Vega deal all but lost, Saville offers to bet five pounds that Wilder will revert to his original speech. *"John Wilder's never thrown away anything in his life that could be to his advantage!"* Henderson accepts the bet, convinced that Wilder is acting on principle.

In the TV studio, Patrick Wymark builds the tension, pausing at the point where he has to decide which version of the speech to deliver, before reverting to the original; *"I feel sure that it was right. It was the only way to make us more competitive."*

As Saville collects his fiver from Henderson, the live TV interview ends, although the programme continues. As Wilfred Greatorex describes it: *"Wilder stalks out from the set. He catches Miller's eye. There is a moment of truth between them. Wilder stalks past him. A moment of defeat - but he's still Napoleon. He is shushed as he goes for making too noisy an exit."*

Originally titled *"Strings in Government"*, the 12th episode of the series was rehearsed between 12th and 23rd November, and recorded on 25th November 1963, for transmission on 3rd December. Wilfred Greatorex's script strengthens the understated relationship between Wilder and his secretary Kay Lingard. The stage direction says, *"As Wilder passes her on his way out he pauses, expecting her to vet his appearance. She plucks some tiny speck from his jacket shoulder and he mumbles what might be taken for a thank you."* On screen, Patrick Wymark straightens his tie, raises his neck and turns his head away as Norma Ronald brushes his shoulder three times. Wymark looks down at himself, smooths his lapels and smiles at her before grunting, *"Hmnh.."*

The script notes that, *"Kay pretends not to notice Henderson's hurt pride"* when Wilder tells him to try making a decision for himself. As Wilder leaves for his meeting with the Minister, Don Henderson complains to Public Relations Officer Steve Miller that the meeting is more important to Wilder than the Vega sale, then quietens down as he notices Miss Lingard pointedly pretending not to hear his criticism of their boss. Don Henderson is standing next to Miss Lingard as Steve Miller hands her the article about Wilder he's arranged in advance of the TV interview. Jack Watling glances down at the paper as if trying to read it. Norma Ronald turns to look at Watling who glances up, realising she's seen him as she pulls the paper away. *"Perhaps you'll be interviewed on television one day, Mr Henderson,"* she says with a warm smile. The scene builds the picture of Kay Lingard as the firm but humane support for Wilder. This will reach its peak in *The Power Game* episodes where Pamela finally leaves Wilder and Miss Lingard holds Wilder's personal life together.

The episode sees strong performances from Wymark and Henderson, as well as Richard Vernon playing the enigmatic MP. Wilfred Greatorex describes Saville as, *"45, sharp of eye. A man of the world who is suspicious of it. A restless contact man travelling the uneasy boundary between politics and business. Haunted by a fear of self-corruption. Zealous, ambitious and has a conscience."* Saville has referred obliquely to Wilder at a Ministry reception as a *"pompous little Napoleon"* saying the industry needs men of "integrity and foresight", while Wilder is suspicious of backbench MPs with other interests *("I'd like to see him make out on £1,750 a year"* Saville retorts (the equivalent of about £38,300 a year in 2021 – MP's actually received around £81,000 in 2021). In some ways Saville seems less of a stand-in for the self-satisfied Sir Gerald, and more of a prototype for Peter Jeffrey's character in the third series.

As well as Saville, Wilder has to deal with other politicians. There is the "territorial MP" for Scott-Furlong, the opposition (ie Labour, at this time) back-bencher whose constituency has the factories and the 20,000 jobs for which Wilder is responsible. Wilder also charms the Minister Geoffrey Drake (George Woodbridge). This is a different character from the aviation minister played by Robert Sansom in the first episode. Possibly the Junior Aviation Minister*, called Geoffrey Hawkins in the draft script and described as, *"52, a stylish West Countryman with the brisk managerial flair of the new generation of Minister of the Crown. He clearly has much in common with Wilder."*

* The actual Junior Aviation Minister at the time was Neil Marten MP.

One point of interest is that the character of Tony Maccabee returns from *Any More For The Skylark*, played once again by Malcolm Webster, an actor with a disconcerting resemblance to Jack Watling. In the script, the character is *"Robin Chapman, salesman prone to making ghastly boobs"*, which sounds a lot like Nigel Carr from The Old Boy Network.

This episode sees the first mention of Scott Furlong's new chairman when Wilder's secretary Miss Lingard tells him that he has an appointment with Sir Gordon

This episode also sees the first mention of Wilder's son when he tells Vega that his son is away at school. Vega asks if it is a grammar school. Wilder says, *"No, no, it's a public school. Grammar School's tend to produce a different type. More ruthless."*

Many thanks to Victoria Bennett of the BFI Library Special Collections for arranging to view the rehearsal script from the Wilfred Greatorex Collection.

10 December 1963 *The Best Of Friends*

Writer Lewis Davidson Director James Ferman.

"There isn't time to repair anything these days. If something doesn't work you just chuck it out and get a replacement unit" Henry Forbes

Reginald Marsh (Arthur Sugden). Robert Urquhart (Henry Forbes). Bernard Brown (Simon Wanleigh). Zena Walker (Anne Wanleigh). Brian McDermott (Terry). Fred Ferris (Sam Adams).

Co- pilot Simon Wanleigh's marital stress triggers an eye injury which almost causes a crash when he misreads the Sovereign's altimeter. Where should a manager draw a line between the professional and personal?. Air crews look out for each other but Henry Forbes feels he's spent his life being *"a combination social worker and money lender."*

Bernard Brown had played Wanleigh in the first episode, and would go on to appear in countless TV series including *Out of the Unknown,* and two episodes of *Inspector Morse.*

Zena Walker was married to Robert Urquhart at the time. She would play Elizabeth Cromwell opposite Richard Harris in *Cromwell* (1970).

17 December 1963 *How Do You Vote?*

Writer David Weir. Director John Cooper.

"Wilder's no fool. Popularly he's the wonder boy of British aviation. He wants to gamble on the difference between solid commercial success and a spectacular winner." Sir Gordon Revidge.

Patrick Wymark. (John Wilder). Jack Watling (Don Henderson). Alan Tilvern (Dr. Katz). Norman Tyrrell (Sir Gordon Revidge). Anthony Sharp (Lord Teddington). Martin Wyldeck (William Keeble). Douglas Muir (Tom Bancroft). Tom Macaulay (Reginald

Cunliffe). Dennis Ramsden (Lt. Commander Cooke). Eric Thompson (Phillip Hammond). Norma Ronald (Kay Lingard).

With fifteen of the first thirty Sovereigns unsold, Wilder wants to borrow money from Elbertson's merchant bank to build another twelve. Scott Furlong will only break-even when forty-two Sovereigns are sold. It would have been too great a risk to build that many at the start. Thirty Sovereigns was a compromise between the limit of their capital and credit and the break-even figure. Even now, the additional debt would be crippling unless Scott Furlong can sell forty-two planes. Wilder says the extra twelve planes will put them ahead of their French competitor. *"There can only be one winner in a race like this."*

This audacious episode from "Series Story Consultant" David Weir brings back rival directors Keeble (Martin Wyldeck) and Cunliffe (Tom Macaulay) and the clueless Lieutenant Commander Cooke (Dennis Ramsden) from Wilder's first episode *Too Much to Lose*. Weir also introduces the new Chairman, Sir Gordon Revidge (Norman Tyrrell). From *A Question of Sources*, Press Relations Officer Simon Stride is referenced while Douglas Muir returns from that same episode, as Technical Director Tom Bancroft. Weir creates a sense of *The Plane Makers* becoming an integrated series rather than a collection of one-off plays.

Wilder sacks computer programmer Philip Hammond (Eric Thompson) after an altercation at an office party. Hammond's section head is Doctor Katz (Alan Tilvern) a board member previously in favour of Wilder's plan to build more Sovereign's. Telling Wilder that, *"I hire and dismiss my own people"* the scientist insists on bringing Hammond's case up at the Board meeting. As tempers flare, the disagreement escalates into a vote of confidence in Wilder's leadership.

Revidge is introduced in a meeting with Lord Teddington (Anthony Sharpe) of Elbertson's Merchant Bank ("Teddy" was played by Dennis Cowles in the first episode *Too Much to Lose)*. Following

Lord Elbertson's death in *The Thing About Auntie*, neither Wilder nor Sir Gerald Merle succeeded him to the Chair of Scott Furlong. Instead, Revidge (who already represents the bank on other boards) has been put place as "Wilder's safety valve."

The bankers' conversation reminds us there are three companies in the Scott Furlong group and the balance of power is very delicate. Revidge acknowledges that Wilder is "a very valuable man", but warns Teddington that if the Scott Furlong board agree to ask for the money, refusal by Elbertson's would cause bad feeling and be used as an excuse for any lack of success with the Sovereign.

48-year-old Norman Tyrrell had made his stage debut aged 18 in a production of *Murder in The Cathedral*. In the 1950's he appeared in several Bristol Old Vic productions before starring as Sid Kittle in R.F.Delderfield's 1956 BBC series *The Recording Angels* . After *The Plane Makers* Tyrrell appeared in a number of film and TV productions such as Jim Allen's *Days of Hope*. He also performed with the Royal Shakespeare Company, playing Bardolph in the 1979 production of *The Merry Wives of Windsor* (with John Woodvine as Falstaff). One of his last TV roles was as a witness, Mr Harbin in the 1997 *House Calls* episode of *A Touch of Frost*.

Tyrrell makes a quiet but firm contribution to the board room scenes. When Wilder shouts that, *"I run this company"* Revidge smoothly corrects him; *"WE run this company – the directors."*

Weir explores several issues in the board room scenes which fuel the explosive confrontations. For Dr Katz there is a humanitarian issue of whether Hammond should lose his job because of an off-duty argument with his managing director. Married to this is his own pride as to hiring and firing his section staff and the possible impact on his own productivity of losing a key employee. For Wilder the issue is one of respect – in this he is supported by fellow director Keble who says, *"The authority of the Managing Director is very important. I don't think Wilder is morally right, but I support him."* Ironically, although Revidge uses his casting vote to support

Hammond's dismissal, Wilder has been swayed by the opposing view. Once he has won the vote of confidence, Wilder proposes to apologise to Hammond and reinstate him. At this point Weir sharply underlines Revidge's formality. As Chairman he enforces the Board's decision and refuses to let Wilder go back on his decision to sack Hammond.

The role of Doctor Katz provides a rare opportunity to see Alan Tilvern playing something more sustained than the heavies he was usually cast as. Katz is a technical specialist who is well aware that he has made millions for the company and is unafraid to speak his mind. During the boardroom scenes, director John Cooper shoots Katz in isolation, from above, whilst Wilder is seen from a variety of angles in conjunction with other directors. The effect lends Katz a magisterial air, deliberately pressing home his points while Wilder struggles to brush the issue under the carpet.

Weir and director John Cooper also deliver a compelling scene between Martin Wyldeck as the poker-faced Keble and Patrick Wymark, when Wilder tries to win his support for the extra planes before the board meeting. Sitting on opposite sides of the aisle in an empty plane, Keble accuses Wilder of, *"Only telling me now because you've heard I'm opposed to the idea. Otherwise you'd have done your usual trick of pushing ahead and asking afterwards."* Wilder concedes this is true, but tells Keble, *"I ran this firm long before it was part of a group – and very successfully. The Sovereign is a result of what you call my pushing. Somebody has to make decisions. A lot of people's livelihoods depend on it. And I'm very good at it!"*

Weir and Cooper give us a taste of the ebb and flow of argument around the table without going into so much detail that it becomes tedious. We are reminded that this is not so much an argument about building the planes as an argument about asking Elbertson's to lend more money. Sensing a tactical mistake by Revidge, Wilder glances at his watch and pauses to phone his son's school and pass on the message that he won't be taking him out for tea.

Wilder had been anxious to conclude the Board meeting before 2.30 as he planned to drive over to his son's new boarding school. It's two months since he's seen Nigel (first mentioned in *Strings In Whitehall*) and while Pamela thinks he's too young to live away from home, *"He needs a crammer if he's going to stand a chance with his common entrance."* Wymark quietly illuminates what seems like a chink in Wilder's armour as he confides to Henderson with a blend of pride and embarrassment that Nigel has already won a prize during his first term. But when Henderson enthusiastically asks what for, Wilder admits the prize is for painting. Half-humorous, half-serious, Wilder reassures Henderson *"He'll get over it (painting).... He'd better!"*

Wilder's son Nigel is never mentioned in subsequent series of *The Plane Makers* and T*he Power Game*".

24 December 1963 *One Out All Out.*

Writer Leslie Sands. Director Peter Sasdy.

"He's as sharp as a knife is our John Wilder. One of these days he'll cut his own throat." Arthur Sugden

Patrick Wymark . (John Wilder). Reginald Marsh (Arthur Sugden). Norman Tyrrell (Sir Gordon Revidge). Anthony Sharp (Lord Teddington). Tom Macaulay (Reginald Cunliffe). Dennis Ramsden (Lt. Commander Cooke). John Junkin (Dusty Miller). Bruce Beeby (George Chadwick). Royston Tickner (Nobby). Oliver MacGreevy (Charlie).

In the Christmas Eve episode, Wilder tells Sugden to start negotiations with the union over cancellation of the Red Major guided missile project. A small number of skilled men will be redundant, but they will soon find jobs elsewhere. Most of the men will be redeployed on the expanded Sovereign line. But when Elbertson's bank refuses to lend money for the Sovereigns, all 400 men from the Red Major project face redundancy.

Wilder admits to Sugden that the Red Major cancellation did not have Board approval *("I cut a few corners.")* They must work together to survive by provoking the threat of a strike by the whole workforce. The company is committed to deliver Sovereigns on contract, and cannot afford a strike. The Board will have to agree to move the 400 workers to the expanded Sovereign range, and Elbertson's will have to provide the cash to protect its existing investment.

At the board meeting, Cunliffe criticises Wilder for cancelling the Red Major project, rather than waiting for the Government to do so (as happened with the real-life Blue Streak and Black Prince rockets). This means they will get less compensation from the Government. Wilder argues that losing some compensation was a necessary cost of moving the workforce onto the project.

At the union meeting, Oliver MacGreevy (Housemartin in *The Ipcress File* and Santa Claus in *Tales from The Crypt*) is seen as Charlie a representative of the *"British Freedom Party"* haranguing the members. Union Convenor Dusty Miller (John Junkin) returns from *The Cat's Away.* Responding to a complaint from Nobby (Royston Tickner) about union inactivity over the draft in his workshop, he challenges him to volunteer for the union. *"You wouldn't, would you? Because you can't spare the overtime! Two hours a week, me, filling in forms for blokes like you!"*

George Chadwick (Bruce Beeby), a paid union employee, warns the members against taking official action because that is now union policy – talk first, strike only if necessary. John Wilder explains to Sugden that, *"There's a General Election looming. The kid gloves are on. You and I are in support of very different parties, but mine are not the only image makers."*

This episode shows a more diabolical aspect of Revidge when Lord Teddington (Anthony Sharpe) tells him that a lot rests on his decisions; *"Whenever someone like you pauses to strike a match, someone's livelihood depends on it."* And Revidge considers the match and then strikes it with delight.

The sub-plot of this episode deals with Margie (Elizabeth Begley), Sugden's secretary who is trying to conceal a disabling joint problem in her hand. In a previous episode we learned that she now faces an hour's bus journey after Sugden's relocation to head office. Asked about her Christmas plans she says that she usually goes with Norah Grant from accounts to the Grey Timbers Guest House in Warwickshire, which runs a house party. While expensive, *"It's worth it when you've no home of your own."* When Sugden forces her to see a Doctor, she's diagnosed with sinovitis (an inflammation of the joints) and is immediately sent for an operation.

In this Christmas Eve episode, there is no fake snow (as is now de rigueur in any TV show set at Christmas) possibly because the long freeze of 1962/1963 had removed any romanticism about snow. Balloons and streamers are seen on the canteen walls and Christmas cards can be glimpsed on shelves. Sugden persuades the Board to postpone any layoffs until after Christmas and also invites Margie to spend Christmas with his family. The episode ends by zooming in on a company Christmas Card from Wilder to Sugden.

31 December 1963 *Loved He Not Honours More.*

Writer Raymond Bowers. Director Hugh Rennie.

"I could not love thee dear, so much, loved I not honour more"
Richard Lovelace, Royalist poet.

Patrick Wymark (John Wilder). Barbara Murray (Pamela Wilder)
Jack Watling (Don Henderson). Robert Urquhart (Henry Forbes)
Norman Tyrrell (Sir Gordon Revidge). William Devlin (Sir Gerald Merle). John Wentworth (Telliter). Harold Innocent (Bessiter).
Norma Ronald (Kay Lingard).

This New Year's Eve episode begins in early December as Revidge and Merle plot to remove John Wilder. They know that if Wilder is awarded a knighthood in the New Year's Honours list, it will be politically impossible to remove him. So Revidge plans to remove Wilder before the honours list is published, gambling that it will cause the offer of a knighthood to be withdrawn. So confident is Sir Gordon that he declines an invitation to Wilder's party, saying, *"Executioners seldom accept invitations from their victims, John."*

Revidge proposes to offer Wilder the Chairmanship of a subsidiary out in Australia so it looks like a promotion instead of a sacking. If he refuses the bank will starve Scott Furlong of funds and Wilder will inevitably be removed by a vote of no-confidence.

Wilder tries to stave off any Scott Furlong board meeting until after the 19th December, the latest date when he can expect to receive a letter the offer of a knighthood. If Wilder does not receive an offer, he must keep that knowledge from Revidge long enough to develop some alternate defence. After New Year's Day, when the honours are announced, it will be open season on Wilder (protocol over such matters was then observed by political parties and the press).

Revidge confronts Merle over an article on Scott Furlong in left wing newspaper *The Globe*. Sir Gordon infers from the way Wilder's photo has increased in size between the first and final edition that the editor has been told to boost Wilder. Merle denies any involvement but Wilder is visited by union chief James Bessiter who implies that he influenced the newspaper article.

The cherubic Harold Innocent depicts Bessiter as a feline moderniser in a modish striped shirt. Calling Wilder, a *"beloved enemy"*, he credits Wilder with averting redundancies in the previous episode. When Wilder says Revidge believes that Wilder's actions could have ruined Scott Furlong, Bessiter characterises Sir Gordon as a witch doctor. *"Like all money men. He expects to find portents in statistics. He's no different from a stone age soothsayer, breaking bones, throwing the bits up in the air and expecting the Gods to blow them down in prophetic patterns. What Sir Gordon failed to consider was the driving power of determined men. He preferred to listen to some rattletrap gibbering computer"*

Bessiter expresses his support for Wilder. *"I know you're no philanthropist. You're a man whose whole record points to a man who gets things done by a kind of selfish brute force. A brute force that means constant dividends for shareholders that I don't give a damn about and constant wage packets for men that I do care about."*

Wilder tells Don Henderson that both union chief Bessiter and Merle the Labour MP are "old Wykehamists" (i.e., educated at Winchester College, the oldest public school in England) which he thinks *"a terrible waste of private money."* In reality, Hugh Gaitskell, former leader of the Labour Party, had been educated at Winchester, as had Richard Crossman and Sir Kenneth Younger (Labour MP for Grimsby when Wymark lived there). This reflects the reality that a privately educated elite were represented across the political spectrum in the 1960's, although perhaps not as dominantly as today.

Although Merle is a Labour MP, he and Bessiter have opposing views on the Honours List. Bessiter says, *"I believe men should honour one another individually and personally, not by some feudally derived committee."* Merle replies, *"I accepted mine, Jimmy, because I thought it less ostentatious to accept."* Bessiter then pointedly tells Revidge and Merle that if we are to have an honours system, he insists as a representative of half a million union members that he should influence who should be on it.

Barbara Murray had originally been offered only three episodes of *The Plane Makers* as Pamela Wilder, but once the future of the character was secured, she set about fleshing out the character. Wilfred Greatorex confirmed that, *"We'd hold long discussions about how the character would be expanded. Barbara suggested that we add a sense of humour, and that a woman like Pamela*

Wilder would want to improve her existence instead of sticking in her shell."

In this episode Pamela's initiative delivers a positive outcome for her husband. Wilder holds a quarter of a million pounds worth of shares in Scott Furlong, but had also made Pamela a gift of £3000 worth of shares ten years ago in exchange for the money to put a deposit on their house. Telliter (John Wentworth) a financial advisor recommended by Henry Forbes, informs her the shares are now worth a quarter of a million pounds. Together, she and John Wilder own 15% of the Scott Furlong stock. Wilder had earlier told Pamela that Elbertson's have a controlling 27% interest in Scott Furlong – both a strength and a weakness if the share price falls. If his back is against the wall, he will start selling his shares in order to depress the price. Seeking to defend her own unexpected fortune, Pamela instructs Telliter to sell her shares as quickly as possible. This sudden sell-off unnerves Sir Gordon who thinks he has misjudged Wilder's recklessness and agrees to back down. 21st Century viewers might be appalled by the unliberated portrayal of Pamela - the fact that she has been kept in ignorance and is like a child playing with a new toy. But, the picture of a woman discovering her power is heartening, and the overall comic effect of Barbara Murray's scenes with Patrick Wymark lift the episode. Pamela's final dissembling line to Wilder, *"Doesn't that make me your boss?"* hints at more to come.

7 January 1964 *A Bunch of Fives.*

Writer Peter Nichols. Director James Ferman.

Jack Watling (Don Henderson) Robert Urquhart (Henry Forbes) Glyn Houston (Colin Stock) Wendy Craig (Jane Gaunt) Barrie Ingham (David Fleet) Anthea Wyndham (Pat Henderson) Frederick Bartman (Christopher Chappell) Fred Ferris (Same Adams) Freddie Earlle (Mac) Neville Smith (Ken Mason)

A relatively rare contribution by playwright Peter Nichols to someone else's format, this was written before the staging of his 1967 hit, *A Day In The Death of Joe Egg*.

With his last sales effort a failure, Don Henderson (Jack Watling) leads a sales team into Europe. Henderson is unamused when company Stewardess Jane Gaunt (Wendy Craig) becomes the focus of romantic rivalry between Co-pilot Glyn Houston and publicist Barrie Ingham

To sell the plane, Henderson needs engineers to explain the technical aspects (including Neville Smith, who would go on to write the 1971 Albert Finney movie *Gumshoe*), salesmen, a publicist to drum up interest, pilots to fly the plane and a stewardess to dispense hospitality.

Co-pilot Colin Stock (Glyn Houston) is generally competent and genial, but apt to threaten and dispense the bunch of fives at various points throughout the episode. Stewardess Jane Gaunt (Wendy Craig), who becomes the focus of his stifled extramarital longings, is a young widow now trapped at home with her mother in a premature middle-age.

Publicist Barrie Ingham - part of the new, upwardly mobile working class, dispensing champagne to the press of Milan - may seem the most enviable but even he reveals hidden insecurities. He is acutely aware of having no real marketable skill compared to pilots like Stock, part of a class that, "*spends all our time trying to keep our jobs or trying to get someone else's.*" Stock's volatility puts his job on the line, but (In a reflection of how things were in the 1960's) Jane is warned by Henderson to keep Colin happy for the duration of the trip.

7 January 1964　　　*The Smiler*

Nb: transmission time moves from 8pm to 9pm replacing The Naked City.

Writer John O'Toole.　　Director Bill Stewart.

Patrick Wymark　(John Wilder). Reginald Marsh (Arthur Sugden). James Villiers (Harvey Graves). Patrick Magee (William Breen).Elizabeth Begley (Margie Thomas). Sheila Raynor (Mary Sugden). Norma Ronald (Kay Lingard). Ray Mort (Jack Brough). Pat Nye (Miss Fitzmeyer). Gabriella Licudi (Lamorna). Ronald Ibbs (Jamieson). Allan McClelland (Jephson).

"He's good natured. He's cheeky and he's brilliant. And I like him. But he's got to go!" John Wilder

Wilder orders Sugden to find a role for Harvey Graves, nephew of the hapless Wing-Commander Cooke, who has been let go from a rival aircraft maker. Wilder thinks Graves knowledge from his previous employers would be useful. Although regarded with suspicion by workforce and managers, Graves quickly begins making practical suggestions to improve production.

Sugden dislikes the manner in which men of his background *"don't just come out and say they want a job. They become available"*, but he is won round when Graves uses his connections to get through to a civil servant who has been avoiding Wilder.

Harvey is smart enough to detect *"the normal procedure for an unwanted man,"* when Breen tries to fob him off on supervisor Jack Brough (suspecting that Brough will pass him on to someone else) and demonstrates natural authority in turning the tables on Breen. Within a couple of days, Harvey has an office and a secretary, is wandering around the factory suggesting improvements and begins dating Wilder's formidable secretary Kay Lingard (Norma Ronald).

Eventually, Wilder himself suspects that Harvey may still be working for his former employers, having used his guileless uncle as a route into Scott Furlong's trade secrets.

Urbane RADA graduate James Villiers plays the charming and ambiguous title role. He gets the most interesting line in the show when he stops short of revealing some gossip about *'poor Johnny Wilder'* to Miss Lingard, only saying Wilder *'has more guts and push than anyone I know. But John feels he's not quite accepted. We all have our dreams and John feels his spiritual home should be with the landed gentry.'*

John O'Toole had turned full-time writer in 1961 after a career in industry. His fourth play, *The Big Ride* (1962), had been set in an aero engine factory against a background of industrial unrest, so it's not surprising his expertise would be welcome in *The Plane Makers*. O'Toole would later write for the BBC soap opera *The Newcomers*.

21 January 1964   *In the Book.*

Writer Arthur Swinson.   **Director Dennis Vance.**

Patrick Wymark (John Wilder). Reginald Marsh (Arthur Sugden). Michael Gwynn (Jeremy Dobell). Anthony Marlowe (Sir Frank Bennington). Sheila Raynor (Mary Sugden). Elizabeth Begley (Margie Thomas). Norma Ronald (Kay Lingard). Noel Davis (Neil Ponsonby). Margaret Gordon (Corinne Dobell)   Alan Baulch (John Dobell) John Garvin (Mr. Evans). Julie Martin (Melanie). Geraldine Newman (Miss Fergusson).

"This isn't just an aircraft company you're dealing with. This is people's lives... reputations!" Arthur Sugden.

Jeremy Dobell has been commissioned by John Wilder to write a history of Scott Furlong. Wilder is pleased with the proof *("He's certainly got me taped")* but Arthur Sugden challenges the chapter about the Questor, a plane built in the 1930's when Sugden was an apprentice. Dobell has credited K.G Bennington with the project, but Sugden says the plane was the idea of works manager Arthur Hedges and Bennington fought against it. Unfortunately, Bennington's brother is managing Director of Anglo-Continental Airlines and Wilder hopes to sell five Sovereign's to the airline.

Arthur Swinson wrote over 300 radio, TV and theatre plays and over 30 books including *Writing for Television*, a 1955 textbook covering documentaries and talks as well as drama. Swinson wrote and produced the TV series *Private Investigator* (starring Douglas Muir - Tom Bancroft in *The Plane Makers*) and would go on to publish novelisations of ATV's *'Sergeant Cork'* as well as non-fiction such as *'The Great Air Race'*. At the time of *'In the Book'*, Swinson had just written *'Scotch On The Rocks'*, an account of the wartime wreck of the SS Politician on which *'Whisky Galore'* was based. He was therefore well qualified to write an episode which explored the difficult path of identifying a version of the truth which would be satisfying to all.

28 January 1964   *Miss Geraldine*

Writer John Gray.   **Director John Cooper.**

Marie Lohr (Miss Geraldine). Patrick Wymark (John Wilder). Robert Urquhart (Henry Forbes). Jeremy Burnham (Nigel Carr). Ruth Kettlewell (Harriet Duval). Norma Ronald (Kay Lingard).

Wilder takes personal charge when 69-year-old Miss Geraldine Pettifur (Marie Lohr) refuses to sell her family home so that Scott Furlong can extend its runway.

This very slight episode has Shakespearean or Chaucerian overtones as unstoppable force meets immovable object. Immensely rich, Miss Geraldine is nevertheless part of that generation of women whose dreams were shattered by the loss of a sweetheart in World War One. Her many complaints and battles with the neighbouring airfield are her sole amusement.

Wilder realises that he must be open and honest with Miss Geraldine. Giving her a tour of the airfield and her first flight on a plane, he tells pilot Henry Forbes that they must 'woo her'.

There appears to be an in-joke relating to the effects of Wymark's success as he declines milk for his tea, telling Miss Geraldine that he has recently realised he has to watch his weight.

The episode ends with the clear implication that Wilder has touched Miss Geraldine's heart and her head, as she negotiates a hard deal to sell her property and then phones her broker to put all her capital into Scott Furlong.

Australian-born Marie Lohr had a long stage career but had also starred in films such as *Went The Day Well* and *'South Riding*. Her godmother was Dame Madge Kendal, who had been the most successful actor to come out of Grimsby before Patrick Wymark.

4 February 1964 A *Condition of Sale*.

Writer Tony Williamson. Director James Ferman.

Reginald Marsh (Arthur Sugden). Norma Ronald (Kay Lingard). George A. Cooper (Sam Westcott). Lloyd Lamble (Geoffrey Lewis). Jack Watling (Don Henderson). Elizabeth Begley (Margie Thomas). Charles Lamb (Ted Castle). Douglas Blackwell (Jack Wilks). Douglas Hayes (Dave Richards). Raymond Mason (Bill Fenham). Paul Gillard (Jimmy). Walter Sparrow (Charlie). Michael Stainton (Smithy).

Wilder tells Arthur Sugden to have new and untested Mark Seven engines fitted to a Sovereign so that it can be flown to Rome for a demonstration. A flu epidemic has reduced the workforce, and Sugden must prepare the factory for this rush job before travelling to Manchester with Kay Lingard to negotiate with the engine manufacturers.

Sugden's secretary Margie succumbs to the flu, which has hit the Scott Furlong factory. With Wilder in Rome, his secretary Kay Lingard sends Margie home, offering to cover for Margie until personnel can sort out a replacement.

Sugden and Miss Lingard take the train to Manchester to negotiate with the sub-contractors, Sam Wescott (George A Cooper) and his technical director Geoffrey Lewis (Lloyd Lamble). Their objections are logical; Scott Furlong gave no indication that the engines would be needed so quickly. Crane Wescott have other customers who they need to supply. Their staff are tied to scheduled work. Above all, Crane Wescott has a reputation for quality. The engines need 600 hours of static proving on a test bed before they can be fitted to an aircraft.

Sugden proposes that they ship the engines back to Radley Heath, fit them onto the Sovereign and test the engines on the plane, but Wescott asks why they should risk their reputation to make Scott Furlong a quick profit.

When Sugden learns that Lewis has made a pass at Miss Lingard in her bedroom, he confronts Lewis who laughingly tells him to stop being so sanctimonious. Enraged, Sugden uses tactics previously suggested by Henderson, telling Wescott that unless they fit the Mark Seven engines, the firm will be out of the running for the military modification of the Sovereign. Ironically, while Lewis correctly guesses that Sugden is bluffing, Wescott suspects that John Wilder is behind the threat and takes it seriously.

Director James Ferman would go on to become Secretary of the British Board of Film Classification, so it's interesting to see how he deals with the assault on Miss Lingard. Earlier on, at the Crane Wescott factory, Lewis has taken Miss Lingard to his office to phone the hotel and book a table for dinner. As Miss Lingard moves to leave the office, Lewis discretely half blocks her path, saying it's a pity she and Sugden are staying only one night. There's a brief downward glance of displeasure on Norma Ronald's face before she smiles up at Lewis, continuing forward and telling him, *"Now we wouldn't want to out-stay our welcome, would we?"*

Later on, at the hotel restaurant, Sugden suggests she takes a break from minuting the meeting, so that he can continue the negotiation with Wescott off the record. Lewis suggests they go for a walk and accompanies Kay to her room so she can collect her coat. Lingard is confident enough to invite Lewis in while she repairs her lipstick, and ignores his attempt at flirting. When Lewis nods to the telephone and suggests they have drinks sent up to her room, Miss Lingard firmly rebuffs him saying, *"I don't think so."* As she tries to walk to the door, Lewis grabs hold of her and kisses her. At this point, the action cuts back to the restaurant with Sugden failing to convince Wescott.

As Sugden goes to reception to phone Henderson, we see Lingard and Lewis coming separately down the stairs. *"You've got a good girl there"*, Lewis sneers, *"Saving it all up for you."* When Sugden demands to know what Lewis meant, Miss Lingard tries to laugh it off, saying Lewis" made *a bit of a nuisance of himself."*

Although Sugden is outraged (enough to lie to Wescott about the military modification) Miss Lingard downplays the event on the train home. Lewis was, *"a little gentleman compared to some"*, she tells Sugden, *" It's all part of the job, isn't it? I HAVE been on these trips before."* And then seeing Sugden's reaction she adds, *"But thank you all the same."*

Bearing in mind the episode, *'A Bunch of Fives'*, where Wendy Craig's stewardess is warned by Henderson to keep a male character happy during a sales trip, and the off-handed comment in *'Loved He Not Honours More'* that Lingard is *'busy vamping a client'*, it's clear that this was, to some extent, viewed as all part of the job (when Sugden first phones Crane Wescott we see Lewis pawing the arm of his secretary). However, the question is what control the women have within that context.

Kay Lingard is not being depicted as ruthless. She is caring enough to see that Margie is suffering with flu in the opening scenes and tries to bring it to the notice of the oblivious Sugden before taking control and convincing Margie to go home. On the train up to Manchester, she is playful when Sugden says it's a far cry from trips to Rome, saying, *"Oh, I've BEEN to Rome with Mr Wilder, but I've never been to Manchester with you."* And she innocently links arms with Sugden in the hotel foyer as they walk towards the restaurant (when the dastardly Lewis then takes Lingard's elbow, escorting her into the restaurant, it's shown dispassionately with no special emphasis). But, in her own words, Kay Lingard is clearly as 'capable of looking after herself' as *The Avengers'* Cathy Gale.

In a final irony, while Sugden is still negotiating with Wescott, Don Henderson receives a phone call from Wilder to tell him that the Italians have agreed to buy the Sovereign without a demonstration of the new engines.

Manchester born Tony Williamson would become best-known for writing ingenious takes on action-adventure series like *'The Champions'* and *'Counterstrike'*. Ironically, he would also write the first treatment of Gerry and Sylvia Anderson's *'Doppelganger'* which featured both Patrick Wymark and Norma Ronald playing 21st century versions of their *'Plane Maker'* characters. In this episode, however, Williamson shows that he was equally adept at finding a new angle in the more pedestrian setting of Scott Furlong.

18 February 1964　　　　*A Paper Transaction.*

Writer Stanley Miller.　　　**Director Bill Stewart.**

Patrick Wymark (John Wilder). Jack Watling (Don Henderson). Jack May (J. Ashley Pender). Naomi Chance (Joyce Pender). Robert Urquhart (Henry Forbes). Norman Tyrrell (Sir Gordon Revidge). Norma Ronald (Kay Lingard). Noel Trevarthen (Davies).

" Like everything human, (the Sovereign) must fall short of perfection." J Ashley Pender

Jack May guests as J Ashley Pender, an accountant who Sir Gordon Revidge has installed to find efficiencies in Scott Furlong. Wilder sees Pender as a threat to himself advising Henderson to *'Pass it around the grapevine that he might be responsible for redundancies if people talk too much'.*

May portrays an emotionless surface for Pender, but we gradually realise he is eaten up by the knowledge that people assume his success has come from his marriage to Sir Gordon's wealthy god daughter, Joyce (Naomi Chance).

During a meeting with 'Uncle Gordon' Revidge, Wilder casually proposes that the Pender's come on a test flight with Sir Gordon. Naomi Chance conveys the desperate search for an excuse before she says they will be viewing a house at the same time. Wymark raises an eyebrow and offers to postpone the flight by an hour. Mrs Ashley Pender's frozen-mouthed look and confusion when her husband agrees, convinces Wilder that *"Our Pender is scared stiff of flying."*

Pender accepts a seat on the Sovereign proving run, but panics during a stall test (where power is cut and the plane loses momentum) and tries to open the emergency exit. Because he expected Pender to back out (or because he himself is scared of test flights), Wilder is meeting a client at London Airport and doesn't see Pender's hysteria.

After his breakdown, from the quiet of a private hospital bed, May's delivery is much more naturalistic as he objectively admits he could never be like Wilder and Sir Gordon. *"When a chosen instrument breaks down, men like him don't weep salt tears. They throw them on the scrap heap and get another one that works."*

The aftermath shows Wilder increasingly isolated as test pilot Henry Forbes, Don Henderson and even the normally unflappable Miss

Lingard are appalled by Wilder's callousness. But as predicted by Ashley Pender himself, Wilder doesn't much care and continues with his paperwork.

This was the only contribution by Stanley Miller, who would go on to write episodes of Rediffusion's *The Rat Catchers* and adaptations of *'Thirteen to Arcturus'* for *Out of the Unknown* and *'Carmilla'* for *Mystery and Imagination.*

25 February 1964   *A Job for the Major*

Writer John O'Toole.   Director John Cooper.

Reginald Marsh (Arthur Sugden). Jack Watling (Don Henderson). Peter Copley (Major Mortimer Crabbe). Fulton Mackay (Bob Gorman). Anthony Sagar (Stan Wallace). Elizabeth Begley (Margie Thomas). Sheila Raynor (Mary Sugden). Pauline Devaney (Shivaun Crabbe). Michael Segal (Ted Amber). Ray Mort (Jack Brough). Gabriella Licudi (Lamorna). George A. Saunders (Jimmy Coyne). Desmond Llewelyn (John Webb).

'I had to contend with dumb insolence from the supervisors and intelligent neutrality at this level of management' Mr Crabbe

Wilder installs former army major Crabbe (Peter Copley), to improve Scott Furlong's systems. Undeniably efficient, Crabbe's management style provokes resentment among the supervisors and Arthur Sugden has the job of keeping the peace.

Mr Crabbe (who issues a notice to the effect that he is now a civilian and does not wish to use his military rank) attempts to impose military efficiency, telling the line managers that he will control access to works managers Sugden and Gorman. Although his system is proven correct when analysed by the computer, his 'task management' style, is imposed too quickly on men who *'left the army behind ten years ago.'*

A scene where Crabbe helps a young apprentice with a proposal for the staff suggestion scheme shows his basic benevolence (the apprentice wins a cash reward he needs to get married). However, his attempt to control the weekly supervisor's meeting in the manner of Frank Savage in Twelve *O'Clock High* (telling them he has drawn up a list of replacements and asking at the start of the meeting if anyone cares to resign) does not address the underlying resentment and his victory is short-lived.

3 March 1964   *A Question of Priorities.*

Writer Raymond Bowers.   Director Eric Price.

Patrick Wymark   (John Wilder). Margaret Rawlings (Marion Brown). Jack Watling (Don Henderson). Georgina Ward (Dawn Rossiter). Ingrid Hafner (Kate Barber). Douglas Muir (Tom Bancroft). James Kerry (Jeff Rossiter). Norma Ronald (Kay Lingard). Kathleen St. John (Mary).

"I want her back home and I want her back today!" John Wilder

Wilder's mother-in-law Marion Brown (Margaret Rawlings) tells him that Pamela is suing for divorce. As he tries to save his marriage, Wilder also schemes to stop Jeff Rossiter (James Kerry) a member of the design team from taking up a job in America.

In *Loved He Not Honours More*, Pamela Wilder referred to John as a *"semi-detached husband'*. Now, her mother reveals that Pamela has employed private detectives to follow Wilder and Kate Barber. She has enough evidence to apply for a divorce, a prospect that outrages Wilder.

"Whatever I've done - whoever I've done it with – has been completely aside from my marriage. It's been like a busy man taking time out to go to the pictures."

When Wilder complains that he is planning a lot of important business dinners that only Pamela can arrange, her mother offers to step in, saying she wants to see their marriage survive. *"As the widowed youngest daughter of the youngest son of a baronet, I know just how much I owe to my daughter's marriage."*

Unfortunately, Wilder puts himself in a weaker position by wining and dining Dawn Rossiter (Georgina Ward), whose designer husband has flown to New York to discuss a new job. Rossiter says he can't be bought (the career prospects are what attracts him to America) but Wilder hopes Dawn can influence her husband to stay. His scheme backfires in two ways. First because Wilder's mother-in-law manoeuvres Kate Barber into visiting the restaurant. Mrs Rossiter tells Wilder that *'a woman in a suit came in – took one look at us- and walked straight out again.'*

Wilder's scheme also backfires because when Rossiter learns about Wilder's overtures, he sends a telegram from New Work to Bancroft, the technical director, saying he resents personally and professionally, *'Wilder's approaches to my wife'* Wilder concludes that Rossiter *'knows how to stir up gossip'*

Curiously, James Kerry (Jimmy Rossiter in this episode) also played the identical character of designer Jimmy Shaw in *A Question of Sources.*

Bowers gives Wymark and Watling a fine Machiavellian scene as they discuss the technical director Tom Bancroft (Douglas Muir). When Henderson refers to *"Old Bancroft?"* Wilder asks, *'Why do you call him old? He's only just over 50,"* Henderson avoids the question and Wilder then calls Bancroft in to explain a technical report. Bancroft passes off the work of Rossiter as his own, unaware that Rossiter had already told Wilder about the problem and the solution. Henderson says that every executive lives off the back of his staff – *"Why not? He's got the responsibility"*. Wilder counters that *"Any executive who passes off another man's work as his own, know he can't do the job as well as the man he's robbing."*

Henderson asks what Wilder thinks about Rossiter, who is prepared to stich up his own boss. *"He's a man with somewhere to go."* Wilder replies, *"Bancroft is a man trying to stay where he is."* But, when Henderson asks when Wilder is going to get rid of Bancroft, Wilder replies that *"the Sovereign is a proved aircraft now, needing only routine management by routine people. A new technical director now may prove more loyal to the chairman than to me."*

This episode marks the end of Wilder's relationship with Kate Barber as she tells him, *"I feel like your wife – used and then not used."* Wilder appears devastated at first, although the final scene, in which Wilder orders events to his own advantage is a supreme example of what Wilder would later describe (in *The Power Game*) as *"rearranging the pieces to make sure they form a pattern that suits you."*

It's not clear if the character of Marion Brown was introduced as a last-minute replacement for Barbara Murray. Patrick Wymark certainly seems disconcerted in her first scene, when Mrs Brown gives him Pamela's photo which she found in the drinks cabinet. *"Yes,* "Wymark says, *"Barbara would put it in the drinks cabinet."*

Margaret Rawlings was apt casting as the strong-willed mother of Pamela Wilder. A founder and Vice President of Equity, the actor's union, she was also Lady Barlow, wife of Sir Robert Barlow, chairman of the Metal Box Company (described as "autocratic, ruthless, cunning and devious").

She had starred in London and Broadway in Charles Morgan's *The Flashing Stream* (1939) as one of two passionate and sexually experienced mathematicians suppressing their desires to perfect a new missile to defend England. On film she appeared in *Roman Holiday (1953)* and also played the medium Madam Bullard who explains the plot in *Hands of the Ripper* (1971).

Georgina Ward, who plays the ambiguous Dawn Rossiter *('I give that marriage two years'* Wilder predicts) was ironically the daughter of the Honourable George Ward, who had been an MP and Secretary of State for Air from 1957 to 1960. She appeared at the Shakespeare Memorial Theatre, and in *The Avengers, Gideon's Way* and *Danger Man*, and later in two episodes of *The Main Chance* (1970) written by David Weir.

10 March 1964.   *Bancroft's Law*

Writer Geoffrey Stephenson.   Director Bill Stewart.

Reginald Marsh (Arthur Sugden). Jack Watling (Don Henderson).
Douglas Muir (Tom Bancroft). Elizabeth Begley (Margie Thomas).
Norma Ronald (Kay Lingard). Derrick Sherwin (Adrian Cantlow).
Jerry Desmonde (Gordon Vallin). Frederick Peisley (Richard
Marsham). Richard Arthure (Rogers).

*"Bancroft's Law; The risk to the head of any department grows in
direct proportion to the ability of your most talented assistant."* Don
Henderson

Metallurgist Adrian Cantlow (Derrick Sherwin) has devised a new
test which suggests the thrust reversers on the Sovereign will
succumb to metal fatigue within three years. His report has been
sitting on the desk of technical director Tom Bancroft (Douglas
Muir) for weeks, so Cantlow takes matters into his own hands and
phones the sub-contractor, Crane Wescott.

Bancroft asks Arthur Sugden to reprimand Cantlow for exceeding
his authority, but when Sugden learns about the report and Crane
Wescott's Gordon Vallin (Jerry Desmond) supports Cantlow's
findings, Bancroft is left desperately trying to recover the situation
before Wilder returns from the Bahamas.

This episode marks the final appearance of Douglas Muir as
technical director Tom Bancroft and underlines the fact that not all
workplace politics is carried out by the smooth and agile. Bancroft
only bursts into life when he suspects his own job is at risk, shifting
the blame onto subordinates and seeking to shunt Cantlow out of
sight.

Cantlow is played by Derrick Sherwin, who had a parallel career as
a writer and would produce *Doctor Who,* and *Paul Temple.*
Cantlow' single-mindedness seems to be justified, but we see him
berating an elderly lab assistant as incompetent and worthy of the

scrap heap. Sugden reminds Cantlow that, *"We'll all be 60 someday"* and suggests that he learns to make allowances. Sadly, in the 21st Century, the Cantlow viewpoint seems to be in the ascendant.

Although no longer transmitted live, it was still expensive to cut the videotape recordings at the time of *The Plane Makers*. So, the actors soldiered on as if it was live. In one scene, Sugden picks up his phone and the 'works' fall out of the mouthpiece. Reginald Marsh calmly pushes the bits back inside the phone and holds them in place as he speaks

17 March 1964   *The Homecoming*

Writer David Weir.   **Director John Cooper.**

Reginald Marsh   (Arthur Sugden). Norman Tyrrell (Sir Gordon Revidge). Jack Watling (Don Henderson). Fulton Mackay (Bob Gorman). Wensley Pithey (Bill Ingram). Anna Wing (Molly Ingram). Elizabeth Begley (Margie Thomas). Sheila Raynor (Mary Sugden). Roy Holder (Charlie Ferris). Peter Layton (Alan Sugden).

"You're a friendly face in a sea of rivals" Don Henderson to Arthur Sugden

Arthur Sugden's six-month trial as General Works Manager is coming to an end when old friend Bill Ingram (Wensley Pithey) offers him the job of Managing Director of his engineering firm in Yorkshire. With Wilder using every opportunity to obstruct Sugden at Scott Furlong, the offer seems like the perfect solution.

The first of two concurrent scripts by Series Story Consultant David Weir, this episode explores Sugden's character by presenting him with a dream job. Bill Ingram is a former Scott Furlong employee who left to set up his own engineering company. By offering Sugden the job of Managing Director he presents an opportunity to return to Yorkshire and avoid the final conflict with Wilder. As

Sugden's dentist son is hoping to buy a practice in Yorkshire, everything seems to fall in place.

But when he asks his secretary Margie (Elizabeth Begley) to consider following him to Yorkshire, she says it's a dream, pointing out that he left when he was a young boy. *"All your roots are down here. Home is where your friends are."*

The reaction to Sugden's news is varied. Don Henderson (Jack Watling) is genuinely upset at the thought of Arthur leaving, saying even Wilder *"knows your value as a works manager."* By contrast, Bob Gorman (Fulton Mackay) is visibly excited by the prospect of stepping into Sugden's shoes, hinting that he'll cut corners if Wilder demands it. Gorman, who was seen as newly arrived from Radley Heath in *A Job For the Major* makes it plain that he intends to do more than 'caretake' the General Works Manager's job, despite being warned that Wilder will want his own man in the position.

When Sir Gordon Revidge learns of Sugden's offer, he sounds him out about taking Wilder's job. Wilder, says Revidge,*" has placed the bank in an invidious position. Wilder cares for only one thing - winning on his own terms. The man is too much of a risk."*

Arthur refuses the offer saying, *"I don't pretend to get on with Wilder. Nobody does. But he's a brilliant man. Nobody could run this company or any other aircraft company better than John Wilder. The industry's needed someone like him for a very long time, and I'll have no part in stabbing him in the back."*

This conversation comes back to haunt Sugden when he learns that Ingram has heart problems. Ingram needs to slow down, but also suspects his days are numbered. That's why he needs Sugden to take over as Managing Director. Ingram confesses that rather than see his life's work broken up, he intends to go public. Sugden says this changes thing. When Ingram dies, they'll bring in another chairman. *"Now I've met some chairmen and I can't play their kind of politics. They'd have me out of here before you could blink."*

Sugden's devotion to Scott Furlong is illustrated by the sub-plot of Charlie Ferris (Roy Holder), whose railwayman father wants him to give up his poorly paid apprenticeship and find a better paid job.

(*The Industrial Training Act was introduced in March 1964 in the hope of improving the poorly paid apprentice system. An engineering apprentice only earned around £2/19 shillings a week, equivalent to £65 in 2020, compared to £8.00 (£175) for an older worker. The Government hoped to regulate apprenticeships with a better paid training allowance financed via a compulsory levy on firms but unfortunately, the scheme was never a great success*).

Charlie tells Sugden he wants to stay as an apprentice because he left school before he had a chance to sit his GCE exams and this is his only chance to better himself. In contrast to Bob Gorman, who tells Charlie that *"rules are rules"* and that he can't interfere in a personal family matter, Sugden tries to find a solution. Remembering how the company once helped him as a youngster from a poor family, Sugden offers to break the rules by arranging for Charlie to be paid more than an apprentice's wages.

The episode ends with Sugden deciding to stay, despite knowing the Wilder wants him out. The sub-plot with Charlie Ferris illustrates Sugden's paternalist streak, as did his comment in *Bancroft's Law* that the company should accommodate older, less able workers. Sugden tries to interest Revidge in a diversification programme to find alternative employment for the men once work on the Sovereign is scaled down. Despite his zeal for creating planes, Sugden believes that the company exists to provide employment. At the same time, he is realistic enough to believe that the company needs a man like Wilder at the top to drive it forward.

Actor Roy Holder, who played Charlie Ferris, had hazy memories of this episode when he appeared at a convention in 2014. However, he did recall sharing a couple of scenes with Fulton MacKay as Foreman Bob Gorman and surprisingly, *"I've never seen such a nervous actor. He used to shake before the scene started."* Roy (who later starred in Ace of Wands) had also worked with (and could still do an impersonation of) Patrick Wymark in the 1963 ITV play, *The Paleto Confession.*

Revidge notes that Sugden's contract is "up for confirmation on the 31st." March 31st was the scheduled transmission date for the final episode of *The Plane Makers.*

24 March 1964   ***Sauce for the Goose***

Writer David Weir.   **Director Eric Price.**

Patrick Wymark   (John Wilder). Barbara Murray (Pamela Wilder). Robert Urquhart (Henry Forbes). Jack Watling (Don Henderson). Murray Hayne (Al Bonner). Georgina Cookson (Laura). Daniel Moynihan (Eric Rushton). Betty Henderson (Mrs Cooke). Alan Curtis (Jean-Pierre).

"It's Paris in the Spring, John" Pamela Wilder

Wilder negotiates with French rivals at the Paris air show, and Pamela's old friend Laura (Georgina Cookson) introduces her to Al Bonner (Murray Hayne), a handsome young American.

David Weir's concluding script gives Barbara Murray a chance to explore Pamela Wilder's frustrations. Grateful to have married out of a "county" background where *"nobody ever lost their temper,"* she denies that Wilder meets the stereotype of the businessman with ulcers, saying he loves what he does too much to suffer. Only when Forbes repeats gossip about Bonner being a gigolo, does Wilder becomes jealous. Pamela, who has accepted a night on the town with Bonner, tells Wilder, *"I wanted to pay you back."* When Wilder demands, *"What for?"* She replies, *"For not knowing 'What for'".* Pamela ultimately denies Wilder's accusation that Bonner is a gigolo telling Wilder that, *"He was too nice to use. If he had been any less of a good person, I WOULD have slept with him."*

"(The French) must have jumped for joy when old 'Morality' Merle suggested a solution to their problems" Wilder says, recalling the

twist from *The Trouble with Auntie*. Wilder reminds us that the deal involves the French getting out of the civil market, leaving it open for Scott Furlong, in exchange for the French getting a NATO contract for their military plane. Weir nudges matters in Wilder's favour when one of the French airline executives confirms that his gamble in *How Do You Vote?* was justified. *"Building that extra dozen aircraft gave you a lead we could not afford."*

Murray Hayne (playing Al Bonner) was the real-life son-in-law of Douglas Muir (Tom Bancroft). Georgina Cookson, as his companion Laura, was the occupant of Patrick McGoohan's old flat in *'The Chimes of Big Ben'* episode of *'The Prisoner'*.

31 March 1964   *How Can You Win If You Haven't Bought A Ticket?*

Writer Edmund Ward.   Director Rex Firkin

"It's the beginning of the big squeeze. You'd better get that desk cleared for a hand-picked Wilder yes-man." Arthur Sugden

Patrick Wymark   (John Wilder). Reginald Marsh (Arthur Sugden). Barbara Murray (Pamela Wilder). Robert Urquhart (Henry Forbes). Jack Watling (Don Henderson). Alan Tilvern (Dr. Wolfgang Katz). Elizabeth Begley (Margie Thomas). Sheila Raynor (Mary Sugden). Peter Madden (Gilbert Cory). Fred Ferris (Sam Adams). Norma Ronald (Kay Lingard). Norman Tyrrell (Sir Gordon Revidge). Martin Wyldeck (William Keeble). John Henderson (hotel porter).

As Arthur Sugden's six-month trial period nears its end, he detects a number of snubs and obstacles being placed in his path by John Wilder. He learns by memo that production meetings are being relocated to Wilder's office and is given only one day's leave instead of the three he's requested to attend an aero engineer's conference where Sugden is delivering a paper (Confirming that the snub is real, Wilder tells an astonished Miss Lingard to pp the memo, claiming that he has writer's cramp).

Wilder himself is frustrated by Sugden's refusal to shorten production schedules for a modification to the Sovereign. Wilder is hoping to sell Sovereigns to the Anglo Air Company. *"If we can unload six Sovereign's on a domestic airline like Anglo, it's as good as a royal warrant."* Wilder plans for Henderson and himself to waylay Anglo's Gilbert Corey at the aviation conference. However, Wilder is for once surprised to learn that Corey and Sugden served together in the RAF during the war.

This final episode of *The Plane Makers* sees the resolution of the conflict between Wilder and Sugden. In the second episode Wilder opposed Sugden because of his background, *"His technical experience is beyond question. But every man has his personal ceiling."* In this episode, Wilder tells Don that, *"I admire his Northern millstone integrity and all that, but the Sugden's of this world are obsolete. Like bed socks. He's just a big boy scout."*

Sugden's refusal to produce a production schedule giving timescale's he believes are impossible is an illustration of his failings in Wilder's eyes. *"There's all the difference in the world between the times that you can promise and the times that you can actually deliver in. That's what contracts are for."*

In other words, Wilder needs a production schedule that will sell planes rather than build planes. When Sugden says the other directors, Keeble and Katz will support his findings, Wilder replies, *"They may or may not support you. But they don't need these faster production times. I do. And in the final analysis Sugden, the general works manager can only be on one side. MINE."*

Indeed, the two other "technical high priests" Katz and Keeble are willing to try and give Wilder the figures he needs when they learn the prospect of selling to Anglo. Chairman, Sir Gordon Revidge still expects unity in the command chain. He tells Keeble (Martin Wyldeck) that the end of his six-month trial is hardly the time for Sugden to disagree with his Managing Director. When Keeble says

Sugden may be right, Revidge replies *"I hardly see that being right is relevant."*

However, the public conduct of the company is still a concern for Revidge. When Wilder snaps, **"what do you want – ethics or aeroplanes?"** It never occurs to him that someone might want both. Or that unethical behaviour may tactically weaken his position against a chairman who wants the board to remove him.

By contrast we learn how respected Sugden is in the aviation industry. When Wilder introduces himself to Gilbert Corey (Peter Madden) at the aero engineer's conference, Corey says, *"I suppose you're here for the Sugden paper. Now there's a man who knows what he's talking about."*

Wilder also learns the effect of leaving an opponent with no hope at all. Sugden refuses to give Wilder revised production figures to discuss with Corey, reminding him, *"I'm on a day's leave. That's all I was allowed."* When Wilder tries to pressure him by asking if he thinks this is going to improve the chances of his reappointment, Sugden snaps, *"What chances?"*

Compounding the error, Wilder confirms he won't be recommending Sugden's reappointment. With two alternatives; be demoted back to his old job at Radley Heath or resign, Sugden meets with Corey, asking if there's a job for him at Anglo. Corey guesses that there's a conflict with Wilder but confirms that Sugden's level of expertise would make him difficult to place. *"There's nothing big enough for you."* However, while negotiating the aircraft sale, Corey tells Wilder that his board would insist on continuity of supervision. *"If I do recommend Sovereigns it's going to be pretty difficult to put through with your works manager being fired."*

Sensing that it's a deal-maker, Wilder confirms that Sugden will stay. When he says he expects that Sugden and Corey were good friends in the RAF, Corey replies that he tried to get Sugden court martialled. Sugden insisted on thorough checks of the Lancaster's and Corey wanted as many planes as possible up in the air. Eventually, Sugden overstepped the mark and Corey saw a way of removing him. But soon after, there was a crash killing scores of men. *"I don't like Sugden. But by god I trust him."*

Barbara Murray is given an opportunity to illuminate Pamela Wilder's fears. She is appalled by the prospect of her husband triumphing over Sugden, saying Arthur is *"vulnerable. Because he's an honest man."* She sees herself as a *"frequent adjunct at business dinners. Highly polished to impress."* Pamela wonders how much longer she will be required, telling Wilder he is, *"a charming destructive little boy. At the moment you're on top of the world and I'm part of it"*. However, Pamela also questions how much longer she can stay by his side. *"Perhaps it's not enough through. Perhaps I'm tired of being a bystander at his Roman triumphs."*

Sugden's appointment is confirmed by the board and Wilder offers him the cigar he refused at the end of *No Man's Land*. He also offers Sugden some advice. *"A man once said how can you win if you haven't bought a ticket. You've just bought a ticket but that doesn't mean you're going to win. You see. We've all got tickets."*

There is no director credit on the transmitted episode. It is possible that producer Rex Firkin directed this final episode (as he would do in *The Power Game*). In the early days of television and single plays, the producer *was* the director.

The series had made a star out of Patrick Wymark. In *The Homecoming*, even Sugden had to admit that Wilder was *"a brilliant man."* The combination of excellence and single-minded selfishness (both professionally and personally) made Wilder a complex lead character who Wymark brought vividly to life.

Case Study Three:

The Plane Makers Series Three

Producer Rex Firkin   Script Editor Wilfred Greatorex

"You can't stand still. Not in this business." John Wilder

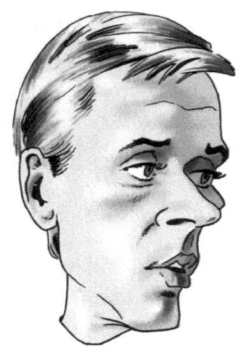 

Alan Dobie as Corbett   **Patrick Wymark as Wilder**

Developing the third series of The Plane Makers, Rex Firkin and Wilfred Greatorex took a bold move. Usually, a TV series will build on a success by delivering more of the same. Perhaps mindful that *The Plane Makers* had succeeded in its second series by breaking away from what had gone before, the third series moved even further away from the shopfloor stories, and gave Wilder a new opponent.

Contrasting with Arthur Sugden's humanistic approach, David Corbett is a single-minded technician, lacking in social or political graces. Corbett would be forced to learn and develop the political tactics needed to resist Wilder. Born in Wombwell, Yorkshire, Dobie had been a fellow student of Patrick Wymark's at the Old Vic Theatre School. While still an 18-year-old student, Dobie had been 'discovered' by BBC producer Naomi Capon who had cast him in

The Earl of Skipton (1953). In 1958 he played Bennett Hatch in Capon's adaptation of *The Black Arrow* (with Patrick Wymark as Will Lawless) . Capon said Dobie was already making a reputation for asking if he could cut his lines and replace them with a look. *"Believing as she does, that a small facial expression can be of the greatest value, she invariably says yes.".*

In 1961 Dobie appeared as Donald Howard in the stage version of CP Snow's *The Affair* starring Alec Clunes. Dobie reprised the role for a BBC TV adaptation at Easter 1963, where the "dignified truculence" of his character was applauded (is it too fanciful to suspect that this led to his casting as the abrasive David Corbett?) Dobie appeared with Wymark again in 1961 in Jacques Gillies' *The Takers* , and in 1963 played the Revenue Solicitor Frank Fragg, persecuting Wymark's Joseph Ransley in the Disney movie, *Dr Syn, Alias The Scarecrow.*

A second newcomer was James Cameron-Grant MP. A former pilot, the ambitious back-bench MP runs his own public relations company and is approached by Wilder to lobby on behalf of the VTOL project. A rival both to Wilder in the board room and Sir Gerald Merle in his ambition to become Minister of Aviation, Grant becomes the audiences' guide to the twists and turns of the plot, decoding the plots of Wilder and Sir Gordon Revidge.

In the episode, *The Golden Silence* it is revealed that Grant was awarded the Distinguished Flying Cross. We learn in the episode, *The Salesmen*, that Grant was in Korea with the son of the MOD permanent secretary when he died. This would suggest that Grant served in the Fleet Air Arm, giving him practical knowledge of jet fighters and short take-offs from aircraft carriers.

Grant was played by Bristol-born Peter Jeffrey, a member of the Royal Shakespeare Company, who had played Delio in *The Duchess of Malfi* (1960) opposite Wymark as Bosola. Jeffrey had also taken over the role of de Laubardemont in *The Devils* (1961) from Patrick Wymark, when Wymark took on the role of Father Barre. In a busy career, Jeffrey would go on to play Inspector Trout in the *Dr Phibes* films and Oliver Cromwell in *By The Sword Divided* (1983).

Laura Challis represents an attempt by Greatorex and Firkin to develop a more proactive female lead than Pamela Wilder. Representing the minority of women able to carve a career into the early 1960's society, Laura Challis mirrors the intellectual prowess of Mary Goldring (then Aviation correspondent of *The Economist*). A former financial journalist, Laura Challis is the new personal assistant and gatekeeper to Sir Gordon Revidge. Despite Pamela Wilder's suspicions, she warns Wilder in *The Salesmen*, that she's made it a rule never to have an affair with someone in the same industry. She has a key to Cameron-Grant's flat and acknowledges that he regards any business move she makes in his favour as, *"a kind of unsolicited dowry."* Just as Cameron-Grant decodes the various political manoeuvrings for the audience, Challis explains some of the financial realities (see *Only A Few Millions*).

Playing Laura Challis, Holbeach-born Wendy Gifford was a member of the Royal Shakespeare Company and had appeared in *The Taming of the Shrew* (1960) and *Two Gentlemen of Verona* (1960)with Wymark. Among multiple TV appearances, she had already played another character is the first series of *The Plane Makers*, and would go on to appear in the thriller serial *The Man In The Mirror* (1966) and *The Troubleshooters* (1966)

Where the first two series of *The Plane Makers* had been set against the background of the commercial aviation industry, the third series took a new direction with a focus on the military Vertical Take-Off and Landing jet.

The Korean war had proved the flexibility of helicopters which could land and take-off without the need for conventional air strips, but the next goal was for jet planes, either fighters or troop carriers, which could fly fast (preferably at supersonic speed) without need for airstrips.

NATO had put forward a specification for a light tactical support fighter, which the member nations were competing to produce. Britain's Ministry of Supply had commissioned Short Brothers in Belfast to produce the SC1 research craft in 1953. Powered by four vertically mounted Rolls Royce engines, it was shown at the biennial Farnborough Air Show's in 1958 and 1960 and the Paris Air Show in 1961, but never went into full production.

In 1957, Hawker Siddeley began developing the subsonic P1127 VTOL in 1957, followed by the supersonic Vertical SHORT Take Off and Landing P1154. Both jets used Bristol Aircraft's Pegasus engine with four swivelling exhaust nozzles. Both prototypes were privately funded, without Government support, although once the jets had proved themselves, the Conservative Government made development grants. In addition, Hawker Siddeley began work on the HS681 VSTOL transport, designed to meet the NATO specification for a troop carrier.

This background is reflected in the second episode, *Other People Own Our Jungles Now* when James Cameron-Grant MP questions why the Government should fund another VTOL from Scott Furlong when the UK already has two in development.

The fortunes of the VTOL reflect the danger of writing up-to-the-minute drama. Not only did *The Plane Makers* have to accommodate a General Election days before its first episode, it also had to be aware of an incoming Government's tendency to cancel the work of its predecessor. In February 1965, the Labour Government cancelled the more adventurous P1154 VSTOL and HS681 troop carrier on grounds of cost. However, Hawker Siddeley *did* win a contract to continue the P1127, which formed the basis of the Harrier jump jet.

Of course, other countries were developing their own VTOL jets. The original VTOL engine concept had been a French innovation, and Dassault had produced the Balzac V, protype for the supersonic Mirage jet programme. Aviation enthusiasts detect a similarity between the Balzac and the VTOL developed for *The Plane Makers* (a similarity which was alluded to by a fictional French competitor in the episode, *The Golden Silence*).

The VTOL mock-up for the TV show was designed by Ronald Fouracre's team with advice from technical advisor Michael Jolley. Costing £4,000 and taking 2,000-man hours to construct, the 48 foot long, 35 foot wing span mock-up was used for publicity at the Biggin Hill Battle of Britain display. Strangely, no secret was made of the fact that the VTOL jet was hoisted on a crane, with the *TV Times* running a picture of the set-up in Dermod Hill's introductory article *Supersonic Rat Race*.

One jarring comment in the story is Hill's declaration that, *"The Predator is no mere word in a script"*. Ironically, this is true. While studio publicity calls the plane *"The Predator"* to distinguish it from *"The Sovereign"*, the TV scripts constantly refer to the plane as the *"Veetol"*.

The Vertical Take Off and Landing Jet shown in the title sequence is the brain child of David Corbett (Alan Dobie). Ryan Airframes is part of the same group as Scott Furlong. Bill Ryan (John Wentworth) and Corbett are passionate about the VTOL project, but their main income is sub-contracting work for Scott Furlong.

Their Works Manager, Bob Fraser (Duncan Bannatyne) is a former Scott Furlong employee, acutely aware that they're missing deadlines for delivery of Sovereign tail assemblies. John Wentworth as Ryan is very different from Telliter, the fey financial advisor to Pamela Wilder he played in the previous series episode *Loved He Not Honours More*. Ryan is the human side of the partnership, commanding the loyalty of staff and spending hours negotiating with the *"bone-headed civil servants"* Corbett cannot abide.

A *TV Times* article introducing the new series listed returning favourites like Reginald Marsh and Robert Urquhart and in the final line noted *"Pamela Wilder played by Ann Firbank"*. In his memoir, *High Drama*, Rex Firkin says he had forgotten to engage Barbara

Murray and she was already committed to the BBC's *The Indian Tales of Rudyard Kipling* (July-December 1964) when the new series began. Ann Firbank is an excellent actress, and if this had been the first time we had seen Pamela Wilder, she would have made the role her own. In a long running stage play, actors move on or understudies have to step in at the last moment. For some audiences, the character is defined by the understudy. But in a continuing television series, the audience has a physical memory of the previous actor. It's not known whether anticipation of this audience reaction led to Pamela's role being considerably reduced in this series.

The first episode of the new series attracted an estimated 13,061,400 viewers (5,937,000 homes) , making it joint 12th in the TAM ratings with the BBC's *Z Cars* and *Steptoe and Son*. Viewers actually grew in succeeding weeks with 7,040,000 viewers watching Arthur Sugden's final episode *It's A Free Country – Isn't It?* In January 1965, the series was still attracting 14,665,200 viewers (6,666,000 homes) *for A Hoopla of Haloes.*

The series was also attracting industry praise with Sydney Newman, BBC head of drama writing in November 1964 to congratulate Firkin on David Weir's *A Lesson For Corbett.*

Internationally, *The Plane Makers* was creating a passionate following in Australia, with episodes sold to Sydney's TCN-9 by ATV's sales arm, ITC.

For Patrick Wymark, Wilder was already creating a dilemma. As David Hope noted in The Stage in November 1964, *"The thing that has happened to Patrick Wymark over the past few weeks I believe he neither wholly likes or perhaps fully understands. The ruthless incisive character of John Wilder has now been indelibly stamped in the mind of the public on the character of Patrick Wymark."* He had become an, *"institution in the public domain, common property."*

On Tuesday December 15th, 1964. Patrick Wymark was presented the Best Actor award by Honor Blackman on behalf of the Guild of

Television Producers and Directors (now BAFTA). He took the opportunity to announce that this series of *The Plane Makers* would be his last. Rex Firkin was also presented with the Best Series award for *The Plane Makers*.

In addition, Wilfred Greatorex, Raymond Bowers and Edmund Ward were presented with the 1964 Writers Guild of Great Britain, Best Dramatic Serial/Series Script awards at the Dorchester Hotel on 11 March 1965.

Tuesday Oct. 20, 1964   *Empires Have to Start Somewhere*

Writer Edmund Ward.   **Director Peter Collinson**

Patrick Wymark (John Wilder). Reginald Marsh (Arthur Sugden). Jack Watling (Don Henderson). Alan Dobie (David Corbett). Robert Urquhart (Henry Forbes). Norman Tyrrell (Sir Gordon Revidge). William Devlin (Sir Gerald Merle). Norma Ronald (Kay Lingard). Elizabeth Wallace (Harriet Evans). Duncan McIntyre (Bob Fraser). Alan Browning (Co-pilot Douglas Bradley). John Wentworth (Bill Ryan). John Cater (Charles Atkinson).

Discussing sales of the Sovereign, Wilder tells Don Henderson, *"We broke even three months ago - with orders still to come. Now we take the profit - just sit back for two years of gravy."*

"Well, we've earned it, "says Henderson.

"No Don," Wilder replies, *"You can't stand still. Not in this business."*

Ryan Airframes, part of the same group as Scott Furlong, earns its income making tail-assemblies for the Sovereign. But they're late on delivery because the attention of Bill Ryan and David Corbett is focussed on their VTOL project.

Ryan and Corbett have asked Elbertson's bank for an extra eight million pounds investment in the VTOL. Sir Gordon Revidge is already sceptical about putting more money into the project, when

Wilder arrives with a plan to invoke a penalty clause on Ryan Airframes and bring the tail assembly work in-house. He then reveals that Bill Ryan has been pushing himself too hard and could be dead within a year, with all his vital knowledge and contacts locked in his head. Wilder knows because the company doctor had held Ryan out as a warning to Wilder!

Revidge forces Ryan to take a golden handshake spread over five years for tax purposes. Ryan tells Corbett he could only defy Revidge if Corbett threatened to take his technical expertise away. Corbett considers it for a second and then says, *"I've spent six years working on this. I can't throw it away for loyalty, politics, anything. I can't. It's too important. I'm sorry. I can't compromise continuity of work with wilful personal interference."*

This tongue-twister of a speech really defines Corbett, described by Henderson as, *"Very technical. Drinks lemonade. Not really my type."*

The share price of Ryan Airframes plummets with the news of Bill Ryan's departure. Wilder offers to save the company by sharing facilities and cutting the cost of the investment Corbett needs to develop the VTOL. Revidge agrees to make Wilder managing director of both Scott Furlong and Ryan Airframes, if he can get Corbett to agree to work with him.

When Corbett asks why he should work under Wilder, he is told, *"It's either me or the Revidge's and Merle's. Their idea of achievement is a balance sheet without a blot on it...I take risks!"* Wilder tells him news has already leaked of Wilder's appointment. He asks Kay Lingard to check Ryan's share price: it's stopped falling and has gone up by four shillings a share. Corbett confirms that he will have technical independence and agrees to work under Wilder. *"A man can be anything he chooses – after that it's just a matter of concentration."*

Don Henderson is finally made a member of the Scott Furlong Board in this episode, as part of Wilder's deal with Revidge.

Reginald Marsh returned as Arthur Sugden after starring the previous night as Albert Tufton the leader of miners striking to get new pumps installed in their pit, in *Undercurrent*, Rediffusion's *Play of the Week*.

John Wentworth would go on to play Henry Castleton, solicitor David Main's Leeds-based partner in Edmund Ward's 1969 series *The Main Chance*.

Tuesday Oct. 27, 1964   *Other People Own Our Jungles Now*

Writer Raymond Bowers   Director John Nelson Burton

Patrick Wymark (John Wilder). Ann Firbank (Pamela Wilder). Peter Jeffrey (James Cameron-Grant MP). Wendy Gifford (Laura Challis). Jack Watling (Don Henderson). William Devlin (Sir Gerald Merle). Norma Ronald (Kay Lingard). Kathleen St.John (Maid). Huw Thomas (interviewer). Lord Francis-Williams *(panellist).

*Frank Williams was editor of the Daily Herald until World War 2, when he became Controller of Press Censorship at the Ministry of Information. After the war he became Downing Street Press Secretary and later a governor of the BBC.

"Election promises – like naughty girls – should be made but not kept." James Cameron-Grant MP

This series of *The Plane Makers* premiered four days after Harold Wilson's Labour Government came to power. Obviously written and recorded before the election was called, the script treads a fine balance to anticipate all possible outcomes. When Sir Gerald Merle (William Devlin) tells Wilder that his job is to fight an election and of his conviction that his party will come to Government, Wilder retorts, *"If only I was sure which party you represent!"*

Don Henderson (Jack Watling) returns from Rome jubilant after having sold four more Sovereigns. But Wilder tells him to hand his prospects over to a deputy and concentrate on selling the VTOL jet. *"How do I sell a military jet?"* Henderson demands, *"The Government orders what it wants and that's that surely?".* Wilder disagrees. He's got Sugden and his men ready to pull Corbett's prototype apart and get it ready for production by January. To Wilder, the Sovereign is a declining product. *"This time last year you were talking about 32 possible sales.".* Wilder reminds Henderson that the airline industry exists on other people's money, and those who control the money are interested in potential.

Raymond Bowers uses several spheres of influence to introduce two new characters into the mix. Former journalist Laura Challis (Wendy Gifford) is the new personal assistant to the board of Elberdson's merchant bank - or more directly the Chairman, Sir Gordon Revidge. She takes some time to convince Wilder that he will now need to go through her before he gets the chance to lobby Sir Gordon. When Wilder fails to win the support of Sir Gerald Merle (William Devlin), she suggests he try James Cameron-Grant MP. As a former pilot, *"He can at least fly a plane."*

Like Merle, James Cameron-Grant (Peter Jeffrey) is a Labour MP, but the men are antagonistic in every way. Wilder needs Grant to win Government support for Scott Furlong's VTOL plane. Merle has his eyes on the post of Aviation Minister. Development of the VTOL had been funded by a Conservative administration (with Merle's unspoken agreement) and he does not wish to jeopardise his prospects in a Labour government by being seen to pursue further funding for a firm he is a director of. Grant is shrewd enough to unpick Wilder's motives. Revidge and Merle would prefer Corbett to produce the VTOL at Ryan Airframes. That way there would be no personal success for Wilder. Wilder needs to win Government funding to produce the VTOL at Scott Furlong. If he can pull it off, the Government would be grateful and that would be Wilder's way into the House of Lords. *"No hustings for you!"* But Wilder needs to have the funding in place before the election.

Possibly for the first time, the public saw how Members of Parliament are bought. Grant runs a public relations firm and he tells Wilder he cannot be hired to lobby for the VTOL. Instead, he suggests that Scott Furlong retains his public relations firm to promote the Sovereign with *"an unconditional budget not all of which I need spend"*

Grant tells Wilder that he will act straight away by accepting an invitation to take part in a political talk show. One where Sir Gerald Merle is also on the panel. The sequence gives a good insight into what the ATV studios looked like devoid of scenery.

Everything seems genteel, with Sir Gerald cracking a few jokes, until real-life TV journalist Huw Thomas poses an obviously planted question about the costs of the VTOL. While Merle does a slow burn, Cameron Grant points out that Merle is a director of the group which is developing the VTOL. Grant acknowledges that the UK already has two VTOL jets in development. He asks what use the UK has for a third VTOL. He says it's a plane designed for use in areas without conventional landing strips such as jungles but, *"other people own our jungles now"*. Grant says he will object to any future development of the VTOL. Sir Gerald is backed into defending himself, saying he had to balance the interests of the nation against any potential conflict of interest when considering the funding of the project and declaring that he will move heaven and earth to see that production funding is directed to the VTOL.

Wilder has got what he wanted, but knows that Grant could be either a formidable ally - or rival.

The middle act of the episode is devoted to an uncomfortable weekend at the Wilders'. Taking up Laura Challis' suggestion, Wilder instructs Pamela to invite Grant over for a social weekend. Grant had earlier made a strong impression on Pamela and both she and Wilder are surprised when widower Grant brings divorcee Challis as his guest. Unfortunately, Pamela Wilder has discovered that Wilder dined with Challis earlier in the week and suspects that

Laura Challis is Wilder's latest conquest. She spends the whole dinner laying verbal traps for Wilder.

Ann Firbank delivers a vigorous performance. It's also unfortunate that Bowers' waspish script casts Pamela in an unattractive aggressive light, especially since Wilder is, for once, innocent of her suspicions *

When we last saw Pamela, she had just stepped back from leaving Wilder, appalled at his treatment of Sugden, *"tired of being a bystander at his Roman triumphs."* In this episode she goes on the offensive, circling to catch Wilder and Challis out in what she thinks is the beginning of an affair, undermining her husband at the dinner table and saluting Grant when he shows himself to be a match for Wilder. Seen in the context of the previous series, Pamela's behaviour is understandable. But divorced from that context, in the body of a new actress, Pamela comes across as sarcastic and undermining – like something out of Edward Albee's then current *"Who's Afraid of Virginia Wolf"*.

Patrick Wymark delivers some first class sulking as Wilder sees his plotting undermined by Pamela's mischief. Having failed to weave his web around Cameron-Grant, he is distrustful when the MP shows that he has anticipated Wilder's offer to lobby for the VTOL. His one sign of pleasure is when Grant deduces that Wilder is enthusiastic about the VTOL because Government funding will put him outside the control of the bank and Sir Gordon Revidge.

John Nelson Burton delivers an adventurous opening sequence. Returning from Rome, Don Henderson (Jack Watling) drives his sports car up the runway at Scott Furlong, suddenly spots Wilder gazing up at the VTOL. Cuts to a POV shot zooming up to Wilder and the jet. Wilder tells Henderson to concentrate on selling the VTOL, and while Henderson is mid-answer he turns to see Wilder already being driven off in his limo.

*Ann Firbank would be given a more sympathetic role as the wife of a Labour MP played by Tony Britton in *The Nearly Man* (1975).

Tuesday November 3, 1964   *A Lesson For Corbett.*

Writer David Weir   **Director Quentin Lawrence**

Alan Dobie (David Corbett). Peter Jeffrey (James Cameron-Grant MP). Wendy Gifford (Laura Challis). William Devlin (Sir Gerald Merle). Robert Urquhart (Henry Forbes). Alan Browning (Douglas Bradley).Philip Latham (Eric Styles). Duncan McIntyre (Bob Fraser). Garfield Morgan (Clifford). Elizabeth Wallace (Harriet Evans) Clement McCallin (Marlow). Frank Mills (Scotty Elllis).

David Weir showcases two of the new characters in this episode as David Corbett invites James Cameron-Grant to watch a test flight of the VTOL. It's hard for director Quentin Lawrence to disguise the fact that the VTOL mock-up is actually being suspended from a crane, but before this becomes too apparent, the jet wobbles precariously as it comes in for a landing.

Corbett rages at Henry Forbes (Robert Urquhart) for potentially damaging the jet through incompetence, but Forbes replies that the instability is a known problem (some of the real-life VTOL jets had big problems hovering, sometimes resulting in the death of their test pilots). Driving away from the airfield, Corbett tells Cameron Grant that the VTOL is not ready for production, and that if production was suspended and he was given another development grant he could iron out the problems and turn the VTOL into a world-beater. Grant asks if Corbett couldn't solve the problems during production and upgrade the first outputs, but Corbett says this would be wasting taxpayer's money. Grant suspects that Corbett's real objection is that putting the VTOL into production now would be a victory for Wilder, whereas delaying production for a year might mean that Wilder is gone.

Corbett meets up with journalist Garfield Morgan from *The Globe*, and feeds him information about the VTOL's flaws. When the story is published, Cameron-Grant suspects that Corbett is the source of the story. Grant convinces Sir Gerald Merle but when they confront Corbett he flatly denies it. However, the story spirals out of control when antagonistic MP Philip Latham (Klove in *Dracula Prince of Darkness*) follows it up. Soon there are concerns at ministerial level about the viability of the whole VTOL project .

Alan Dobie takes full advantage of an excellent script by Weir which displays the single-minded character of Corbett. In the first episode, Bill Ryan (John Wentworth) warned Corbett that he could only survive by fighting the Wilder's and Merle's on their own terms. Weir shows Corbett has taken this advice to heart. We see him openly strategizing against Wilder on two fronts; he encourages his works manager Bob Fraser (Duncan McIntyre) to dispute the new production layout designed by Arthur Sugden, and attempts to undermine Henry Forbes' position as Chief Test Pilot, setting him against the younger Douglas Bradley (Alan Browning) who Corbett continually reminds people has *"been with the VTOL project from the start"*.

Weir also gives an edge to the characters on the receiving end of Corbett's schemes. Bob Fraser is like a less effective version of Tom Bancroft from the second series. He makes a half-hearted attempt to pass the new production layout off as his own initiative but is almost immediately contradicted by Corbett. Douglas Bradley is torn between ambition and loyalty to Forbes, while Forbes himself preserves what Corbett calls his *"aging vanity"*. When a Ministerial delegation arrives to see the VTOL in action, Forbes has a telegram from Wilder endorsing Forbes' decisions as Chief Test Pilot. Corbett wants Bradley to fly the VTOL, worried that Forbes will not be able to handle the unstable jet, Forbes is determined to take the lead until Corbett realises that shouting orders won't work and tells Henry he'd *"be very grateful"* if Bradley flew the plane. Forbes agrees to let Bradley take control, but after the successful demonstration, the Minister asks why Bradley flew the VTOL. *"We wanted you to see that it didn't need a senior test pilot to fly it"* Henry improvises charmingly.

Weir also gives Sir Gerald Merle a more constructive role as director of Scott Furlong. Without compromising Merle's established characteristics, he shows him working with Grant to protect the company interests. Peter Jeffrey also gets to demonstrate the persuasiveness of James Cameron-Grant, convincing MP Philip Latham that the problems with the VTOL have been exaggerated, and ensuring that Corbett feels the full force of the press interest in those problems.

As the political pressure on the VTOL project grows, Corbett retreats into the technical issues like a child hiding under the blankets on a stormy night. Eventually it is Cameron-Grant who convinces him that he must confront the most immediate threat to his brainchild – the political threat of his own creation. If the essence of drama is change through conflict, *"A Lesson For Corbett"* is a textbook example. The final shot is almost a retread of Lawrence's closing of the previous season's *"Too Much To Lose"* – only instead of the whisky-drinking Wilder realising how close he's come to a career-killing physical disaster, the tomato-juice drinking Corbett greets the end-titles with the realisation that he's only averted the cancellation of the VTOL by learning to compromise.

Philip Latham would later play Willie Izard, company secretary of the Mogul Oil Company in BBC 1's *The Troubleshooters*, for which David Weir would become a principal writer.

Tuesday 10 November 1964   *The Golden Silence*

Written by Raymond Bowers   **Directed by James Ferman**

Peter Jeffrey (James Cameron-Grant MP). Wendy Gifford (Laura Challis). Jack Watling (Don Henderson). William Devlin (Sir Gerald Merle). Norman Tyrrell (Sir Gordon Revidge).Robert MacLeod (Camile Tonelier). Carleton Hobbes (Samuel Hesterby MP). Henry McCarthy (Evrais).

"Whenever I encounter a one-way street in France, halfway down I hesitate. I so often find myself the only driver obeying the sign." Sir Gerald Merle.

Camille Tonelier (Robert Macleod), Minister of France's newly constituted Bureau for the Integration of Expenditure, has a radical solution to the rivalry between Britain and France.

Both Britain and France are developing VTOL fighters. NATO will buy only one. If they have to choose between two aircraft, NATO will delay and this will give the Americans time to present their VTOL *("and being newer, it will seem better")*. Tonelier arranges a meeting with several British back-bench MP's with aviation expertise including Merle and Grant.

Tonelier offers to share -without strings- the details of Evrais Aviation's VTOL (Evrais reluctantly handing out personally assigned copies of the specification). Tonelier proposes that the French and the British should agree which plane is better. Only one will go forward to production, but the other nation will then have no competition in developing NATO troop carriers. Sir Samuel Hesterby (played by Carleton Hobbes, the former radio Sherlock Holmes) jokes that, if they can agree on this, *"there'll be no need to go into the Common Market"*.

When Sir Gordon Revidge learns of the French offer through a press leak, he is eager for David Corbett to examine the French specification as soon as Sir Gerald Merle can hand it over. But Sir Gerald piously reveals that he refused to accept a copy of the report because it would be a conflict of interest with his commercial responsibilities as a director of Scott Furlong. Revidge angrily criticises Merle for not thinking of his duty to the bank.

With Wilder travelling around Europe's capitals, staying out of touch (but phoning Don Henderson on a daily basis) Revidge is in control. He believes there is no future in military contracts and wants Scott Furlong to continue making commercial aircraft but *if* the Government *insists* on giving out money to develop the VTOL, he would prefer the money to go to Ryan Airframes. James Cameron-Grant later decodes this as, *"Revidge is fighting Wilder to remain top dog. He finds Wilder uncontrollable, so Wilder must go."* A development contract for the VTOL at Scott Furlong would be a success for Wilder making him difficult to remove. But if the contract can be delayed long enough, Wilder can be removed.

Grant exploits his copy of the French specification, negotiating (with Wilder, via Henderson) an extension of his PR contract with Scott Furlong. He also forces Revidge to offer seats on the boards of both Scott Furlong and Ryan Airframes.

Bowers delivers a neatly flirtatious scene between Peter Jeffrey and Wendy Gifford. Laura Challis is cooking partridges in the rotary grill of a "wood façade oven" when Grant enters his apartment. Laura's key is stuck in the lock and he tells her," I'll *get you another one cut"* . Grant hands her a perfume box saying Tonelier brought presents for everyone's wife. *"You're a widower"* she points out, but Grant replies*, "As a Frenchman he felt that was no circumscription."*

References to the recent election suggest that this episode was written or made before the result was known. Sir Gordon Revidge tells Sir Gerald Merle that*, "Before the election you expected – win or lose- that your party would promote you to its front bench – it hasn't !"*. And at a meeting in Paris, Tonelier congratulates the back-bench MP's on surviving the election.

Director James Ferman has several loving close-ups of William Devlin as Sir Gerald Merle doing slow burns in this episode – such as when Grant reveals that Wilder has offered him a directorship of Scott Furlong, and then when Sir Gordon replies that it is more likely someone less adventurous, *"some seat warmer"* will be chairing the company.

Jack Watling is nicely flustered as Henderson, being caught out by both Revidge and Cameron-Grant over whether he does or doesn't know Wilder's whereabouts. Revidge tries to make Wilder distrust Henderson by ensuring Don is present when he negotiates with Grant. He also tempts Henderson (made a director of Scott Furlong as part of Wilder's deal in the first episode) to join the Ryan

Airframes board saying that Wilder eventually gets rid of "Wilder men". He says, *"Eventually, Wilder feels under some compulsion to return their loyalty – at such moments he ceases to feel like Wilder – and he gets rid of them. Being on the board of Scott Furlong never helped any of them."*

Tuesday 17 November 1964   *The Island Game*

Written by Wilfred Greatorex   Directed by George More O'Farrell

Patrick Wymark (John Wilder). Reginald Marsh (Arthur Sugden). Jack Watling (Don Henderson). Alan Dobie (David Corbett). Robert Urquhart (Henry Forbes). Wendy Gifford (Laura Challis). Norma Ronald (Kay Lingard). Elizabeth Wallace (Harriet Evans). Duncan McIntyre (Bob Fraser). John Harvey (Aviation Minister*). Laurence Hardy (Bourne). Peter Cartwright (Dunnett). Jack Lambert (Group Captain Meylor). John Boyd Brent (Air Vice Marshal).

* The Minister of Aviation (in charge of military aircraft supply, as well as civil aviation) was Julian Amery, until 16 October 1964 when Roy Jenkins replaced him following the general election.

"Why does power turn men into little boys?" Henry Forbes

When the Ministry of Defence expresses concern about temperature control in the VTOL cockpit, Wilder sends Henry Forbes and the VTOL out to Tripoli for low-level flight tests. Corbett only learns about the tests after the VTOL has returned to England, and Wilder orders Don to ensure that Forbes' report is sent to the MOD without Corbett seeing it..

Wilder attempts to play his "island game", isolating Corbett from the information flow but Corbett fights back. He engineers a meeting with the Minister so that he can beg a lift to a demonstration that Wilder had tried to freeze him out of. Henry

Forbes observes that he hardly looks stranded. Indeed, it's Wilder that's beginning to look ragged. At one point, when Corbett has ignored his calls to the phone, Wilder tracks him down to one of the aircraft hangars. When Wilder accuses Corbett of wasting time, Corbett replies, *"You're the one who's been driving around all morning trying to find me."*

Wilder also attempts to neutralise Bourne (Laurence Hardy), an obstructive civil servant, Wilder tells Henderson, *"I want Bourne bought over, won over, or discredited"* and finally makes a crude attempt to buy Bourne off with an offer of a job at Elbertsons Merchant Bank. *"I'm all for creaming off top civil servants into industry."*

The rivalry between Arthur Sugden and Bob Fraser grows, leaving a team of 30 men waiting for instructions over the new production line. Sugden and Fraser still disagree. Wilder instructs Corbett to mediate between the two, but Corbett perceives this as means of keeping him busy and off-handedly instructs Sugden to use Fraser's plans for the new production line. Wilder is at first disinterested, but then countermands Corbett's order. Whatever the merits of either plan, the new production line becomes a sideshow for the bigger struggle.

Late at night, Wilder leaves the office doors open and summons Corbett to a confrontation, but the news that the production contract has been won postpones the showdown.

Another sub-plot is brought into play when Don Henderson remarks to Wilder that he's pushing himself too hard in the conflict with Corbett. Wilder looks older in this scene – his hair grey at the sides – although it's hard to tell if this is make-up or a consequence of the studio lighting and quality of telecine reproduction in this scene. Henderson says, *"Corbett's young enough to take this kind of stress. It's beginning to show John"*

Wilder insists that, *"I'm not losing weight – and I sleep very well – I've taken nothing stronger than an aspirin for months!"*. But after winning the production contract, he declines to join Don in the pub for a celebration. As the end titles begin, Wilder takes a bottle of pills from his pocket and knocks one back. We recall that in *Empires Have To Start Somewhere*, Wilder said the company doctor had given Bill Ryan as an example of what can happen when you push yourself too far.

Tuesday 24 November 1964 *It's A Free Country - Isn't It?*

Writer Edmund Ward. **Director John Cooper**

Patrick Wymark (John Wilder) Jack Watling (Don Henderson) Reginald Marsh (Arthur Sugden) Sheila Raynor (Mary Sugden) Meredith Edwards (Greening) Cyril Raymond (Major Farrell) Norman Tyrrell (Sir Gordon Revidge) William Devlin (Sir Gerald Merle) Bryan Mosley (Frank MacKenzie). Edna Landor (Monica Parsons) Keith Anderson (Bob Langhorn) Duncan McIntyre (Bob Fraser). Howard Goorney (Peter Skinner). Helen Cotterill (Sandra Wilson) Anthony Dawes (Minister's Emissary).

"I saw my own security file at Gregson's once...and they knew more about me than I did myself. They never asked me a single question. Every stupid thing I'd ever done was listed and I couldn't argue because nobody ever asked me." Don Henderson

Ministry of Defence investigator Greening arrives at Scott Furlong to review security. A classified file is missing from Arthur Sugden's office (his rival Bob Fraser has taken the file for work purposes). Sugden refuses to let Greening's men search his home for the missing file. Even when the file is found, Greening is unsatisfied. The file, *"is meaningless in itself – all documents are – it's the effect they have on people (that's important). The file was a keyhole and we shall look through it and see a whole room!"*.

After investigating Sugden further, Greening decides to remove his provisional security clearance. Arthur's professional association tell him he can't fight because the security people don't have to give a reason for removing his clearance. The Scott-Furlong board sees Sugden's continued presence as a threat to the VTOL contract. Corbett says by telegram that Sugden's job is not important enough to jeopardise the VTOL project. Ironically, Wilder resists because he doesn't want civil servants interfering in his business. But even Wilder can't win this one. Sugden is given two options – work under Fraser as deputy works manager producing Sovereign parts, or resign on health grounds with three years pay and 70% salary. But he must also agree to keep silent about the real reason he left.

"There's one thing I learnt from my father, " Sugden says, *"Principles don't pay the rent. "* He agrees to resign.

Don Henderson drives Sugden home and breaks the news to Mary. *"He's done nothing, "* she says, *"He's not broken any law. "*

"There isn't any law, " Henderson says, his voice breaking, *"They make their own. "*

In Edmund Ward's 1969 series *"The Main Chance*", his lawyer hero David Main is advising a company which has just taken over a factory that employs an industrial agitator called Grady (Anthony Bate). Grady joined the firm just after takeover talks were announced and they suspect his target is the wider conglomerate. Main suggests his clients transfer Grady to a production line doing classified work for the Government, *"And then get him thrown out as a security risk. It's a branch of the law where there's no legal comeback."*

In, *"It's A Free Country- Isn't it?"* that same law triggers Arthur Sugden's downfall. Scott Furlong's security officer Major Farrell (Cyril Raymond) reminds Wilder, *"As part of all defence contracts, Ministry security have the right to check on all arrangements and personnel."* To smooth the way for the VTOL project, Trade Union officers with *"affiliations"* (to the Communist party) have already been moved with *"no fuss."* Even so, Ministry investigator Greening (Meredith Edwards) says, *"Industry always regards security as a quiet matter – above a certain level that is. A file left in a taxi by a director usually creates far less fuss than when a workman steals ten pounds of lead."*

Reginald Marsh's final appearance in the series draws together several themes: Wilder's original prejudice that Sugden did not have the right background for the job of General Works Manager is echoed by Greening who says, *"The profile, as our American colleagues would call it, is not a very impressive one from a security standpoint."*

The self-belief (or arrogance) that led Sugden to challenge Gilbert Corey during the war (*How Can You Win If You Haven't Bought a Ticket?*) becomes part of the circumstantial case against Sugden. The fact that Corey tried to have him court martialled is pulled from Sugden's RAF record but Sugden's was vindication is ignored. His attitude antagonises Greening, but also triggers events. Sugden refuses to let Bob Fraser *"pick his brains"* over armament weights for the VTOL. As he exits the office, Sugden tells Fraser, *"You might pick up something from those books over there on the shelf. That's how I learnt about it. Late at night mostly."* Fraser flicks unenthusiastically through one of the manuals before spotting the security cabinet where Sugden has a file on *"Vibration Dampers for Armament Mounting"*. Unknown to Sugden, Fraser has a key to the cabinet and borrows the file, resulting in it being missing when Farrell and Greening make their check of signed out documents.

Greening and Farrell begin to search Sugden's office for the file but he makes them stop. Later, Sugden refuses to let Mackenzie (Bryan Mosely, the "big man" from *"Get Carter")* search his house.

In the second series episode *"No Man's Land"*, Wilder opposed Sugden's appointment because he didn't have the right background. Now Greening makes the same assessment. When Major Farrell excuses him saying, "A lot of people regard our job as interfering," Greening qualifies; *"Yes. Workers. Labourers. But General Works Managers – No. I should have expected full and automatic co-operation from a General Works Manager."*

Greening takes into account Sugden's background and acknowledges, *"The usual working class resentment of police action. A dogmatic resentment of encroachment of privacy."* But Sugden should have risen above this. *"He is a man of some authority and as such he should understand some of the problems of authority. If he hasn't got this understanding, then he's not a fit person to have security files at his disposal."*

Meredith Edwards brings a lugubrious gravitas to the role of Greening, who introduces himself to Wilder by saying, *"People don't like security officers and this is a feeling I like to encourage. We're not engaged on a convivial activity."*

There is a certain irony to the casting of Edwards. The son of a coal miner, he worked as a factory lab assistant before becoming an actor. As a conscientious objector on religious grounds in World War Two, he served in the National Fire Service in Liverpool before being drafted into the Non-Combatant Service with the "Army Tropical Theatre" in Palestine. (*"Is Sugden religious?"* Greening asks Mackenzie . *"No. Didn't act like a pacifist either."*) A strong-minded Welsh nationalist who later stood for Plaid Cymru in the 1966 general election, he persuaded director Leslie Norman to let him play his death scene in *Dunkirk* (1958) in Welsh.

The file on Arthur Sugden is consistent with what we've seen before. Sugden's father was an activist in Ossett, not popular with the employers. His brother, played by Jerome Willis in *No Man's Land,* is a fierce union man. Sugden had been a union convenor before becoming a manager. From his RAF record we learn that Sugden refused reserve duty for Korea, stating that he saw too many lives wasted during World War Two. Greening concludes that they have a *"circumstantial but valid case"* to withdraw Sugden's security clearance.

Given that John Wilder opposed Sugden's appointment as General Works Manager throughout the second series of *The Plane Makers,* Edmund Ward makes his defence of Sugden convincing. *"I don't even like the man."* He tells Greening. But he believes in him. As he tells the Scott Furlong Board, *"I've had his Northern integrity shoved down my throat til I nearly gave him a hymn book."* Perhaps unconsciously he's echoing Gilbert Corey at the end of the last series when he said, *"I don't like Sugden. But by God I trust him."*

It's made more convincing when Sir Gordon Revidge announces that he's already cabled David Corbett, who thinks the matter is not important enough to threaten the VTOL project. The fact that Sugden is now perceived as *"a Wilder man"* makes it seem right that Wilder would take an opposite view to Corbett. When the Board wants to remove Sugden, Wilder challenges Sir Gerald Merle; *"I thought you were supposed to be the unswerving champion of the individual."*

Shiftily, Merle replies, *"On security matters I've always found it wisest to support the proper authorities,"* and then retorts, *"I'd have thought YOU were hardly a staunch advocate of democracy."*

"I'm not," Wilder replies, *"But I will not have a greasy little man threatening me in my office!"*

Wilder's pride highlights another common theme in this episode. Wilder prides himself on fighting to retain Sugden rather than standing with the *"grey, little men".* Greening has pride in his instincts, on ensuring that the highest levels of management are treated equally with the labourers and on getting his boot on the throat of industry. It could also be argued that Sugden's downfall is triggered by pride and the rivalry with Fraser. The episode opens with him leaving for work early, telling Mary that, *"Whatever time I get in, Bob Fraser's there an hour earlier. It gives him time to think up all the questions so he can pick everyone's brains."* We later see Fraser complaining to Wilder that Sugden won't share his knowledge about armaments weights *("He did a lot of this work during the war and I didn't")*. Wilder is unsympathetic, *"All the details are down on paper. If you don't understand them, that's your look out."* Sugden could have helped Fraser, but instead –with a touch of pride – reminds him of all the study he put in. Fraser, perhaps not wanting to look stupid with Wilder's words fresh in his ears, helps himself to the file in Sugden's security cabinet.

Fraser only has a key to the secure cabinet because it came from Ryan Airframes where Fraser was works manager. Fraser got the spare key because *"Bill Ryan was fed up with the red tape applying for spares"*

The second series episode *"A Question of Sources"* by Wilfred Greatorex also dealt with a conflict between a vital technician whose son is a communist, and an officious security officer. In this episode, Scott Furlong's security officer Farrell (Cyril Raymond) is more personable, trying to make Wilder understand that he has to co-operate with Greening before he arrives. He's also the one who has to make the full impact of Greening's decision clear when he collects the security files from Arthur's office. Sugden says he'll need the files and Farrell says, *"I think they're taking you off VTOL work – I'm sorry."*

Even after repeated viewings, *It's A Free Country – Isn't It?* still has impact. Reginald Marsh's exhausted slump into his armchair at the end sums up all we've learned about Arthur Sugden – his passion for plane making – *"we create"* – his reputation within the industry – now all lost. Modern TV shows come up with ever inventive methods of "killing off" characters, but no-one has yet destroyed a character as thoroughly as *The Plane Makers* did with Arthur Sugden.

Tuesday 1 December 1964   *A Question of Supply*

Writer Arthur Swinson   **Director Josephine Douglas**

Alan Dobie (David Corbett). Robert Urquhart (Henry Forbes). Jack
Watling (Don Henderson). Peter Jeffrey (James Cameron-Grant
MP). Wendy Gifford (Laura Challis). Elizabeth Wallace (Harriet
Evans). John Harvey (Aviation Minister). Geoffrey Chater
(Nightingale). John Crocker (Hunt). George Waring (Lockett) .
Peter Cartwright (Dunnett). Michael Collins Sir Henry Manning).
Frank Tregear (Assistant Secretary). Sidney Gatcum (Barman).

*"I don't think that moral philosophy is going to help us. We're
technical men and we've a technical problem to face! Let's get on
with it!" David Corbett*

During low-level tests in the VTOL, Forbes has to seize control
from the autopilot narrowly averting a crash. At Radley Heath
airfield, Corbett accuses Forbes of almost wrecking the plane, but
Henry angrily defends himself and Dunnett, his observer saying the
radar failed. *"There were no red lights flashing. It's a system
fault."*.

Corbett finally accepts that there's a fault in the radar when he gets
confirmation from the Ministry of Defence that parallel tests at
Boscombe Down have had the same problem. The radar is an
American design, made under license by a British firm. Corbett
meets with the Ministry officials; Nightingale (Geoffrey Chater)
who is anxious that the VTOL is delivered to the RAF on schedule
and Hunt (John Crocker) who argues the radar is fundamentally
sound. Corbett wants to replace the radar and when Hunt says the
only British alternative is too large for the VTOL and doesn't work
at supersonic speeds, Corbett argues that they should go direct to the
American manufacturer, Field Connor.

Nightingale warns Corbett that taking the contract from Browning's
may cause hardship in a high unemployment area. In the House of

Commons, James Cameron-Grant is approached by Sir Henry Manning, Conservative MP for the constituency containing Brownings, who asks him to use his influence as publicist for Scott Furlong. *"Work's hard to come by up there, lad."*

Both Henderson and Cameron-Grant warn Corbett that this technical problem has political elements and that he should leave the problem to Wilder (who is in Paris). Corbett is determined that nothing should delay the VTOL and meets with the Minister (John Harvey) to push for the American deal. A radar is flown over from America and performs perfectly in a test flight. However, the Americans then say they can't supply in quantity for 12 months. As Corbett and the civil servants meet to try and find a solution, Sir Henry Manning breaks the story in the House and the Minister comes under attack for betraying British industry.

The answer finally comes from Lockett (George Waring), a Scott Furlong technician who has stripped down the British and American radars for comparison. There was a small modification to the American set which wasn't incorporated in the British set. He thinks overheating caused the radar to drift. With the low-level radar reassembled to specification, Forbes and Dunnett take the VTOL back up to repeat the near-fatal test. This time the auto-pilot avoids the ground without intervention. As the VTOL flies past the airfield, Corbett orders three bottles of whisky from the board room. One each for Forbes and Dunnett, the third for Lockett.

Written by Arthur Swinson, who had contributed the impressive episode *In The Book* to the previous series, *A Question of Supply* is directed by Josephine Douglas, who had directed *6-5 Special* and *Emergency Ward 10* for ATV and would go on to produce *Dracula AD 72* for Hammer. As a 16-year-old, Douglas had joined the RAF during the war and trained as a radar wireless mechanic, which made her uniquely qualified to direct this episode (information from *Little Shoppe of Horrors* #7).

Douglas handles a complicated episode well. With Forbes and Dunnett's faces obscured by helmets, she has to resort to shooting

Forbes face on, and Dunnett from the side to differentiate between the two. While opening the episode in the middle of the test is dramatically reasonable, it gives the viewer very little time to take in the fact that Forbes is not holding the control stick because the VTOL is on auto-pilot.

The conclusion of the episode is played out much better. With Corbett now *"the most popular man in British aviation"* and awaiting Wilder's return from Paris, the test-flight with the upgraded radar is his last chance. The scene is played out with a close-up of Corbett's face listening to Forbes over the intercom, and then a look between Corbett and Lockett as his body language acknowledges that Lockett has saved him, and then a call to his secretary to get the Ministry on the phone and bring down the three bottles of Scotch.

The acknowledgement of the bottle of whisky to Lockett shows that Corbett is learning he can't do it all by himself. By pushing forward and involving the Minister, he has jeopardised the VTOL project. He has also refused to hear out Grant who has learned from Laura Challis that the American deal was brokered by Wilder because he was selling Sovereigns to a subsidiary of Field Connor *"..and they dropped a hint or two. Wilder signed up a nice package deal in London with the Ministry."*

Geoffrey Chater, who played the public relations officer in A *Question of Sources*, here plays Nightingale, the civil servant whose main concern is that the VTOL is delivered on time, *"The RAF will be hopping mad if it's late into service"*

Elizabeth Wallace, as Corbett's secretary Harriett Evans has an amusing line when Corbett watches Cameron-Grant walking to his car and says, *"When I came into this business when you hired someone, you also hired their loyalty."* Wallace says under her breath, *"That was before you came into this business."* However, they do later share a touching scene later on when the Minister has come under attack in the House and Corbett is avoiding the press and any other callers. She brings him a cup of coffee, and he stops as if to see her for the first time and thank her.

Tuesday 8 December 1964

The Flying Frigates

Writer Raymond Bowers   Director Eric Price

Patrick Wymark (John Wilder). Jack Watling (Don Henderson). Alan Dobie (David Corbett). Peter Jeffrey (James Cameron-Grant MP). Wendy Gifford (Laura Challis). William Devlin (Sir Gerald Merle). Anthony Newlands (Tony Tilling MP). Elizabeth Wallace (Harriet Evans). Chip Coveney (Trilby).

"Nobody joins me conditionally. You join me in ignorance or not at all." John Wilder

Wilder organises a demonstration of the VTOL for representatives of the German Air Force. Although it is 20 years since the end of World War Two, the arming of the Luftwaffe is still a sensitive subject. No-one is sure what Wilder is up to, but his enemies see a potential chance to remove him. In *The Golden Silence*, Sir Gordon Revidge offered directorships in Scott Furlong and Ryan Airframes to Cameron-Grant. Now the MP must decide which seat will further his political career.

An intriguing script by Raymond Bowers with its roots firmly in the politics of 1964. It's worth reminding ourselves that Wilder's visitors are from the "Western" half of a divided Germany. The Federal Republic of Germany was a member of the capitalist North Atlantic Treaty Organisation, while the German Democratic Republic was part of the communist Warsaw Pact. Following the disarming of German forces at the end of World War Two, the West German Luftwaffe was established in 1956 when the FDR joined NATO.

As Don Henderson (Jack Watling) tells Laura Challis (Wendy Gifford) people are often trying to tempt him away from Wilder with all kinds of plans. The thing about Wilder is that no-one ever knows what he's planning until he's done it.

Laura Challis says the merchant bank has two concerns. Now that the Government is funding the VTOL, the bank can use the money put aside for the VTOL elsewhere. Sir Gordon thinks the bank could invest in production facilities at Ryan Airframes. If NATO buys the VTOL, Corbett could hand over home production to Scott Furlong and build an improved VTOL at Ryans. If NATO buy the French version, Sir Gordon sees more profit in a civil design which Corbett has shown him.

As the speculation continues, Eric Price has fun with the exterior shooting. Wilder stands in his jeep waving off the convoy of limousines as someone remarks that Wilder looks like *"a warlord reviewing an armoured division,"* and *Ride of the Valkyries* plays over the soundtrack.

The second part kicks off with an amusing but intense afternoon tea on the terrace of the House of Commons as Labour party whip Tony Tilling (Anthony Newlands) discusses Wilder's plans with Cameron-Grant and Sir Gerald Merle. Tilling's concern is that nothing should embarrass the party while Merle and Grant are both seeking the post of aviation minister. As a prospective director of both Scott Furlong and Ryan Airframes, Grant convinces Tilling that he is best placed to investigate Wilder. The verbal fencing between Grant and Merle is amusing but complex. How sad that Bower's script was seen only once – never repeated, never available for home consumption until fifty years later.

Wilder tells Corbett that the Germans like his VTOL, but would like it modified for toss-bombing (where the plane pulls up when releasing the bomb, distancing itself from the blast). Wilder asks how long it would take to provide a modified VTOL. *"Don't say six months, David. Say two months from now!"*

Corbett protests that the German's are not supposed to buy without co-ordinating with the other NATO countries. Still smarting from his experiences in *A Question of Supply,* even Corbett is aware that arming Germany is a political risk. When Wilder protests that the war ended 20 years ago, Corbett retorts that, *"The Spanish Civil war was over 25 years ago, but that didn't stop it blowing up again in Britain when we tried to sell Franco some of our frigates!"*

Corbett is referring to a then-current but now long forgotten episode in British history *(see page 121)

"The scandal of the Flying Frigates, eh?" says Wilder, *"It would make a good headline for the Globe."* And sure enough, with a tip off from Sir Gerald Merle, the Globe's presses are soon thundering with the headline, *"Now Flying Frigates!"*

In a bravura final scene, Corbett, Henderson and Cameron-Grant are waiting to see Wilder when Laura Challis and Merle arrive on behalf of Sir Gordon to demand Wilder's resignation.

"And who has he in mind to take my place?" Wilder asks, *"David there, who has always told the press he has no responsibility? Grant, who has chosen to join a man who by his own admission is not big enough to take responsibility? Or Sir Gerald, who despite his connection with Scott Furlong has already spoken in the House deploring my action – a most honourable and public-spirited gesture!"*

Laura replies that Sir Gordon was thinking of Henderson, but Don jumps in; *"You can dam well tell Sir Gordon that if he hasn't got the guts to come and tip John out by himself, he hasn't got the muscle to lift me in. If John goes, I go!"*

Wilder smiles and says that now they know where everyone stands, he can reveal that his last visitor represents Tonelier, the French Minister for Integration of Expenditure (from *The Golden Silence*). Tonelier has decided that if the Germans are going to buy Scott

Furlong's VTOL, further development of the French VTOL would be uneconomic. The Evray VTOL will be scrapped.

"Tell Sir Gordon I no longer need bank or state finance! I'm being financed Continentally!"

One of the most satisfying episodes of *The Plane Makers* third series, Bowers' script brings together threads from previous episodes and delivers substantial action for most of the major characters. It's particularly rewarding to see Don Henderson react to the temptation of the managing director's chair, and his delighted grin when Wilder tells him to get over to Italy and start selling VTOL's.

Bowers also uses secretaries to reflect the three main characters. Chip Coveney plays Henderson's secretary Trilby, a knowing young woman who laughs at his flustered reaction to Wilder's unannounced return and says of Laura Challis that, "Sir Gordon uses her like a spoon to stir up trouble." The episode opens with Elizabeth Wallace as Harriett Evans growing increasingly annoyed as Corbett makes several false starts dictating a letter. And later on Norma Ronald plays Kay Lingard with cat-like amusement as she watches Wilder keeping Corbett waiting while he signs a series of letters.

* The Spanish Frigates: In the 1960's, both Spain and Britain were excluded from the Common Market. Spain's fascist dictator General Franco, had encouraged tourism in coastal resorts such as Benidorm and even Franco's communist opponents had encouraged British workers to holiday in Spain in order to bring cash into the country.

In May 1964, an MOD press release revealed that Britain's Conservative Government was negotiating with Spain to hand over specifications of the "Leander" class anti-submarine frigate for construction in Spain. While no help to Britain's ailing ship-building industry, it was viewed as a "loss-leader" towards the prize of supplying the whole Spanish navy.

Opposition leader Harold Wilson raised the issue on 17 June 1964 during a debate on foreign affairs. Wilson looked forward to the end of Franco's rule in Spain. *"When that occurs, we shall be ready and willing to welcome Spain into the comity of nations. To supply valuable information about naval vessels... to a democratic Spain is one thing. To supply it to Fascist Spain is quite another. The Government's policy towards Spain should be the same as it is to Eastern Europe and Cuba...Trade, yes... But arms, no."* Wilson then asked the Foreign Secretary, *"Has the right hon. Gentleman received from the Franco Government a withdrawal of their claim on Gibraltar? Has he made that a condition of the arms deal?"*

Rab Butler replied that Gibraltar was not discussed in the negotiations. Wilson's mention of Gibraltar was calculated to win over British opinion. The Spanish broke off negotiations and in November 1964 struck a deal with the United States to build modified Knox frigates at the Bazán El Ferrol shipyard.

Tuesday 15 December 1964　　*Only A Few Millions*

Writer David Weir　　　　**Director John Cooper**

Alan Dobie (David Corbett). Robert Urquhart (Henry Forbes). Jack Watling (Don Henderson). Peter Jeffrey (James Cameron-Grant MP). Wendy Gifford (Laura Challis). Norman Tyrrell (Sir Gordon Revidge). William Devlin (Sir Gerald Merle). Elizabeth Wallace (Harriet Evans). Richard Bebb (Alistair Burton). Malcolm Tierney (Page). Edward Burnham (Louis Heldman). Jack Melford (Cullen).

"Every step of the way, Wilder outwitted us," Sir Gordon Revidge

Although Patrick Wymark does not appear in this episode, Wilder casts a long shadow as the other characters spend the whole episode trying to outguess him. Sir Gordon Revidge and Sir Gerald Merle intend to nominate David Corbett as a director of Scott Furlong. They assume Wilder will oppose him, but learn that Don Henderson has been instructed to vote for Corbett in Wilder's absence.

With Wilder attending a NATO meeting in Paris, it will be up to Corbett to meet with the Ministry of Defence and discuss VTOL costs. Although Corbett believes the meeting is long overdue, he is also apprehensive that costs have risen. *"The Ministry aren't going to jump for joy when they find out the VTOL's going to cost £18 million more than the figure, we quoted a few weeks ago."*

Corbett is suspicious that Henderson and Forbes know more than they're letting on, and presses Henderson to reveal that the MOD expect Scott Furlong to fund the £18 million shortfall. *"Wilder wanted me to look foolish! Floundering in front of the Ministry."*

Corbett is determined to find the extra funding, but Laura Challis explains that (in the 1960's economy) the problem can't be solved by writing some figures on a balance sheet. *"If you borrow £18 million, someone, somewhere has to have £18 million"*

Revidge makes discrete enquiries in the banking community, but can't identify anyone with the spare capacity. When Corbett begins contacting bankers directly, Sir Gordon Revidge is angered and explains that the world of merchant banking is a small one - if a firm controlled by Elbertson's bank starts asking for a loan everyone will know about it, and question why they can't come up with it themselves.

With no funding available, the desperate Corbett's first act as a member of the Scott Furlong board is to commit the company to the £18 million. He explains to Revidge that Wilder would not have set the situation up, without knowing that he could return *to "pull the money from up his sleeve – another Wilder miracle!"*

Revidge realises that the reason he couldn't find out where the £18 million was coming from, was because Wilder was getting it from outside the banking community. Further enquiries confirm that the loan would come from a joint stock company. The chairman was anxious for a Knighthood and the Minister had agreed to broker the deal because it would save the Government having to increase the

VTOL budget . If Corbett had admitted that he didn't know where to find the extra £18 million, the Minister would have told him.

A well-plotted story from David Weir keeps the audience engrossed up to the last minute. If the story has any flaw, it is one shared with films like *Skyfall* which depend on everyone acting the way the grandmaster expects; in this case that Corbett's paranoia will lead him to pressure the "truth" out of Henderson and that Corbett's *"pride and stubbornness"* would prevent him from admitting to the Minister that they didn't have the £18 million.

However, Weir develops the story convincingly. Like the old joke, "just because you're paranoid, it doesn't mean they're not out to get you," Corbett's badgering of Henry Forbes seems over the top at first until we realise that Forbes really does know something that will affect Corbett. The opening scenes about impending board room elections give no hint that the plot will take a right turn into the world of high finance. Weir also enlarges the character of Sir Gordon Revidge as he tells Corbett a parable about his early days as young financier.

Revidge's reaction to Corbett as a non-drinker is typically discrete. Accepting a brandy, Revidge tells him that, *"The first drink of the evening after a busy day is a great pleasure."* By contrast Laura Challis jokingly turns down an offer of a drink at lunch saying, *"You teetotallers seem to think everyone else drinks themselves to death."* (*"Some of them do",* Corbett remarks matter-of-factly).

This episode shows a gradual softening of Elizabeth Wallace who appears as Corbett's secretary Harriet Evans. Having detested Corbett when he took over from Bill Ryan, Harriet now leaps to Corbett's defence when Don Henderson criticises him. *"You don't know the pressures they put on him! Just because he won't do things their way. Just because he's not a yes man."* Wallace would go on to play the White Witch in ABC's 1967 version of *"The Lion, The Witch and the Wardrobe."*

There's an interesting effect during the opening sequence. The camera is looking through the entrance doors of the Scott Furlong offices as Revidge and Sir Gerald Merle arrive in a limousine. The camera cuts outside as Corbett meets them on the tarmac and they walk towards the office and then cuts back in front of the doors as they walk into the office. But it looks very much as if the doors are part of a false wall put outside, just for the Outside Broadcast cameras to film through.

Tuesday 22 December 1964   *The Salesmen*

Writer John Gray   **Director James Ferman**

Patrick Wymark (John Wilder). Jack Watling (Don Henderson). Peter Jeffrey (James Cameron-Grant MP). Wendy Gifford (Laura Challis). Ann Firbank (Pamela Wilder). Norman Tyrrell (Sir Gordon Revidge). Norma Ronald (Kay Lingard). John Harvey (Aviation Minister). Anthony Nicholls (Sir David Carstairs). Olaf Pooley (Walter MacDonald MP). Tony Steedman (Finlay Crowden). John Frawley (Air Vice-Marshal Sloane). Elisabeth Murray (Jane Langham). Ann Godfrey (Cameron-Grant's Secretary).

"You have a distracted quality. Like a boy that's been caught stealing sweets." Laura Challis to John Wilder.

When James Cameron-Grant hears a fellow MP say, *"We may yet cancel the VTOL"*, he takes it as idle chatter. But Wilder is determined to get to the truth. Grant concludes there is a pattern showing that someone at the top wants to cancel the VTOL. Laura Challis' analysis of the Minister's speeches, especially in America, shows that he is against a British VTOL jet. Sir Gordon Revidge agrees; *"The Government has cold feet. There's a chill of compensation in the air."*

"The Salesmen" is a mystery story. Whether or not it's about the murder of the VTOL project is the heart of the mystery. James Cameron-Grant is employed as Wilder's leg man to find out the

truth. The episode is notable in showing a particular vulnerability in Peter Jeffrey's performance; unsure of his relationship with Laura Challis, threatened by the Whip's office, and conscious of intruding on his relationship with Sir David.

Olaf Pooley contributes an interesting performance as the Chief Whip, Walter McDonald MP who is ironically introduced building a house of cards (this was many years before Michael Dobbs created the unstoppable whip Francis Urquhart in the novel and TV series of the same name). McDonald's first approach is mischievous, followed by a laboured parable about a poor man whose bread landed butter side up. Finally, he resorts to direct threats.

This episode also features one of the few appearances in this series of Pamela Wilder, played by Ann Firbank. Once again there is an acid little scene in the bedroom as they discuss previous visitors from the German air force. *"Do they ever bring their wives?"* Pamela asks, *"Or is that what they say about you on the Continent?"*

The climax of the episode comes in a bizarre little scene which opens with Wilder brooding in his office after receiving Grant's warning not to sell to the Australians. He complains to Miss Lingard about the unpalatable sandwiches he's been served. Norma Ronald comes forward to try one of the sandwiches as Wilder takes a phone call from Sir Gordon Revidge. The banker gives Wilder a free hand provided he realises that he's on his own. Delighted, Wilder bites into a sandwich and he tells Kay Lingard to call his Sales Manager, Don Henderson. As she picks up the phone, Henderson (Jack Watling) strides into the room. *"That's the sort of efficiency I like to see at Scott Furlong. You deserve a raise."* He offers Henderson a sandwich and says to Lingard, *"You deserve one, but you're not going to get it."* Norma Ronald laughs and debates whether to eat a sandwich as Wilder tells Henderson they've got the go ahead to sell to the Australians.

The episode ends on a cynical note as Revidge fakes outrage at Wilder's actions and tells Cameron-Grant they will have to "rebuild bridges" with the Government. With Christmas and the pantomime season approaching, Peter Jeffrey fixes Norman Tyrrell with a disbelieving raised eyebrow. Ironically, in the real world, the new Labour Government really was getting cold feet over VTOL projects but no-one at ATV could have known this. Or could they?

Tuesday 29 December 1964 *Appointment in Brussels*

Writer John Gray   Director Peter Collinson

"I'm not lost. I just don't happen to know where I am." John Wilder

Patrick Wymark   (John Wilder). Wendy Gifford (Laura Challis). Ann Firbank (Pamela Wilder). Norman Tyrrell (Sir Gordon Revidge). Gerald Campion (Francis). Norma Ronald (Kay Lingard). Bob Grant (Antique Dealer). Caron Grant (Secretary). Patrick Connor (Expense Account). Robin Ford (Pierre Dagenais). Colette Dunne (Stewardess). Stephen Hubay (Hotel Clerk).

A humorous episode which offers an insight into Wilder's character and features an amusing performance by Gerald Campion as Francis, the English waiter at a Belgian restaurant where Wilder and Challis are stranded.

Sir Gordon Revidge discovers that John Wilder has an appointment to meet Pierre Dagenais (Robin Ford) in Brussels. Dagenais is an old adversary of Revidge's but his business is commercial aviation, not a military plane like the VTOL. Revidge instructs Laura Challis to accompany Wilder, saying he must know what's being discussed at the meeting.

Their plane is forced to land at Ostend due to engine failure. Thick fog shrouds the port and although Wilder hires a car, he ends up driving in a circle back to Ostend. They book in at the Hotel Metropole and spend the evening in a restaurant. The next morning, Laura Challis wakes late and finds that Wilder is breakfasting with Pierre Dagenais.

At the end of the previous episode, also written by John Gray, Pamela Wilder asked, *"Are you using Laura Challis or is she using you?"*. In this episode, Wilder and Challis spend another evening together, with Challis gently trying to uncover Wilder's secrets. This episode opens with Wilder leaving a Harley Street office (laying the ground for the following episode, *"A Hoopla of Haloes"*, which would deal with Wilder's health). During their meal Laura asks, *"How serious was that illness? I heard you'd been sick."* Wilder deflects the challenge saying*: "the World is sick."*

Recorded 1st December 1964 and broadcast between the Christmas and New Year holidays, *Appointment in Brussels* was directed by Peter Collinson, who would go on to make *The Italian Job* (There is a scene of Sir Gordon and Lady Wilder's limousines synchronised to music which seems to anticipate the Mini's in the movie).The episode has comic overtones, but does not inhabit the world of comedy in the same way as *'Costigan's Rocket'*. The opening scene features Bob Grant (pre-*On The Buses*) as an obsequious antiques dealer over-charging Wilder £300 for a Chinese vase (which Pamela Wilder subsequently tips off the bedside table when Wilder cancels her trip to Brussels). There are also some amusing scenes of frustration as Wilder spends three hours trying to drive from Ostend to Brussels, only to end with a fog horn underlining his failure as he comes up against a road sign reading 'Oostende'. The humour underlines the fact that the episode is, on the face of it, a non-event which does not further the ongoing storyline. There are, however, some compensations in an exploration of Wilder's motivations.

As Wilder and Challis dine, a counterpoint is provided by a rude businessman (Patrick Connor) who is obviously aiming to seduce his secretary (Caron Gardner). Where the businessman is dismissive, Wilder and Challis are amused by the unexpected challenge of their waiter. They accept Francis' suggestions for wine, which Wilder thinks it is over-priced *("you get what you pay for"* is the retort) to accompany a three course dinner (minestrone, sole and steak tartare) , whereas the businessman snaps out an order for pizza and Stella Artois, signifying a crude package-tour exoticism.

Francis: "Whisky's a little dreary!" Wilder: "I see there's a touch of tyranny. Perhaps you can suggest something."

The episode is also notable for the casting of Gerald Campion as Francis, the English waiter at *Chez Bichette ("I find the continentals very simpatico"* says Francis when Wilder ventures that it's odd to find an Englishman working in Ostend). Campion had played Frank Richards' schoolboy *Billy Bunter* for the BBC from 1953 to 1961 (he had already been overage from the first episode when he was 29). Just as Patrick Wymark was now becoming a household name through the character of Wilder, Campion had been in demand for public appearances, *"opening fetes and pie factories".*

Campion (who was born in a pub and had a reputation as the *"slowest and rudest barman in London")* had also run a number of drinking clubs for actors – the most recent of which was Gerry's Club in Shaftesbury Avenue. At a time when licensing laws meant "the pubs closed as soon as you were thirsty", private clubs were the only means of getting a drink after the theatres had closed. Remarkably, Campion ran each club from 6pm to 2am while starring in *Billy Bunter*, cooking, serving drinks and clearing up, before reporting to the BBC's Lime Grove studios at 8am for rehearsals and performing live in the early evening.

Gerry's was the third club run by Campion (following the Buckstone and the Key Club), and he later established a number of restaurants devoted to French cuisine. He continued to perform after "Billy Bunter", appearing in films such as *"Carry on Sergeant"* and *"The Comedy Man"* and played Morse Hudson in "The Six Napoleons" opposite Jeremy Brett in *The Return of Sherlock Holmes* (1986). In common with Wymark, Campion had played Mr Toad (1953), and had recently worked with Peter Collinson's former guardian Noel Coward on 29 November 1964 in a BBC tribute to Winston Churchill called *"90 Years On"* (Campion had played Graham Moffatt opposite Wilfred Brambell as Moore Marriott).

Patrick Wymark was a member of Gerry's Club, as were many other show business personalities. Nick Triplow notes in *Getting Carter:*

Ted Lewis and the Birth of Get Carter that it was, "*a regular haunt for those in film, television and media and was used by certain members of the press on the understanding that nothing they witnessed there would find its way into the papers.*" Ted Lewis visited Gerry's Club with actors' agent Peter Crouch and it is likely to have been one of the venues where he quietly observed the "East End boys" who formed the basis of Jack Carter.

The role of Francis is a substantial change to John Gray's original script. The restaurant (*Chez Bichette* in the transmitted version) was originally "*L'Universe*", described as having been rebuilt after the war with "*nothing quaint or antique about it*". In Gray's script the waiter is Armand ("*named after my uncle*") who is initially unenthusiastic when Wilder and Challis walk in. He consults his watch as if to draw their attention to the lateness of the hour and looks pained when Wilder announces that, "*We've come to have a dinner - a very long dinner.*" In the transmitted version, Campion is briskly polite, glancing at his watch to confirm they have time for dinner before leading them to a table. Armand is something of a stereotype - when the second couple enter, he's distracted by the pretty young girl, handing the menu upside-down to her companion. As Campion plays Francis, he is as at best unimpressed, at most disapproving of the couple.

While the rest of the action sticks close to Gray's original, Armand's dialogue is amended to suit the revised character. When Wilder initially orders a Whisky, Armand disapproves saying, "*Whisky does blunt our taste. Perhaps an aperitif*" whereas Francis says, "*Whisky's a little dreary. Wouldn't you prefer an aperitif?*" Where the teleplay does stick to Armand's dialogue, it is generally interpreted by Campion to amusing effect (his uncle was, "*a very peculiar man. He used to drink metal polish.*") Another significant departure is his final scene. In the script, Wilder overpays Armand and the direction is that the waiter struggles with himself whether to admit this, before Wilder asks if Armand discovered his mistake in the change. "*Surely not*" Armand replies, to which Wilder responds "*My mistake*". The direction says that Armand "*accepts the compliment*". In the broadcast version, Challis and Wilder wait at the door for the change. Offscreen, we hear offscreen Campion yelling at the chef, followed by a clatter of pans. Wilder and Challis shrug at each other and agree to leave the restaurant.

Comparison of the rehearsal script and transmitted version also shows that Wilder's illness was downplayed slightly. In the script he takes a pill from a small box while waiting for Miss Lingard to connect a phone call for him, whereas in the transmitted version Wymark pours himself a glass of water without the pill. Similarly, a shot of Pamela Wilder trying to stick together the pieces of the Chinese vase (which she had earlier broken in fury) was deleted from the transmitted version.

As noted above, the episode does not really forward the ongoing storyline and we are left to speculate whether it reveals anything about Wilder. We know that Wilder had originally planned to take Pamela on the trip to Brussels. When he learns that Sir Gordon has also booked Laura Challis on the flight, he has a momentary outburst of fury before deciding there's more than one way to skin a cat and phoning Revidge to thank him for "sending Miss Challis." He then phones Pamela to say it is no longer convenient for her to come (when he previously asked if she wanted to come on the trip, Pamela had said, *"Yes. Very much. Too much."* The vulnerability of Ann Firbank's delivery is the closest we see to the Pamela Wilder of the previous series).

The twist in this tale is that the meeting with Dagenais was personal (to arrange the purchase of a villa from Dagenais). With Laura Challis forced on him, Wilder makes the meeting seem suspicious in order to keep Revidge guessing. It's therefore debatable whether anything that Wilder discloses during their evening meal is truthful.

When Challis probes Wilder as to what drives him, he tells Challis that the prime motivations are survival, goods and comfort. He questions whether power comes next. *"I used to think that power would be sufficient – that when you had it you just pulled the strings and everyone would dance. But they don't do they?"*

He goes on to tell Challis that *"if you're looking for motives it's not money. I have a 'gentle sufficiency'. It's the race that I like."*

"Life is not reward," he says, *"Life is a fact. A process. It can also be an art if you start practicing it early enough. "*

Wilder elaborates – *"The thing that people never expect a man to be anymore is himself."* Wilder says he is a simple man but admits that he has his fair share of vanity and also enjoys a gamble, *"the trouble with taking the simple course is that it's perfectly obvious to everybody what it is except those who are fools."*

Wilder says if he sees an apple, the simple course is to reach out and take it. But the more entertaining course is to order up a bowl of fruit, and offer a pear to one man, a pomegranate to another and then casually reach out for the apple. *"as if it's an afterthought."*

Wilder's thoughts on progress are still relevant today. *"Progress is very useful and a lot of men accept a little of it in the certainty that they'll get some kind of return instead of reaching and gambling for a great deal that's unsure. So you can spoon a little bit of progress into them like gruel and they feel very good."*

Thanks to Victoria Bennett of the British Film Institute for help in viewing the archive copy of the Rehearsal Script

Tuesday 5 January 1965 *"A Hoopla of Haloes"*

Writer Raymond Bowers.   Director Eric Price

Alan Dobie (David Corbett). Jack Watling (Don Henderson). Robert Urquhart (Henry Forbes). Peter Jeffrey (James Cameron-Grant). Wendy Gifford (Laura Challis). Norma Ronald (Kay Lingard). Elizabeth Wallace (Harriet Evans). David Langton (Dr Renkle). Michael Barrington (Finch).

"You are to be my fellow hound, Jim, and we are going to harry Wilder until he drops." David Corbett.

John Wilder has never taken a holiday in his adult life. So Corbett is suspicious when Wilder goes away for two weeks leaving only a Post Restante address in Naples. Learning that Wilder recently visited a Harley Street specialist, Corbett deduces that Wilder is unwell and plans the *"compulsory retirement of a worn-out man."*

In Wilder's absence, Corbett is next-in-line to sign off Don Henderson's expense claim. The sales director has spent the weekend in Amsterdam between business conferences in Rome and the Hague, and what seems like a petty argument is actually an attempt to smoke out Wilder.

Henderson's expense file has given Corbett the clue to Wilder's illness with a claim for a hire car to pick Wilder up from neuropharmacologist, Doctor Renckel. The file also shows that Wilder and Henderson visited a hotel popular with Americans. Rather tenuously, Corbett concludes that they must have been meeting Americans. And that ties in with an anomaly in Henry Forbes' expense file. He flew to Ottawa on a sales trip, but flew back from New York with no audit trail to show how he got from Canada to America.

Corbett suspects that Wilder's Americans and Henry Forbes' return from New York are connected. He freezes Don Henderson's expense account and then orders him on a sales trip around Europe assuming that he'll complain to Wilder and this will force Wilder to get back in touch. Grant points out that, *"You're assuming Wilder worships Henderson as much as Henderson worships him. Wilder only worships Wilder. Indeed his worship of himself only exceeds your worship of yourself in its frankness, which is why it's more tolerable."* However, both Henderson and Forbes see through Corbett's tactics and decline to contact Wilder.

Posing as a potential patient Grant visits Doctor Renckel (David Langton) who explains his discrete methods. The patient tells friends that he's going on a fortnight's holiday leaving a Post Restante address. They stay at a villa where the cook works for Renckel and the "man about the house" is a trained nurse. After two weeks the patient sends a telegram to say he's decided to stay on for another fortnight. At the end of the month he is cured. Grant asks what happens if the patient just needs a rest. Renckel says he offers both rest and treatment – the only difference is which villa you reside in (If this has overtones of *The Prisoner*, just note that Renckel has SIX villas all known by their colour. All we ever learn is that Wilder is staying at the Blue Villa).

Back at Scott Furlong, Henry Forbes is undergoing a simulated change of altitude in a pressure chamber. Rather than sending pilots to use the official pressure chamber at Farnborough, Scott Furlong can test its pilots on site. High altitude produces a condition similar to drunkenness and the scene in which Henry struggles to write a simple list with audibly laboured breath is genuinely unsettling. Grant sees Corbett trick the befuddled pilot into revealing that he and Wilder visited Greater American Airlines. Corbett reasons that the only component of the VTOL that could interest a commercial airline is the pressurisation. He decides to contact the airline and close the deal, snatching the victory from the absent Wilder.

However, James Cameron-Grant turns the meeting with GAA's European Manager to his own advantage when the American takes an interest in Scott Furlong's pressure chamber. The staff doctor is proud of it saying, *"It only takes a jiffy compared to the Farnborough method."* Grant suggests that Corbett demonstrates the chamber. Untrained for altitude, Corbett is unable to complete a simple building blocks test and suffers a headache as an after-effect. After Corbett's reactions have been analysed, Grant confronts him with his medical report which shows that he's very ill, suffering from hypertension. Grant tears the file up saying, *"I'll only exchange this at the right time for one article of furniture – and that's the one you're sitting in."*

Last week's teasing explanation (*Appointment in Brussels*) of Wilder's methods, raises the question of whether Wilder's holiday is one more false trail laid to distract Corbett. Why would Wilder have Henderson collect him from the specialists in a hire car, rather than use his own driver? We saw Wilder taking pills at the end of *The Island Game* after protesting to Henderson that, *"I'm not losing weight – and I sleep very well – I've taken nothing stronger than an aspirin for months!"*. Having pensioned off Bill Ryan on health grounds (following a conversation with the company doctor intended to warn *Wilder* to slow down) Wilder may have gambled that Corbett would jump to the same conclusion.

Laura Challis gives her own verdict on Wilder when she says that you, *"Always know who he is and what he is."* However, that verdict may be tainted as Laura (Wendy Gifford) is trying to understand what her position is with Grant. As an MP and a widower, will there be a time when it is right for him to marry, and will she be the one he marries? Even with Laura, Grant can't be open: *"If I ever needed to marry, I would consider you second...I would consider myself first."*

It's interesting that Corbett is naive enough to assume that Grant is an ally, but Grant is straightforward enough to make his independence clear. After watching Corbett interrogate Henderson over his expense account, Grant tells Corbett that , *"Anyone who questions my expenses puts my dignity at doubt, which I don't mind; but also my ingenuity, which I do."*

Similarly, Grant's distaste after Corbett exploits Henry Forbes suffering in the pressure chamber, is clear to see. It's easy to infer that he resolves to pay Corbett back at this point, although a less charitable conclusion is that Grant has just seen a way to advance his own position.

The most significant scene in this epigram filled episode is the one in which Grant and Forbes play golf while Grant is still trying to discover Wilder's whereabouts. Forbes compares Wilder to Corbett saying, *"One man enjoys fighting and winning. The other simply enjoys winning."*

"Robber Barons are gentlemen," Grant chides, *"But usurping serfs are not?"*

Unimpressed, the pilot replies, *"No. One man knows how to behave. The other simply doesn't want to learn."*

"Yes," the Labour MP replies, *"But some men don't get the chance to go to the right schools. Some men feel under privileged. That, I'm told, enormously increases their appetite as well as their cunning."*

"Good God," Forbes retorts, *"Don't you know what sort of an education Wilder has? He'd never forgive me if I told you."**

Catching on, Grant says, *"You have. Why should he be ashamed of it? Belated snobbery?"*

"No. A disinclination to make excuses for himself. Has it never occurred to you that Corbett's actually glad he went to 'Redbrick' instead of to Oxford? He expects to be forgiven his crudities, tolerated for not knowing any better and he claims advantage from supposed handicaps that Wilder would never even mention. One man always runs from 'scratch' Jim, and the other always claims that the world owes him a start."

Grant is frustrated. *"How disappointing. I thought you were reassuring me that chaps like us are bred for the top but there you are saying that urchins like Wilder can climb up and pass themselves off as to the manor born. Very disturbing. If Corbett suddenly sprouted a halo I wouldn't mind because I've always detested and disapproved of aesthetics and saints. But now Wilder's suddenly sprouting a whole hoopla of the things and it shatters my faith in sinners..."*

*In *The Power Game* episode *The Chicken Run*, Ken Bligh states that Wilder's public school was, *"minor...borderline."*

In his very first episode, Wilder was described by Peter Humphreys as having been, *"climbing all his life and now he's balanced at the top of the tree."*

In the January 1964 episode "The Smiler", the character of Harvey Graves (played by James Villiers) calls him *'poor Johnny Wilder'* and says *he "has more guts and push than anyone I know..but feels he's not quite accepted. We all have our dreams and John feels his spiritual home should be with the landed gentry."*

As the series draws to a close, we learn that Wilder is a self-created man. The question is - how long can he survive?

Tuesday 12 January 1965   *The Firing Line*

Writer Edmund Ward   **Director James Ferman**

Patrick Wymark (John Wilder). Alan Dobie (David Corbett). Jack Watling (Don Henderson). Robert Urquhart (Henry Forbes). Peter Jeffrey (James Cameron-Grant MP). Wendy Gifford (Laura Challis). Ann Firbank (Panela Wilder). Norma Ronald (Kay Lingard). Norman Tyrrell (Sir Gordon). Elizabeth Wallace (Harriet Evans). John Harvey (Aviation Minister). Joby Blanchard (Peter Mollett).

"When those figures are out they'll crucify the Minister and they'll crucify you!" David Corbett.

Corbett obtains proof that the production costs of the VTOL over the next six years will be one hundred million pounds more than Wilder's original estimate.

The decisive final episode of *The Plane Makers* once again keeps the audience guessing until the final moment. The first act implies that we're going to see another board room battle when Sir Gordon Revidge nominates James Cameron-Grant as joint Managing Director of Ryan Air Frames.

However, Wilder sets Miss Lingard to research the clients of Grant's PR company who are also suppliers of Scott Furlong. Wilder then phones the chief executives and tells them, *"Seen from the outside that's the kind of back-scratching job which can do the lot of us a great deal of harm. It's the sort of thing the press are looking out for."*

Faced with the potential loss of £200,000 worth of clients, Grant is forced to withdraw from the nomination. However, he is sanguine. He is well aware that Revidge was nominating him to create *"another pawn in the game against Wilder."* Grant also tells Corbett that, *"Conflict of interest is the first thing you learn to be aware of in the advertising business. But if I quote it, Revidge thinks I'm turning down a ripe plum – he gets offended. If Wilder does it for me, I'm still in the running for next year's harvest."*

Corbett meanwhile, has been using computer programmer Peter Mollett (Joby Blanshard) to analyse the production costs of the VTOL for the next six years. The results are devastating. As Corbett tells Wilder, *"I've always said more development work was needed on the VTOL...much of that work was needed to iron out production costs."*

*"I remember, "*Wilder replies, *"We were waiting for costs and we didn't want to hang around for them.".*

Triumphantly, Corbett tells him that the VTOL costs will total one hundred million pounds more than the original estimate. *"Because you were too greedy to wait. The methods you use may have worked ten years ago. They won't work now! You took an aircraft on day one and sold it. What the customer really wants is something that can compete in year three! You may be able to deliver it, but not at day one prices!"*

Wilder is aware that the Minister's reputation is tied to the VTOL project. After much persuasion by Wilder and Challis, the Minister's been boosting the VTOL in every speech he's made.

Cameron-Grant refuses Corbett's request to start a parliamentary enquiry and Laura Challis is disinclined to pass the report on to Revidge, who is away in Dorset. Pamela advises Laura not to warn Wilder about the report. *"Certain people, like John, don't really feel independent unless they bite the hand that feeds them. You can't help them. They have to do it on their own."*

Challis believes Wilder can't win this battle, but Pamela says he'll try. *"They'll all try. While the wives wait. Patient, familiar bed-warmers. Ful of vitamin pills for the ego. Somewhere to come back and get the next store of energy for the next day's bout of infighting. Corbett, Revidge, James Grant, John. All shuffling round the same board. Manoeuvring. They'll all become old men without ever once getting off the board."*

Grant and Challis decide to bunk off to Kew Gardens* rather than observe the gathering storm, while Wilder sends Don Henderson and Henry Forbes to a sales conference in Milan. *"It's almost as if you're clearing the decks"* Henderson guesses.

Realising he can't dispute the facts in the report, Wilder calls an early morning crisis meeting with Revidge and the Minister. He says their one advantage is that the figures need not have been published for another year. *"The British love the little boy who owns up."*

Wilder suggests the Minister makes a statement in Parliament saying his department had been analysing costs, *"to show your constant vigilance and concern about public funds."* While the figures are Corbett's, *"it's not unusual for two financial things to go on at the same time. The Ministry has full access to the figures."*

Finally, Wilder offers to be the scapegoat, with a letter of resignation waiting to be signed. John Harvey, as the Minister, is

*This was the last appearance of Challis and Grant although Wendy Gifford and Peter Jeffrey would play husband and wife in the 26 September 1970 *Fraud Squad* episode *The White Abyss*.

visibly relieved as he processes Wilder's plan and sees his own career being saved. When Revidge demands to know Wilder's price for signing the letter, the Minister jumps to Wilder's defence. *"I don't think you quite appreciate the magnitude of Wilder's offer! To my mind he's behaving in the best interests of us all. I'm surprised at your tone!"*

Turning to Wilder he tells him that his recognition in terms of public honours is long overdue. And Wilder then presses his advantage, asking for a seat on the Board of Elbertson's merchant bank. *"There's no power there,"* Revidge tells him. *"Don't you think I know it?"* Wilder replies.

That evening, Wilder confronts Corbett in his office. He reads out a news agency report of the Minister's statement about his department's investigation into VTOL costs. Horrified, Corbett hears that the Minister thanked Wilder, *"for his services to aviation"* and that he is, *"tipped to become Sir John Wilder very shortly."*

"You've still got everybody in your pocket haven't you?"

"There's a bit more," Wilder tells him, *"John Wilder has resigned as overall managing director in order to become a member of the board of the Revidge group."*

Triumphantly, Corbett realises that Wilder is out.

"With a certain degree of free will." Wilder tells him, *"I'd rather commit suicide than let you cut my throat. You made one mistake Corbett. You haven't got the stomach for the real knife jobs. When you got those figures, you shouldn't have peddled them around. You should have done your own dirty work. You're still an amateur!"*

The Firing Line brings *The Plane Makers* to a conclusion with Wilder walking out of the office building during the end credits. As

Wilder walks to the lift, the doors close in his face and he turns to walk down the stairs.

Edmund Ward's script provides a satisfying conclusion to *The Plane Makers*. With Patrick Wymark reportedly tiring of the series, it was not surprising to see him walk away from Scott Furlong. However, the conclusion of the rivalry between Corbett and Wilder is surprising. While Corbett thinks he's won, he is left as managing director of Ryan Airframes having to explain the cost over-run. And of course, the far more politically aware James Cameron-Grant is waiting in the wings. What no-one could have known at this point is that within four months the new Labour Government would cancel several military aviation projects. For *The Plane Makers* the end really was near.

Case Study Four:
Front Page Story

Producer Rex Firkin (Pieter Rogers, last 10 episodes)

Script Editor Wilfred Greatorex.

While the final series of *The Plane Makers* was underway, Rex Firkin and Wilfred Greatorex were already working on its successor, *Front Page Story*.

Given a generous run of 26 episodes from 19 January to 20 July 1965, the new series was set in *The Globe*, the popular Fleet Street daily introduced in *The Plane Makers*. A large cast of characters was led by regulars were John Bennett as the obsessively ambitious editor Roy Boscombe. Ace reporter Denny Tarrant was played by Derek Godfrey, who had starred as Antonio opposite Patrick Wymark in the 1961 Royal Shakespeare Company production of *The Duchess of Malfi*.

Godfrey played Tarrant, with a glint in his eye at the scent of scandal. He, *"flattered one, wooed another, insulted a third, all with the same suave ease,"* reviewer Marjorie Norris noted approvingly in *The Stage*.

Supporting characters included Roddy McMillan as news editor Alec Ritchie, Harry Towb as reporter Paddy Lucas, Derek Newark as Tarrant's pugnacious rival Joe Harwood from *The Star* and Chip Coveney as Boscombe's secretary Lucy.

Once again, Rex Firkin avoided the need to employ film crews for location shots, this time employing an outside broadcast spy camera called *Monoculus* which could film actors in Fleet Street without passers-by being aware.

The other innovation was that *The Globe* had a closed-circuit TV system installed so that the editor could exchange glares with other executives from the comfort of his office.

Right from the start, there seemed to be confusion about what kind of show *Front Page Story* was meant to be.

Firkin and Greatorex insisted that this wasn't going to *be The Plane Makers* in a newsroom. While the theme of *The Plane Makers* was the struggle for power, its use and abuse, the theme of *Front Page Story* was, *"The Individual at Bay. The person pursued by Fleet Street and invasion of privacy. On the other hand, the reporter as the defender of private rights being threatened by the law or politicians."*

However, ATV immediately wrong-footed viewers when Edmund Ward's opening episode was replaced on opening night by Raymond Bowers' *The Second Seller*, (originally planned as the third episode). Viewers and critics were perplexed when the heavily promoted characters of Tarrant and Lucas did not appear. The editorial director and proprietor sidled on unannounced. Clifford Davis, in the *Daily Mirror,* commented that, *"Even to someone accustomed to working for (newspaper executives) I found it difficult to determine who was who."*

The sub-plot of night editor Hugh Reamer's (Lloyd Lamble) plotting to unseat editor Boscombe led Marjorie Norris to speculate in *The Stage* that ATV wanted to show that, *"anything nasty Wilder and Co could so, the Globe staff could do nastier."* But Davis conceded that in Bowers script, directed by James Ferman, *"the players acted like real people and they spoke natural dialogue."*

Assistant night news editor Griffin (Norman Rodway) suspects he's about to be sacked. When an ex-cop offers him documents that compromise a prospective university vice chancellor, Griffin buys the documents with £1000 of his own money, intending to charge *The Globe* £5000. In the end Griffin is undone by proprietor Lincoln Ross (Edward Burnham) who orders editorial director Vic Stafford (Ivor Dean) not to buy the document.

Edmund Ward's *The Quiet Load* , directed by Peter Collinson, was broadcast the following week, delivering a more satisfying story in which Tarrant uncovers the truth behind a simple lorry accident that has been clumsily hushed up by the authorities.

Rex Firkin later said it took 13 weeks before he was satisfied with *Front Page Story*. By then the character of tough lobby correspondent Shirley Gray had been introduced in Raymond Bowers' *Command Performance* (9 March 1965). Shirley was played by Paddy Webster, daughter of *London Evening News* sports cartoonist Tom Webster and herself married to a Fleet Street journalist. A reporter for the rival paper *The Star*, Shirley is too expensive for *The Globe* until she comes across a story which threatens a personal impact on editorial director Vic Stafford (Ivor Dean).

David Stone's episode *The Vital Contact* (13 April 1965) introduced Basil Henson as Sandy Warren, the Globe's specialist with high level contacts. Described by one critic as, *"Inscrutable and ultra-suave ...his office is more like a luxury flat with couch, cooking range and creeping plants. He defends his integrity with Roman disdain and remains detached even from the editor."* (1)

Boscombe pits Warren against Shirley Grey to uncover an American takeover bid which the Treasury wants kept quiet. Roddy McMillan had observed that reporters are told, *"Do not intrude",* but with an underlying rider, *"Don't come back without a story."* This ambiguity is teased when Shirley Gray is shown in longshot getting the address of a secret meeting from the wife of a Treasury official, with the viewer left to speculate whether she had posed as a civil servant or let the wife make that assumption.

Despite the assurance that this was not *The Plane Makers* in a newspaper office, the final few episodes concentrated on night editor Hugh Reamer's (Lloyd Lamble) schemes to replace Boscombe. *Drop A Spot of Acid In It* (15 June 1965) by Peter Draper, has a storyline which would still be relevant in post-Covid Britain. Boscombe is approached by Sir Edward Lend (Bernard

Archard) who offers evidence about the awarding of Government contracts. Boscombe is told to stall the story and make it clear that the contract was a mistake not malpractice. Meanwhile Reamer finds a photo of Sir Edward quarrelling with his wife (Annette Kerr) and prints it.

In Raymond Bowers' *Whitehall 14* (29 June 1965), proprietor Lincoln Ross (Edward Burnham) is persuaded by board member Sir Howard Caull (Gerald Cross) to support his campaign against satirical TV show *Whitehall 14*. *The Globe's* TV critic Arthur Widden (David Knight) enjoys the show and refuses to write to order. He suggests to Boscombe that he gets a temporary replacement to review *Whitehall 14* but the editor refuses. *"If you have principles, you must stand up for them and accept either praise or penalty."*

The final episode, *The Shake Up*, was written by Edmund Ward and directed by Rex Firkin. With the circulation falling Editorial Director Vic Stafford (Ivor Dean) is excited by an advertising agency's suggestion that they publish a supplement. Reamer is appointed to edit the supplement after Boscombe refuses.

In the end, it's difficult to assess whether *Front Page Story* was a success. Right from the beginning there seems to have been confusion about what sort of series they wanted Front Page Story to be. As Ries and Trout put it, *"You can't stand for something if you chase after everything."* (2).

Front Page Story was always popular with the viewers – it was number 6 in the TAM ratings for 26 February, with an estimated 7,220,000 homes or 18,884,000viewers. Although it had dropped to number 13 with 5,860,000 homes by April, it maintained that audience into July, with 5,830,000 homes or 12,826,000 viewers.

But numbers aren't everything. Just as the BBC's *Z Cars* had met opposition from the Chief Constable of Lancashire, *Front Page Story* was "slammed" by the Guild of British Newspaper Editors in April 1965. *"The way we are presented in this programme is a complete travesty of what goes on in Fleet Street or any other newspaper office."* (3)

So, while viewers stuck with the series, journalists and their editors, who write the history of what is popular, did not. Certainly, by the time *Front Page Story* ended, Firkin and Greatorex were ready to start production on *The Power Game*.

John Bennett went on to star in ATV's *Market In Honey Lane* (1967-1968) ironically taped in the same backlot that the BBC would later use for the market square in Eastenders.

Nothing more was heard of *Front Page Story*, except for Sandy Warren (Basil Henson), *"the man with connections in the finest corridors of power,"* who returned in the *Power Game* episode *Confound Their Politics*.

Notes:

1 - John Tilley. Newcastle Journal. 24 July 1965.

2 - RIES, AL and TROUT, JACK. The 22 Immutable Laws of Marketing (1993). Harper Collins. Page 31.

3 - Sunday Mirror. 4 April 1965.

Case Study Five   The Power Game   Series One

Producer Rex Firkin Script Editor Wilfred Greatorex

Patrick Wymark as Wilder   **Clifford Evans as Bligh**

By February 1965, while *Front Page Story* was on the air, Firkin
and Greatorex were also in pre-production for *The Power Game*.
*"I'm delighted to say we're being given plenty of time to spend on
getting it set up,"* Firkin told *Television Today's* Marjorie Bilbow in
April, *"We won't start taping until the end of September...this is the
sort of time one should have for setting up a series that is going to
keep up the quality over a staying period."*

Firkin argued that the long gestation period was essential for
producer and script editor to get to know the characters in their
heads and then "brainwash" the writers. Get pre-conceived ideas out
of their heads, *"and get our ideas into their heads. If our
brainwashing works and they become as excited as we are about the
way the series is to go, their creative processes start and they add
all sort of touches that speed the development of the characters."*

To replace Alan Dobie's David Corbett, *The Power Game* pitted
Wilder against a new adversary - Caswell Bligh, played by Clifford
Evans. A film actor in the 1930's and 40's, Clifford Evans had
starred in one of the early ITV crime series *Stryker of the*

Yard (1957) and had recently starred in the Hammer Films *Curse of the Werewolf* (1961) and *Kiss of the Vampire* (1963).

Wilfred Greatorex's initial thoughts about The Power Game were that, *"The Plane Makers was mainly about the struggle for power inside one firm with Whitehall and Westminster the extra battlefield. The Power Game will have Whitehall and Westminster as its main arena, with industry the extra battlefield. The industry itself will be different – civil engineering instead of aircraft."*

In the first draft, the National Export Board was, *"The Royal Commission."* Greatorex noted that, *"Wilder, since the days of Wolfenden and Pilkington, has wanted his own Commission with the inevitable Wilder Report."* The character of Susan Weldon was called Fiona, and Caswell Bligh was plain Bill Bligh (his father was Caswell).

After some thought, it became clear that the name of Caswell Bligh was better suited to Wilder's opponent in the series. Born in Preston in 1907, Caswell was chairman of Bligh Construction Ltd, described as, *"Wealthy and moody. He has a sense of family which Wilder lacks and unlike Wilder he is capable of self-deception: deep down there's a Primitive Methodist lurking."*

Caswell's father, Albert was a monumental mason. *"Caswell built the company up with paving work, tearing up tramlines and road building. He took the company limited and called himself founder."* By the time the series starts, Bligh Construction is involved in construction of roads and bridges in Britain, dams and harbours abroad and has annual profits of £2 million (the equivalent of about £41 million in 2022).

Greatorex reminds us that at the end of *The Plane Makers*, Wilder lost his battle with Corbett and walked out of Scott Furlong. *"He got his knighthood. But it was a shabby honour, the result of a business bargain and part of the price Wilder levied for loss of office in the aircraft industry. He also got a seat on the board of Elbertson's merchant bank."*

"He has his eye on Sir Gordon Revidge's desk, but doesn't deceive himself. His talents are not the obvious ones to impress bank directors. Meanwhile, Revidge sees that Bligh Construction's need for Wilder is greater than his own."

Wilder and Bligh's main battleground is the National Export Board, which Greatorex describes as, *"set up by one of our successive bewildered governments to find ways and means of developing Britain as an exporting nation. The chairman, who is too tired to exhort himself, let alone a nation, is clearly about to leave 'on grounds of ill health.'"*

Caswell's son, Ken Bligh, is managing director of Bligh Construction, described as being born in 1929, *"able, bright, efficient, but short on drive and enterprise. Wilder's thinking is short term (tomorrow's motorway contract), Caswell's medium (heading a new Ministry of Roads). Kenneth has his sights on implementation of the 1963 Buchanan report on Traffic in Towns."*

Pamela *"Still neglected. Determined to keep her husband. Her tidy personal fortune has been removed from Scott Furlong and is ready for a new home."* Susan Weldon. *"Wilder's mistress is not passive like Wilder's former mistress Kate Barber. She is the 28-year-old daughter of a parson."*

Technical advisors for the new series included Conservative MP for Gravesend, Peter Kirk and Labour MP for All Saints, Birmingham, Brian Walden. Both MP's made themselves available to the writers and designers during pre-production and wrote critiques of each script. Kirk also took credit for the idea of the National Export Board. Walden, Parliamentary Private Secretary to the Chief Secretary of the Treasury would later go on to present the LWT series *Weekend World.*

David Weir, story consultant on the second series of *The Plane Makers*, had joined the BBC 1 series *The Troubleshooters* , which went out in opposition to the first two series of *The Power Game* Weir has more of a fan following today for his English dub scripts for the Japanese series *Monkey* but *Troubleshooters* creator John Elliot wrote that Weir, *"brought a new quality and dimension into the series...at a time when it could otherwise have gone cowboy-and-Indian, he helped it to think"*.(Elliott, J. MOGUL: The Making of a Myth, page 193).

Unlike *The Plane Makers, The Power Game* utilised the standard British TV production process of videotaped interior scenes and exteriors generally shot on film. With more of the action taking place indoors, this was obviously a more economic approach.

The title sequence for *The Power Game* was a relative rarity in British drama because it was more like the ITC film series, showing each member of the main cast.

Opening with the fanfare of Wayne Hill's martial theme music, the

camera sweeps across the Westminster skyline towards St Paul's Cathedral. The camera pans down to pick John Wilder striding across Paternoster Square (only recently rebuilt from the devastation of the Blitz). Patrick Wymark's caption shot shows him looking up at the scaffolding-covered dome of St Paul's (the lead was being replaced under the dome). The old London of Wren and the modern world of construction are neatly juxtaposed under the title card. Each of the lead actors walk up, ignored by Wilder but calling to mind Pamela's image in the finale episode of *The Plane Makers, "'all shuffling round the same board. Manoeuvring."*

Wayne Hill (allegedly born Robert Dale) was a composer and vibraphone player who worked with a Dutch-based group of session musicians called *The Noveltones,* producing library music for the De Wolfe music service (Hill's vibra-tone tune *Left Bank Two* had already been heard in a night club scene during *The Plane Makers*). Hill's theme for *The Power Game* would win a sadly posthumous Ivor Novello award in 1967.

The Power Game would attract the ultimate accolade of a parody in BBC 1's short-lived satire show, *BBC 3.* Thought to have been broadcast in April 1966, the sketch features Roy Dotrice and John Bird parodying the mannerisms and delivery of Clifford Evans and Patrick Wymark, while astoundingly Ann Firbank steps back into the role of Pamela Wilder.

13 December 1965   *The New Boy*

Writer Edmund Ward.   **Director Victor Menzies**

Patrick Wymark (Sir John Wilder). Clifford Evans (Caswell Bligh). Barbara Murray (Lady Pamela Wilder). Jack Watling (Don Henderson). Peter Barkworth (Kenneth Bligh). William Devlin (Sir Gerald Merle). Norman Tyrrell (Sir Gordon Revidge). John Brooking (John Courtenay). Peter Hughes (Douglas Maddox). Peggy Sinclair (Jane Redvers). Pauline Loring (Henrietta). John Gatrell (Minister of Transport*) Fred McNaughton (Bisset). Tim Brinton (ITN News Reader).

*The actual Minister of Transport was Tom Fraser until 23 December 1965 when he was succeeded by Barbara Castle.

"Put the megaphone away, Bligh. I'm not one of the terrified mediocrities you've gathered around you!" Sir John Wilder

Less than a year after the end of *The Plane Makers***, the first episode of** *The Power Game* **opens with Sir John Wilder, finally knighted but finding the quiet life** *"beginning to pall a little"***. Apart from a seat on the National Export Board, his only business activity is a directorship with Elbertson's Merchant Bank which is negotiating a finance agreement with Bligh Construction.**

For Wilder's old antagonist Sir Gordon Revidge (Norman Tyrrell), Bligh Construction offers, *"a high profit outlet for our overseas funds."* Caswell Bligh (Clifford Evans) is willing to accept an Elbertson's nominee as joint Managing Director, so long as Bligh maintains control. Bligh has outside interests as President of a lobbying organisation called the National Motorways Council, but still keeps a firm hand on the company which he built up from an excavator in a stone quarry 35 years ago. As one of the Elbertson's Board, Courtney (John Brooking) comments, *"Bligh's a bit of an oik but no matter."*

Elbertson's nominee is Sir Gerald Merle MP, who has used his connections with the Treasury to ensure that the transfer of funds will not be opposed. However, Wilder begins to manoeuvre, inspiring Bligh's son Kenneth (Peter Barkworth) to oppose Merle's appointment.

Wilder then confounds everyone by refusing to accept the nomination on the terms offered by Bligh. He demands full control of the funds allocated by the bank to Bligh construction. Confronting Bligh, Wilder first makes an appeal to logic. The firm's balance sheet is high on "work in hand". While this talks about contracts they hope to win, getting them signed is another matter. Wilder thinks he can close the deals.

Bligh is still dismissive, so Wilder appeals to emotion. Kenneth wants control of Bligh Construction. *"Though he doesn't know it yet, he's got to cut somebody's throat to do it. Yours. Or mine, if I'm here. Which would you prefer?"*

"We had a cat once, who could get into almost any cage you'd care to mention. He'd just study the cage for a couple of hours and then smirk. Just like you..we lost a lot of canaries, but the cat choked to death on feathers." Pamela Wilder to John Wilder.

The New Boy marks an assured transition from the last episode of *The Plane Makers*, which had ended 11 months before. Board room dialogue informs us that Wilder is under-employed and we first see Wilder sitting in his living room in a sweater and open-necked shirt, rather than his customary suit. Don Henderson (Jack Watling) tells Wilder that his former rival David Corbett is *"porridge-faced as usual"* and busy learning French (implying that Scott-Furlong's aviation rivals now have the upper hand). *"When you pulled out the timing was marvellous."* Wilder replies that, *"All good exits are."*

The rules of the Independent Television Authority, which controlled ITV, meant that in the 1960's a TV series could not be about any product that might be advertised during the commercial breaks. Producer Rex Firkin had originally identified ships and aircraft as two products that would not be advertised on TV, but road construction was an obvious third alternative. While aviation was in decline, construction was suffering cyclic problems with Wilder telling Bligh, *"You're in a depressed industry, Every time the Government puts in a squeeze, the construction industry yelps."*

The appearance of Merle and Revidge in the opening episode provides a sense of continuity (with Devlin delivering some fine silent twitching when Wilder's sardonic seconding of his nomination to a badly negotiated appointment hits home during the board room scene). Producer Rex Firkin had learnt from his mistake with the third series of *The Plane Makers* and ensured that Barbara Murray and Jack Watling were available to reprise their old roles. Murray is particularly entertaining as she comments on Wilder's strategies throughout the first episode, telling him that he'll be wearing patched trousers next when she sees that he's proposing to travel to the board meeting in the back of a (*chauffeur-driven*) Mini as a sign of humility.

The ending of this first episode mirrors the final episode of *The Plane Makers* with Wilder making his exit once more in a limousine (although this time in triumph). Wilder's confrontation with Bligh also echoes his final showdown with Corbett (Alan Dobie), particularly in the throat-cutting metaphor. Although he has been leaning forward aggressively throughout the conversation, Patrick Wymark slowly leans back offering his throat to Clifford Evans at this point. The difference between the two conversations is that where Wilder was making the best of a bad situation at the end of *The Plane Makers*, in *The Power Game*, Wilder is gambling on being able to turn the situation round to his own advantage.

The scene where one of the Elbertson board members refers to Bligh as an *"oik"* recalls the disparaging remarks about Arthur Sugden's *"background"* in the first series of "The Plane Makers" The fact that Bligh controls a multi-million pound empire means his background has to be tolerated, whereas for Sugden it was always an obstacle to overcome.

20 December 1965   ***Lady for a Knight.***

Writer Raymond Bowers.   **Director John Nelson Burton**

Patrick Wymark (Sir John Wilder). Clifford Evans   (Caswell Bligh). Barbara Murray (Lady Pamela Wilder). Rosemary Leach (Susan Weldon). Jack Watling (Don Henderson). Peter Barkworth (Kenneth Bligh). James Maxwell (Colin Townley). Norma Ronald (Kay Lingard). Fred McNaughton (Bissett). Ric Hutton (Hopeton).

"Name boards are for the obscure – do you have one?" Don Henderson to Ken Bligh

Director John Nelson Burton opens the episode with a film sequence of Jack Watling as Don Henderson, steering his open-topped sports car through the streets of London, past St Paul's Cathedral and up to the modern offices of Bligh Construction as big band music blares in the background.

As Joint Managing Director of Bligh Construction, Wilder has hired Kay Lingard (Norma Ronald), his secretary from Scott Furlong and appointed Don Henderson as his personal assistant.

A new battle looms with Wilder and Caswell Bligh both being members of the National Export Board. A Government sponsored body tasked with promoting exports, the board is made up of three economists, three trade unionists and three industrialists. With Bligh and Wilder now representing both the same industry and the same company, the press speculates which will have to leave the NEB.

Wilder intends to turn Bligh Construction into an international force, bidding for construction projects around the world. For that he needs to keep his seat on the National Export Board.

Raymond Bowers introduces Susan Weldon (Rosemary Leach), a Higher Executive Officer in the Civil Service who is deputy secretary of the National Export Board. As Henderson tells Wilder, she is also secretary to the Civil Engineering Committee which means that she has *"more information regarding exports than anybody…including the Chancellor of Exchequer."*

Leach plays Weldon as quietly defiant when Wilder tries to get his own way at the National Export Board, innocently and calmly explaining why she can't agree to his orders. Despite some quite aggressive behaviour from Wilder, director John Nelson Burton leaves us in no doubt as to the effect he's had on her, as we see her tugging at the top button of her suit jacket. Wilder's seduction of Weldon is as outrageous in its own way as Michael Caine's seduction of his landlady in *Get Carter*.

Pamela Wilder is shown as omnisciently resigned to events. Even before Wilder has met Susan, his wife has phoned the National Export Board to try and get hold of him. After chatting to Susan for a couple of minutes, she pointedly asks for her name as if she already senses what will happen.

Assistant Under Secretary Colin Townley, the career civil servant in charge of the National Export Board, is played by James Maxwell, who had written the Theatre 59 Theatre Company translation of *Danton's Death* in which Wymark had starred at the Lyric, Hammersmith. Together with Casper Wrede and Richard Negri, Maxwell would later found Manchester's Royal Exchange Theatre. Maxwell depicts Townley as politely anxious to avoid any contact with Board members outside a chaired and minuted meeting.

The contrast between private and public sector is clearly illustrated by designer Peter Roden. Bligh Construction is headquartered in bright, spacious offices with modern art on the walls. Susan Weldon is huddled in her coat over a sputtering electric bar heater, a view of Victorian rooftops out of her window and faded imperial wallpaper creating the subtle image of prison bars.

This office is scene of the first confrontation between Susan and Wilder. Arguing over the procedure for holding an NEB meeting, Weldon says it can only be chaired by the Chairman or Secretary (Townley). Wilder says there is nothing to say another member cannot chair the meeting. *"It's implicit"*, Susan replies. *"THAT, is a matter of opinion,"* Wilder retorts," *What is NOT, is that it's NOT EXPLICIT!"*

Bowers deepens the conflict between Wilder and Caswell Bligh. Where Bligh was personally opposed to Wilder as an interloper, we now we learn that Bligh has political ambitions, as some kind of Minister for Motorways. He therefore sees his seats on both the National Motorway Council and the National Export Board as vital stepping stones. Bligh is in no mood to stand aside from either position.

Bowers does not serve either Henderson or Wilder particularly well in this episode. Henderson is patronising to the Bligh commissionaire who tries to direct him to the visitor's car park, and then begins sniping at Ken Bligh when he tries to welcome him. Although Ken may be Joint Managing Director, Henderson warns him that he is Personal Assistant only to John Wilder. This isn't the first time Henderson has come across as supercilious, but it's certainly more pronounced here than in *The Plane Makers*. Jack Watling has enough charm to carry it off without making Henderson too obnoxious.

Patrick Wymark also plays Wilder very aggressively in this episode. Trying to push through a National Export Board meeting, and later trying to shoot down a newspaper interview* about his membership of the NEB the aggression is certainly more pronounced than in *The Plane Makers*.

Charles Handy (1) observed that the difference between position power and personal power can be observed *"once the power source is withdrawn."* Many managers believe their influence is due to personal power or charisma, rather than position power, *"only to be disillusioned when…removed from his position."* In Wilder's case, he resorts to a combination of personal power (charisma) and physical power (bullying) to replace his lost position power.

The aggression carries over to the final scene where Wilder and Susan Weldon seem to be testing each other. After having sex with her at her flat, Wilder says that it would be a mistake to repeat the experience. But he then picks up some confidential papers, which she invites him to read. Suddenly, Wilder decides he may not have to go home for the weekend after all.

The newspaper trying to run the story on Wilder and Bligh is The Globe, from Firkin and Greatorex's 1965 series, "Front Page Story"

27 December 1965   *Hagadan*

Writer Peter Draper.   Director Quentin Lawrence

Patrick Wymark (Sir John Wilder). Clifford Evans   (Caswell Bligh). Barbara Murray (Lady Pamela Wilder). Rosemary Leach (Susan Weldon). Jack Watling (Don Henderson). Peter Barkworth (Kenneth Bligh). George Sewell (Ken Hagadan). Victor Platt

(Mahanny). Peter Madden (Magister). John Humphrey (Alan Lacey MP).

"London holds on to people, no matter what it does to them." Susan Weldon

Joint-Managing Directors Ken Bligh and Sir John Wilder (Patrick Wymark) are separately backing two competing projects for Bligh Construction. Ken favours an African Dam, while Wilder is pushing for the new M27 motorway. Taking on both projects would leave the company over-stretched, so only one can win.

Pamela suspects Wilder is having another affair, but doesn't know it's with Susan Weldon (Rosemary Leach). Over lunch Pamela tells Wilder that divorce is not an option. In Italy, Wilder hires Frank Hagadan (George Sewell), an ambitious engineer who has plans for a machine which can cut the time (and therefore the cost) of motorway construction.

Returning from Italy, Wilder is seen with Susan at Luton airport by Angela, a friend of Pamela's. When Pamela mentions what Angela saw, as if it was a piece of abstract gossip, Wilder refuses to discuss Susan's identity with Pamela, snapping *"I don't see it's any of Angela's business"*. Wilder brings the newly arrived Hagadan to his house for dinner. The following day, Susan meets with an enquiry agent who tells her that after Wilder took Hagadan back to his hotel, he spent two hours at a woman's flat in Notting Hill Gate. Susan goes to the Bligh Construction office, and accidentally meets Hagadan in the foyer. She agrees to join Hagadan for lunch.

Wilder meets Alan Lacey MP (John Humphrey), Parliamentary Private Secretary to the Minister responsible for the African Dam project, who tells him that Ken previously underestimated Bligh's bid for the Asahi Dam and the project had to be bailed out with World Bank money. Wilder reminds Lacey that because it's in a British protectorate, the UK Government is underwriting the latest Dam project. He hints that he would not want to be associated with a project that has a chance of failure.

Ken thinks motorways are a short-term win; the UK has a finite capacity for new roads. The roads will be built regardless of who wins the contract. Africa, with its much greater area, offers a long-term future in construction. But although Elbertson's got involved with Bligh Construction to finance overseas expansion, Wilder opposes Ken Bligh's African project because he needs success at his co-Managing Director's expense. Wilder exploited Ken's conflict with the domineering Caswell to gain entry to the company, but now has to undermine the son.

After the waspish and brutal overtones of the previous episode, Peter Draper's script packs in more incident, but takes a more elegant approach to exploring Susan Weldon's motivation. Draper and director Quentin Lawrence had earlier collaborated on *The Plane Makers* episode, *Don't Stick Your Head Out* in which Kate Barber (Ingrid Hafner) outlined the parameters of her life as Wilder's mistress.

In this episode, Susan Weldon is less able to take Barber's pragmatic view. She is unhappy with her status (*"whatever the word is, whatever I am"*). When Wilder laughs off a mistake with cooking the evening meal, she says if they were married, he would be irritated by a mistake, and then asks if he is ever going to marry her.

Unlike Kate Barber, who tolerated her position as a mistress because she didn't feel competent in any job, Weldon is a university graduate and high-grade civil servant who has risked dismissal and possible prosecution by passing information to Wilder. Rosemary Leach is totally convincing as an intelligent, successful career woman who is *"inefficient"* in her personal life. She's totally convincing when she tells Wilder, *"I do actually, and in fact love you"*. Ominously, when Susan tells Wilder about her previous affair with a married man, it sounds very similar to Barber's description of her life with Wilder. Susan is unwilling to return home to Dorset. Half the women in her apartment block are separated from their husbands, all unwilling to return home, all drawn to London.

The first part of the episode is like a standalone play as Wilder and Susan move from her flat, to a pub, to an Italian restaurant talking about life. Quentin Lawrence literally goes to town with a surreal sequence filmed entirely from the window of a taxi showing the night streets of London as Wilder and Susan have a conversation entirely in voiceover.

The mechanics of motorway construction are outlined throughout this episode. Wilder compares it to being like a *"jobbing builder"* – the design of the motorway is put out a separate firm with the constructor being responsible only for making it happen. Ken Bligh takes Wilder to their current road-building project. Ken tells Wilder a long schedule is safest. *"The M1 took 19 months to complete and is costing 5 and a half million to put right."* Hagadan tells Wilder that in Italy, highways are built faster (and therefore cheaper) because there are no planning procedures as in England *("In England everyone wants motorways, but not in their back garden. In Italy…if a back garden's in the way, it goes straight through")*.

If it's unlikely that many of the audience would approve of Hagadan's viewpoint, it underlines that there may be a reason why public works always exceed their budget. There is a price to be paid for democracy.

When Hagadan explains his plan for a machine that will compact the foundations of a motorway, Wilder meets with Magister (Peter Madden), whose firm will design the motorway, to confirm that it is possible for a contractor to suggest an alternative schedule with two separate prices. This is the key to Bligh Construction undercutting its competitors. Magister deduces that Wilder is hoping to bring in a new machine, but warns him that if they win on the cheapest bid, Bligh Construction will bear the cost of any cost over-run.

The title character of Frank Hagadan is played by George Sewell, who had made his stage debut aged 35 with Joan Littlewood's Theatre Workshop in *Fings Aint What They Used T'Be*. This led to appearances in films (*This Sporting Life* 1963) and TV (The *Gideon's Way* episode *Boy With Gun*). Sewell's background as a merchant navy steward and travel courier was distinct from that of the classically trained actors in the cast, although his performance as Hagadan is assured.

The scenes between Pamela Wilder and Hagadan are delicately handled. She has confronted Wilder over the identity of his latest *("I saw Joanna yesterday. She said Kate is in America so it isn't Kate")*. She accepts Hagadan's invitation to lunch after her enquiry agent tells her Wilder has spent hours at Susan Weldon's flat.

Even so, she pulls away from a passionate kiss with Hagadan at his flat. He puts her coat on telling her, *"Women like the idea of having lovers, but when they're alone in a room with a man, they're not so sure about it. Eventually they can't wait to get out of that room again, back to where everything is the same as it was before"*

In contrast to the previous episode, Wilder is able to show enough charm for it to seem credible when Susan declares her love for him. At the same time, a very natural flurry of emotions passes through his head as wriggles away from Susan's plea that he indicates there's a possibility of marriage. *"If I was single…if there was nothing in the way…we probably would be married by now."* Later, Wilder declares that Pamela wants him as he was ten years ago and laments that, *"Everything wears out. Living demands the continuous production of waste. We use up people as we use up everything else."* Susan resignedly says *"As you will eventually use me up, 'And throw sweet flowers upon love's grave.' "*

3 January 1966   *The Politician.*

Writer John Bowen.   **Director David Reid**

Patrick Wymark (Sir John Wilder). Clifford Evans   (Caswell Bligh). Peter Barkworth (Kenneth Bligh). Rachel Herbert (Justine Bligh). Ewan Hooper (Alderman Hall). Martin Boddey (Jack Wigan MP). James Bree (Davis, Labour Party agent) . John Abineri (Councillor Mallor). Fred Ferris (Paul Budge). Dorothy Bromiley

(Beryl Ritchie). David Cook (Peter Willoughby). Bryan Magee (TV interviewer).

"Why be an MP when you can buy one for tuppence?" Sir John Wilder

Caswell Bligh (Clifford Evans) makes a bid to be selected as a Labour candidate in a local election, the first step in his vision of becoming a Minister for Motorways. For both Wilder and Ken Bligh, the prospect of Caswell being immersed in politics removes an obstacle to their own plans for Bligh Construction.

With Harold Wilson's Labour government over a year into office, John Bowen's script takes Bligh through the selection process as a Labour party candidate in the suburban town of Fairmile, which has recently been brought to a standstill by traffic problems.

Both Ken and Wilder would benefit if Bligh entered politics. He'd be distracted from Bligh Construction and would have to resign from the National Export Board. Wilder assumes that Bligh would stand as a Conservative and offers to pull strings at Central Office. When Ken says he didn't know he supported the Tory Party, Wilder replies, *"I have no politics, only friends."* In fact, Caswell has retained Labour Party membership for 35 years and claims to have known Nye Bevan. As the Labour Party is in Government, it is attractive to Bligh's ambitions.

The episode introduces Rachel Herbert (Number 58 in the *Free For All* episode of *The Prisoner*) as Ken's wife Justine. An elegant wife and mother, Justine is also unafraid to demonstrate a sharp intellect. When Ken says Bligh had been hoping to achieve his Transport Ministry ambitions by being made a Lord she retorts, *"They don't let an important Ministry like that go to the Lords. Why else do they give up their titles?"* It is Justine, defying her husband's ambitions, who explains the political realities to Bligh and makes him realise that he would be out of his depth as a politician.

10 January 1966.

Point of Balance.

Writer Wilfred Greatorex.   Director Peter Collinson.

Patrick Wymark (Sir John Wilder). Clifford Evans (Caswell Bligh). Rosemary Leach (Susan Weldon). Jack Watling (Don Henderson). Peter Barkworth (Kenneth Bligh). James Maxwell (Colin Townley). Nigel Green (Hartley). David Langton (General). Philip Madoc (Ted Newark). Norma Ronald (Kay Lingard). Fred McNaughton (Bissett).

"It's a problem, Sir John, squaring security with a free society."
Colin Townley

A rare charitable gesture exposes Wilder's relationship with Susan Weldon. Wilder and Caswell Bligh are leaving a National Export Board meeting, when Wilder spots a traffic warden waiting to put a parking ticket on Susan Weldon's car. Wilder rushes over and puts another shilling in the meter before it expires. Caswell asks why Wilder should make such a gesture for a lowly Civil Servant and tells Colin Townley (James Maxwell) that he suspects Susan is passing restricted information to Wilder. Although Townley attempts to downplay the suggestion, Bligh's suspicions interest "The General" (David Langton) who deals with security. The General introduces Bligh to Mr Hartley (Nigel Green) who is interested in the wider area of corruption.

Wilder and Henderson have been secretly compiling a bid for the construction of the Kawanderi Dam. Wilder expects Ken's bid for a different African dam to fail. Wilder instructs Henderson to tell Ken that their bid is guaranteed to be 3% lower than any other bid. As expected, Ken goads his father that Wilder has beaten him on his own ground – the Export Board. Bligh says the only way Wilder could guarantee the lowest bid would be if he got details of the competing bids from Susan Weldon. Bligh cables Desmond, the

Bligh employee charged with hand-delivering the bid. He tells him to withdraw the bid saying he doesn't want the firm dragged down with Wilder and then passes the tender document to Hartley.

Wilder receives a cable from Desmond confirming that Caswell's attempt to cancel the bid has been ignored. Meanwhile, Susan has been ordered to attend an interview with Hartley. Colin Townley attempts to warn off Wilder pointing out that in a relationship like this, *"the Civil Servant, having signed the Official Secrets Act is vulnerable."* Afterwards, Wilder meets with union leader Ted Newark whose father was a friend of Bligh's. He learns that Caswell briefly joined the British Union of Fascists during the 1930's before returning to the Labour party.

Wilder meets with Hartley and reveals that the copies of the tender given to Ken and his father have been filled in with meaningless figures. The actual tender is blank, and Wilder has arranged that the African Minister receiving the bids will fill in a figure 3% below the lowest bid. Hartley passes on the explanation to the General who says Wilder had passed on the information about Bligh's BUF membership in retaliation. Bligh's dossier supports the story that he left the Fascists when he realised what they were about. The General decides to take no further action. He says that Wilder and Bligh can tear each other apart but *"Not with my weapons"*.

Wilfred Greatorex delivers a script which would almost be at home in *Mission:Impossible* or *Hustle* with the whole episode being a well-concealed exercise in misdirection. Underlining just how much attention was required of viewers in the 1960's, this episode was never repeated after its original transmission, but a second viewing on DVD allows the viewer to see just how well the Bligh's have been roped in. When Don Henderson, having watched Wilder put a shilling in Susan Weldon's parking meter, chides Wilder saying he might as well wear a placard, he's unwittingly put his finger on exactly what Wilder is doing. Viewed with that knowledge, the inevitable effect on Susan of Bligh's suspicions only underlines Wilder's ruthlessness.

In his classic analysis of the confidence trick, David W. Maurer said, *"it should be no reflection on a man's intelligence to be swindled. The higher a mark's intelligence, the quicker he sees through the deal, directly to his own advantage. It is not intelligence but integrity which determines whether or not a man is a good mark."* (2)

Rosemary Leach again depicts Susan Weldon as a heart-breaking mixture of perky defiance and convincing self-destruction. Townley tells Bligh that Susan is not *"some naïve child from the typing pool. She has a first-class honours degree in economics and could debate most of our board under the table if she put her mind to it."* But when pleading with Wilder to marry her, she says that while being man and wife would not be a defence in law, it would make what she is doing justifiable to herself.

Director Peter Collinson (*The Italian Job*) attempts some ambitious effects with the studio cameras. He punctuates one scene by zooming in on *"The Penkovsky Papers"*, a 1965 book about a KGB double agent who passed secrets to the West. He also illustrates Susan's desolation when under investigation with film sequences of Rosemary Leach walking forlornly through a rainswept Parliament Square. Finally, a silent studio sequence shot looking in through the "exterior" window of her flat, shows Susan returning home, enclosed by the bars of the window frame and then finally looking out of the window, reacting in terror to something she sees below (a real, or imagined, watcher – we never see).

One effect does not come off quite so well. Susan is talking to Wilder in the kitchen saying she doesn't want to go out for a meal because she's got paperwork to do. Wilder returns to the living room and there is a close up of her briefcase next to the soda siphon where he attempts to refill his whisky glass. Unfortunately, as Rosemary Leach shouts *"See for yourself, I've got a case full of stuff to get through"* the glass overfills and splashes soda over the briefcase. Patrick Wymark grunts and attempts to brush the soda off the briefcase before returning to the kitchen.

Nigel Green gives a suave performance as Mr Hartley. Green had played the humourless Dalby in *The Ipcress File* (1965) but Hartley is more laid back. Although employed to root out corruption, his boundaries obviously end at the English Channel. While Wilder does not admit to bribing Aduba with the £25,000 taken from Bligh's "Information Account", he does answer Hartley's question by saying, *"Stick to your job, it's got a pension."* Green had also appeared in 1965's *The Skull,* as the detective investigating the death of Marco (Patrick Wymark) and as Nayland Smith in *The Face of Fu Manchu.*

James Maxwell delivers another effete performance as Townley, Secretary of the National Export Board who finds the confrontations resulting from the worlds of business and security so distasteful. However, it also becomes clear that behind his delicate phraseology, Townley is determined that there will be no ripples in his pool.

There are several references to the final episode of *The Plane Makers* – Henderson warns Wilder not to underestimate Bligh like he did with Corbett *("Corbett was lucky"* Wilder responds). In a confrontation with the Bligh's, Wilder says he does not involve himself in lost causes and Caswell reminds him about the VTOL *("That was not John's fault"* Henderson interjects). Later, Wilder says Henderson has developed bad habits under Corbett *("You're becoming more argumentative! It spoils you!")*

17 January 1966   *Saturday's Women*

Writer Raymond Bowers.   **Director John Cooper**

Patrick Wymark (Sir John Wilder). Clifford Evans (Caswell Bligh). Barbara Murray (Pamela, Lady Wilder). Rosemary Leach (Susan Weldon). Jack Watling (Don Henderson). Peter Barkworth (Kenneth Bligh). James Maxwell (Colin Townley). Anne Rye (Agnes) Anne Tirard (Enid). Reg Whitehead (Saunders). Garth Adams (Furbisham).

"I think you fluttered to the wrong nest. John's migratory. Not regular in the seasonal sense. Nor consistent. But frequent and versatile." Pamela Wilder

Ken Bligh returns to London, not just disappointed but perplexed. His bid for the African Dam has been rejected but Ken believes he made the lowest bid. He and Caswell still believe that Wilder has been getting details of the competing bids from Susan Weldon. At the same time, Don Henderson returns from a secret trip to Venezuela and learns that Wilder has just secured a UK motorway construction contract.

Caswell tells Ken that he lost the bid because Wilder had primed Alan Lacey MP (in *Hagadan*), to ensure the Minister killed the Bligh bid (the UK Government is underwriting the dam, being built in a British protectorate). Ken knows that his father also met Lacey, and accuses Bligh of also wanting the foreign project to fail saying he is *"motorway mad"*. Bligh counters that his secretary signed for a parcel of tropical clothing for Henderson, delivered after Don had left the country. He warns Ken that Wilder is planning another foreign adventure.

Don arrives at the Wilder home to find Pamela unaware that he had been summoned. She has not seen John since the previous weekend, and as she predicts, he is currently breakfasting in Notting Hill. Susan Weldon challenges him about his plan to return to Pamela for the rest of the weekend and Wilder elects to stay with Susan. He phones his house and instructs Don to show Ken Bligh his research into Venezuela's massive investment opportunities. Wilder has called a board meeting for Friday, but he will now vanish. Wilder will guarantee to deliver a tender with the lowest price so long as Ken takes the meeting and gets the board to support Wilder's bid for a Venezuelan project. Susan, in turn gives Wilder an ultimatum. Start divorce proceedings by Wednesday, or she will end their relationship and leave the National Export Board.

Raymond Bowers lays out Wilder's long-term strategy, explaining the apparent contradictions of previous episodes. The motorway contract gives Caswell more salt to rub in Ken's wounds. Wilder wants to set son against father. *"I don't much care which gets in first, as long as only one is left standing. With blood all over him."* Even the tropical clothes were delivered to Caswell's secretary on Wilder's instructions to get Caswell wondering where Don had gone and perhaps suspect that Ken knew what Wilder was planning.

Patrick Wymark exudes calculated menace as he lays out his plans, *"I want (Ken) to get his own back and I want him to tear out his father's guts to get it."*

But Wilder finds the balance of power shifting to the women in his life. Susan knows that Wilder's plan depends on having access to the contract bids by competitors which pass over her desk at the National Export Board. Wilder protests that, *"I cannot divorce Pamela because I have no grounds. She won't divorce me, although she has grounds."* Susan replies: *"make the impossible happen"* as he has just done with the Bligh's. *"As a Civil Servant I find your attentions dishonourable. As your wife I'd think otherwise."*

Rachel Herbert continues to demonstrate a nurturing charm as Justine Bligh, side-lined to the role of spectator although clearly calm and intuitive. She instructs the new maid on how to make bacon for Caswell's breakfast *("for Mr Bligh, you dip lean slices into boiling lard for 20 seconds"*. The maid says she thought Mr Bligh liked it pressed down on a stickless pan and Justine explains, *"Mr Ken Bligh does, but not Mr Bligh"*). She attempts to discretely defuse the more aggressive exchanges between father and son, but when Henderson arrives, she is dismissed. *"I'll discuss business with Father in front of you,"* Ken says, *"but not with an employee present."*

Peter Barkworth unleashes the deep-rooted resentment that Wilder hopes to exploit. *"When your mother was alive, I told her everything I did. In business, politics, everything."* Caswell says at the breakfast table. *"That would explain her early death."* Ken retorts.

Jack Watling breezes through the episode, providing a sounding board to Ken, Pamela and Wilder and demonstrating the easy charm of a man who *"gets through"* life without too many qualms. A reference to not having a moustache since the Battle of Britain reminds us that these men may have spent their formative years in a life and death struggle

Wilder says Susan's demand is *"Poppy Bloody Nonsense"* - With the rise of Mary Whitehouse's National Viewers and Listener's Association in 1965, ATV was obviously worried about one of its stars saying "cock" on national TV (although it was the "bloody's" that Mrs Whitehouse tended to count).

24 January 1966   *The Switch*

Writer Edmund Ward.   **Director David Reid**

Patrick Wymark. (Sir John Wilder). Clifford Evans   (Caswell Bligh). Rosemary Leach (Susan Weldon). Jack Watling (Don Henderson). Peter Barkworth (Kenneth Bligh). Alfred Burke (Joe Panton). James Maxwell (Colin Townley). Philip Madoc (Ted Newark). Peggy Sinclair (Jane Redvers). Norma Ronald (Kay Lingard). Fred McNaughton (Bissett).

"All disasters leave a few pieces behind. The secret is to shuffle the pieces into the pattern that you want. "   Sir John Wilder.

Lord Scaife, the unseen Chairman of the National Export Board retires and Caswell Bligh sees himself as the natural successor. Meanwhile, Sir John Wilder plans to acquire a plant hire firm on behalf of Bligh Construction. The owner, Joe Panton (Alfred Burke) is a long-time friend and supplier of Caswell Bligh, but Elbertson's bank wants a short-term return on its investment. Buying the plant-hire firm will improve Bligh's cash-flow.

The episode is a bit of an anti-climax. Alfred Burke starred as private detective Frank Marker in ABC's *Public Eye* but the prospect of Wilder versus Marker never really comes off. Burke sports the grizzled beard which he habitually grew as soon as a series of *Public Eye* ended, but Panton seems like a plaything of fate. Although he vows to be awkward, he knows that his fate is sealed.

Wilder shows Panton a copy of his own profit and loss account, amended to show what would happen if Bligh's took their business away. When Panton tells him that civil engineering is in a recession, Wilder says that why Bligh's must diversify or cut down on sub-contractors' costs. Since plant hire is one of the highest costs it makes sense to own a plant division. Panton counters that Bligh's could set one up, but Wilder replies that he would sooner have one ready-made. *"We could still supply the rest of the industry profitably. If we set up our own division, you'd lose two thirds of your income anyway."* Wilder ends the argument by saying, *"Accept gracefully and we'll talk figures. Otherwise, you're beating your head against a stone wall...it's your head. I just provide the wall."*

Although Ken Bligh publicly supports the take-over, he would prefer to see Elbertson's investment capital diverted to a Central American Strategic Highway project. He advises Panton how to sink the take-over deal. Peter Barkworth seems slick and convincing when he outlines the plan, although when it later threatens to go wrong it's noticeable that Barkworth once again wears the high-collared coat and bowler hat that makes him seem like a cross between a tortoise and a little boy.

Jack Watling shares an amusing scene with Rosemary Leach when Don arrives at a pub with apologies on behalf of Wilder. Ordering a pink gin he describes himself as, *"in my usual capacity – a trusty but drunken go-between."* Susan observes, *"It's like something in a comic opera. Second Act, Baritone Aria; 'My beloved Master is detained on business."*

At the retirement party for Lord Scaife, Pamela finally comes face-to-face with Susan Weldon, reminding Susan that they spoke once on the phone when Pamela was looking for Sir John (*Lady for a*

Knight). Barbara Murray glances pointedly at Jack Watling as she says the party is, *" a marvellous opportunity to meet people one has only HEARD ABOUT."*

In his final appearance as Colin Townley, James Maxwell surveys the aftermath of the party, *"Empty glasses and full ashtrays. The remains of tribute."* He warns Susan that they must stay neutral in the jockeying for the Chairmanship. Bligh thinks the position is his, but an unseen character called Gillingham has also shown an interest. The Civil Service provides continuity during regime change, *"Whatever happens WE are involved. Not the self-seekers; the Gillingham's, the Bligh's...the Wilder's. US – the agenda compilers, the writers of minutes. Gillingham understands this – I doubt the others do."*

31 January 1966   *The Crunch*

Writer Peter Draper.   **Director John Cooper**

Patrick Wymark (Sir John Wilder). Clifford Evans (Caswell Bligh). Barbara Murray (Pamela, Lady Wilder). Rosemary Leach (Susan Weldon). Jack Watling (Don Henderson). Peter Barkworth (Kenneth Bligh). George Sewell (Ken Hagadan). Rachel Herbert (Justine Bligh).

"Out of the seven nights that go up to make a week of my loosely-termed married life, I tend to find myself alone on at least four of them for one reason or another. Does it surprise you so much that I should go out, now and then, to find someone to talk to?" Pamela, Lady Wilder.

Wilder returns home unexpectedly one evening to find Pamela out. He suspects that she is having an affair and is oddly distressed. As gossip spreads that Hagadan is Pamela's lover, Susan sees a chance for Wilder to divorce Pamela and marry her.

Patrick Wymark shows a rarely-seen aspect of Wilder, perplexed, hurt and bewildered; Not knowing who to trust or suspect, not willing to ask the right words for the answers they might bring.

Hagadan's road-building machine will prepare foundations *"at half the time and considerably less cost"* than conventional means. It needs further adjustments to make it economic, but will be able to put on a convincing demonstration on some waste ground outside Bligh's HQ. Hagadan and his machine will be introduced to the trade at a cocktail party on Friday.

Wilder tells Hagadan that their competitors say he won the M27 contract with unrealistic figures, and predict that Bligh's will fall down on the job. *"They don't like being undercut. And they don't like being undercut by so much. It makes them look foolish at best. And at worst that their figures are seriously far out."*

Caswell Bligh tells Ken that if Hagadan left before his machine was complete, Bligh's would still have to deliver the M27 at the bid price. *"The premature departure of Hagadan would be more of a cost to Bligh's than the loss of Lady Wilder's chastity."*

Visiting Pamela , Caswell offers to put his country cottage at Pamela's disposal, if she and Hagadan agree to be discrete for a few weeks. *"I'm not making a moral judgement. As far as I know your relationship may be completely innocent."*

Peter Draper also explores Wilder's culinary preferences, when Wilder order for both during a post-concert meal with Susan. Gazpacho, Waterzooi and Coeur a la Creme for dessert telling the waiter they'd better prepare it now, *"I don't want it with cream and sugar. I want it with finely chopped chives."* Susan chides him for being *"excessively masterful."*

Jack Watling has an opportunity to make Don Henderson both touching and amusing as he confronts Frank Hagadan over two halves of bitter. *"It has come to my ears,"* he says, in best public-school manner, *"That you've been seeing rather a lot of certain lady. It's got to stop. I'm not prepared to stand by and see her name dragged through the mud."*

"And you'd rather you were getting it than me," Hagadan retorts, leaving a chastened Don sipping at his beer as Frank tells him to get stuffed. But later, comparing notes, Pamela and Hagadan agree to put their affair on hold. Pamela knows that Wilder would try to blacklist Hagadan in the UK and Hagadan would go back to another highly paid contract in Italy.

Unaware of this, Susan is angry that Wilder will not divorce Pamela and marry her. *"If you divorce her, there's still me. And if you don't divorce her, there's still me. What about me? I am not incidental to you. I'm not one of your employees. And I'm not your whore!"*

Wilder finally confronts Hagadan at Bligh HQ as their construction rivals gather for the cocktail party. When Hagadan admits that he loves Pamela, Wilder prepares to explode; *"I brought you here..."*

"Don't start that with me," Hagadan snaps, *"You didn't take me out of the gutter. You took me from one highly paid job to another highly paid job."*

Wilder threatens to finish him, but Hagadan retorts, *"No you won't There's more people against you than for you, and most of them are in that room there. I can get a job in ten minutes under your nose. And they'd do it just to see the look on your face."*

They agree that Hagadan will finish his contract on a project in Libya after the machine is complete. He won't see Pamela again. As Wilder introduces Hagadan to the cocktail party, he turns to look at Pamela who silently toasts him. For now, in the game of marital power, Wilder has won, but his confidence has been shaken.

Unfortunately, the set designers weren't prepared for Patrick Wymark's flourish as he enters his office to confront George Sewell. He slams the door shut, only for it to slowly fall open. Hanging his coat on the hook, Wymark calmly pushes the door shut as he turns to glare at Sewell.

7 February 1966   *Late Via Rome*

Writer Wilfred Greatorex.   Director Peter Collinson

Patrick Wymark (Sir John Wilder). Clifford Evans (Caswell Bligh). Barbara Murray (Lady Pamela Wilder). Rosemary Leach (Susan Weldon). Jack Watling (Don Henderson). Peter Barkworth (Kenneth Bligh). George Sewell (Ken Hagadan). Rachel Herbert (Justine Bligh). Ian Holm (Sefton Kemp). Ralph Michael (Bob Gillingham). John Tate (Billy Straker). Llewellyn Rees (Economic Affairs Minister). Jean Trend (Stewardess). Deborah Watling (Jennifer). Norma Ronald (Kay Lingard). Fred Naughton (Bissett). John Quayle (Straker's assistant).

'You're lowering, John - frowning menace.' Kenneth Bligh

Kenneth Bligh returns from Africa on a delayed flight as rumours spread in London that his airport construction project has encountered problems which will drive up the costs. Meanwhile, the Minister has appointed a new secretary to the National Export Board, Sefton Kemp. Susan Weldon suspects that Kemp will try to have her transferred on security grounds, while Wilder and Bligh speculate whether the new chair will revive attempts to remove one of them from the NEB.

One of two episodes directed by Peter Collinson, (*The Italian Job) Late Via Rome* opens with some adventurous camerawork in the meeting of the National Export Board. As Wilder ponders a mysterious note, the camera passes over his shoulder to meet the stares of new chairman Gillingham (Ralph Michael) and secretary Sefton Kemp (Holm). They have noted that both Wilder and Caswell Bligh have been receiving and ignoring messages about Ken Bligh's North African airport construction project during the meeting.

Throughout the episode, Collinson alternates between sociable wide shots and tight close-ups as characters group and plot. After Ken Bligh has shown unexpected independence during one meeting, Wilder and Henderson look down at the office car park. *"Ken's taken to driving himself lately"* Jack Watling observes as they see Bligh swapping places with his driver in the car park. *"So I've noticed"* lowers Wilder.

Deborah Watling, daughter of Jack, plays a precocious fellow aeroplane passenger of Ken Bligh on his return flight to England. *"You're much cleverer than you pretend, aren't you?"* she says, after he solves one of her crossword clues. And her words are significant. Until now, Ken has been the fall guy. But for once Wilfred Greatorex allows Ken to turn the tables on the vultures circling over the failed African construction contract. The final scene reveals Ken delayed his return to give time for inaccurate rumours of his failure to spread. This smokes out a profitable reaction from their partners in the joint venture.

The replacement of James Maxwell's Colin Townley as secretary to the NEB is explained in a couple of lines as Ministerial manipulation. Kemp, who was 'weaned on protocol at the Treasury' has come over from the Board of Trade. Townley was serenely protective of Susan Weldon, but Kemp will remove anyone capable of doing his job. He displays irritation at the *"singular diffidence"* of his predecessor in expanding the powers the NEB and reactivates the question of the Official Secrets Act while making it plain to Susan that he will not object to her relationship with Wilder so long as it works in favour of the Board. Ian Holm, who had played Verges to Patrick Wymark's Dogberry in the Royal Shakespeare Company's *Much Ado About Nothing*, reactivates the question of whether Bligh or Wilder should leave the NEB. If the sudden replacement of Townley has unsettled Susan Weldon, she doesn't show it, with Rosemary Leach making her almost cockily self-assertive in front of the new chairman. Ralph Michael (*Dead of Night*) brings an amused gravitas to the role of Bob Gillingham, an Imperial Engineering executive who moves effortlessly between private industry and the Civil Service *("cross-fertilisation"* Kemp calls it).

Like Patrick Wymark, director Peter Collinson was born in Cleethorpes, although in vastly different circumstances. The unwanted child of performers, Collinson was placed in the Actors' Orphanage at the age of eight. At the time, Noel Coward was president of the Orphanage and discovered Collinson weeping in a corner after his father failed to visit him. As dramatised in Marcy Kahan's radio play, *Mister Bridger's Orphan* (2013), Coward was moved by Collinson's plight and took up his cause, eventually becoming his godfather. Coward arranged for Collinson to get his first job in the theatre and by 1967, Collinson was directing movies. In 1969 he offered Noel Coward the role of Mr Bridger in *The Italian Job*. Although he didn't need the money, Coward accepted, as if to acknowledge how far Collinson had come.

14 February 1966   *Persons and Papers*

Writer Peter Draper.   **Director David Reid**

Patrick Wymark (Sir John Wilder). Clifford Evans   (Caswell Bligh). Barbara Murray (Lady Pamela Wilder). Rosemary Leach (Susan Weldon). Jack Watling (Don Henderson). Peter Barkworth (Kenneth Bligh). George Sewell (Ken Hagadan) Rachel Herbert (Justine Bligh). Ian Holm (Sefton Kemp). Ralph Michael (Bob Gillingham). Norma Ronald (Kay Lingard). Peter Hager (Sam Bell). Alan Gerrard (Bill Clavering). Benjamin Whitrow (Customs Officer). Mary Griffiths (Betty).

"Do you think it would be easier for me to never see you again? Do you think it would be easier for me to destroy Pamela – her whole life and part of mine? Or you? When you say to me 'I love you'.... why does everyone think I have all the answers?" Sir John Wilder

Wilder negotiates a joint-venture with rival company Infells on the M27 road construction project. Despite being joint Managing Director, Ken has not been consulted. Instead of being exasperated,

Ken replies, *"It fascinates me. The last time I mentioned it you decided we couldn't handle it on top of all the other things."*

But Wilder is distracted. He takes a rare four-day skiing holiday with Pamela. Wilder looks forlorn in a tightly fitting 1960's ski jumper as they discuss Pamela's affair. She assures him it's over and he asks, *"Is that because Hagadan is in Africa and you may never see him again or under any circumstances? How do I know when you're with me you're not thinking about him?"*

Pamela asks how he really expected her to keep on loving him when his life was moving further away from her and she seemed to have no part in it. She recalls what he was like at 35. *"I sometimes think the only reason you really want other women is to prove to yourself that time is not rushing past quite as fast as you think it is. And if I can just hang on, you'll realise it rushes past just as fast for me."*

Back in England Susan berates Wilder for going on holiday with Pamela saying the business with Hagadan disturbed him, *"And you were surprised you were disturbed. It changed you!"*

Back in England, Wilder is shocked when he meets the Infells negotiating team. Hagadan is Infells new project manager. Hagadan had given notice to Bligh's African office which has been slow to update head office.

The confrontation between Wilder and Hagadan works dramatically although it's also amusing. The argument starts over a seven-mile stretch of land which Hagadan says is the most difficult area. If they get it wrong, they won't make a penny profit on the deal. Sam Bell (Peter Hager) from Infells, asks what Hagadan would do. *"Well, I should think we'll have to swamp shoot for about three miles* (Bell narrows his eyes and draws on his cigarette*) ...that won't be too difficult* (Bell nods in agreement*). Then we lay three feet of hardcore over the peat and run the vibrator over it....*(Hagadan looks across the table at Wilder) *What would you think about that?"*

Wilder: *"Well...I usually leave that to my technical people..."*
Hagadan: *"You do know what swamp shooting is?"* Wilder: *"This is
a preliminary meeting...."* Hagadan: *"At which we hardly seem to
know what we're discussing. Now if you like we can go and measure
it together by slack chaining...you do know what slack chaining is I
suppose."* Wilder: *"I DO know what slack chaining is"*

Finding an excuse to come out of the meeting, Wilder tells Ken to
drop the joint venture. *"If it starts like this, it'll end in open bloody
warfare before we've got a skip of dirt out of the ground."* But Ken
decides that as joint managing director he has the right to see the
deal through, and that he will lack Wilder's emotional involvement.
At the end of the episode, we learn that Sam Bell has inevitably
taken Hagadan off the job – no one man (or two men) is going to
stand in the way of a lucrative joint venture.

Now that Hagadan is back in London, Wilder urges Pamela to meet
Hagadan and tell him their affair is over, *"Now he'll do anything he
can to see you. A letter doesn't work. Tell him to his face. Leave no
doubt in his mind."*

Meanwhile Sefton Kemp prepares to reactivate the security
investigation into Susan Weldon unless she assures him that her
relationship with Wilder is over. But Wilder is unwilling to break
off the relationship. When Susan protests that the previous security
investigation (*in Point of Balance*) found nothing because there was
nothing to investigate. *"You tell me there was nothing to
investigate"*, says Kemp, *"I have only your word for it. If you were
lying you might well tell me the same thing"*

Ironically Susan is saved at the end by Gillingham, who decides that
he doesn't want Security back in the NEB. If security is called in too
often people will think there's an ongoing problem with the NEB
and that (it is implied) will reflect on Gillingham.

Although the term *"Persons and Papers"* was mentioned by
Townley in *The Switch* and will be defined in the following episode
Trade Secret, it is hardly relevant here since it refers to the powers

Kemp and Gillingham seek to make people give information to the NEB.

Like Patrick Wymark, Peter Hager (Sam Bell) would appear in *The Battle of Britain (1969)* as Field Marshall Albert Kesselring.

21 February 1966   *Trade Secret*

Writer John Bowen.   Director Quentin Lawrence

Patrick Wymark (Sir John Wilder). Clifford Evans (Caswell Bligh). Barbara Murray (Lady Pamela Wilder). Rosemary Leach (Susan Weldon). Jack Watling (Don Henderson). Peter Barkworth (Kenneth Bligh). Rachel Herbert (Justine Bligh). Ian Holm (Sefton Kemp). Ralph Michael (Bob Gillingham). John Tate (Billy Straker). Llewellyn Rees (Economic Affairs Minister). Philip Madoc (Ted Newark). Fred Ferris (Paul Budge). Philip Brack (James Fielding MP).Mark Burns (Minister's PPS). Robert Raglan (Fulton).

"Don't call me darling. I don't like it. I don't like love words." Sir John Wilder to Susan Weldon

In the House of Commons, the question of Bligh and Wilder both being members of the National Export Board is revived. The Minister defends Bligh and Wilder (without naming them) saying they have contributed so much. Sefton Kemp and Bob Gillingham continue to press for the NEB to extend its powers to compel any firm or body to give evidence. Caswell Bligh is opposed, saying it would compromise secrecy. But the NEB has asked for an explanation of Bligh Constructions' success in the communist controlled state of Matabelia and if Bligh does not answer it will compromise his position on the Board.

The probe into Bligh Construction's success winning contracts in Matabelia highlights the contradictory relationship between the West and Iron Curtain countries during the cold war. Formerly "Milner's Land", the "independent" Matabelia now runs on state aid from the East Germans. We learn from Ken Bligh that during the war, his father entertained a lot of visiting socialists, and one of those East German friends now controls Matabelia.

Wilder continues to probe and discovers that Caswell has been using an underhand procedure to evade sanctions against communist East Germany. Caswell finally accepts that Wilder's knowledge will force him to resign from the NEB. But the Minister tells Gillingham that he's just stood up in the House expressing confidence in both Wilder and Bligh. If the evening papers announce Bligh's resignation, he'll look a fool. *"Tell Bligh if he still wants to resign in six months' time he can develop a weak heart or prostate trouble. But at this moment in time he'll bloody well stay where I want him."*

Bowen revives the character of Paul Budge (Fred Ferris) first seen *in The Politician*. Although Bligh dominates Bligh Construction, Budge is the man in charge of overseas contracts. The episode *The Politician* showed that while Caswell publicly embraced the Government's export drive to cut the balance of payments deficit, he privately stifles Bligh's overseas projects because he wants his name visible on UK construction sites. Wilder had tempted Budge to feed him information with the prospect of becoming a Director. Budge tells Wilder that he's realised he'll never be put on the Board. *"When a man of my age knows he can't go any higher, he concentrates on simply staying where he is for as long as possible by not taking sides."*

When the NEB starts asking questions about Matabelia, Caswell Bligh tells Budge that Ken has suggested they move him to Geneva. What would be an exciting prospect for a younger man, is a threat to Budge. His arguments are prosaic but heartfelt. He's finally got the plantain weeds out of his garden after seven years and his wife is active in the local townswomen's guild. Although Caswell relents, Budge realises that his knowledge about Matabelia is dangerous to Bligh and perceives that the safest way to neutralise that danger is to let Wilder bring it out in the open. Budge drops a broad enough hint for Wilder to start digging.

Rosemary Leach shows more assertiveness from Susan Weldon when she tells Wilder she's asked for a transfer from the Civil Engineering Committee. Wilder says he needs her on the Committee and she replies that, *"Having a mistress in 1966 means more than buying expensive meals and jewellery.... There are a lot of other things involved. Like consideration and affection. I won't say love. So I'm telling you my darling. If you really want a mistress it's time you started working at it."*

There's a nostalgic scene of 1960's domesticity – Ken Bligh can't sleep and sits up in bed lighting a cigarette. Justine wakes and he offers her a cigarette. *"Can I have one of mine?"* she says, *"They're on the dressing table."*

This was the last episode of the series to be shown for four months as Prime Minister Harold Wilson announced a General Election on 28th February – the date when the even more politically charged *"The Man With Two Hats"* was scheduled to be broadcast.

Monday 13 June 1966   *The Man With Two Hats*

Writer Wilfred Greatorex   Director John Cooper

Patrick Wymark (Sir John Wilder). Clifford Evans (Caswell Bligh). Barbara Murray (Lady Pamela Wilder). Rosemary Leach (Susan Weldon). Jack Watling (Don Henderson). Peter Barkworth (Kenneth Bligh). Rachel Herbert (Justine Bligh). Ian Holm (Sefton Kemp). Ralph Michael (Bob Gillingham). Michael Goodliffe (Geoffrey Packard). Anthony Newlands (Alan Norton). Norma Ronald (Kay Lingard). Eric Dodson (Davis). Fred McNaughton (Bissett). Lockwood West (Hon. Member). John Scott Martin (Bernard). Sidney Dench (Stan Calder). Marilyn Gothard (Deirdre). Adrian Drotsky (Howard). Janice Hoy (Amanda). David Aldridge (Paul).

"It's not for me to judge men, Sir John. Only their books." Davis, the auditor (Eric Dodson) *"By their figures ye shall know them. And knowing them dig their graves, eh?"* Wilder

Caswell Bligh cuts short a holiday in Barbados when he learns that Sir John Wilder has called in a firm of auditors and has hired public relations consultant Geoffrey Packard (Michael Goodliffe) to promote Wilder through Bligh's. Caswell arrives to find his father's memorial stone removed from the lobby to make room for a map of the company's international projects, and is just in time to save his bronze bust from being removed.

Following the revelations of Bligh's sanctions busting in the previous episode, Wilder has an excuse to bring in the auditors, although his real target is evidence of the wartime fiddles (revealed in *Late Via Rome*) on which the company was founded. Wilder sends Don Henderson to track down what he thinks is the Clerk of Works "fixed" by Bligh and Billy Straker during the war, but even Wilder is surprised when Don finds out that Bligh Construction has been making secret payments to the local Conservative Party. Wilder concludes that the famous Socialist millionaire (who earlier stood for selection as a Labour MP) has been laying off against the prospect of a Conservative government. But Ken Bligh declares that he authorised the payments without Caswell's knowledge.

*"**WILDER (Stopped by the General Election) FIGHTS AGAIN"***
said the *TV Times*, introducing the final two episodes of *The Power Game*. As Anthony Davies explained, *"this was the story which should have been seen on March 1, the day after Mr Wilson announced the election date. But because it is concerned with payments by a big industrial company to Conservative Party funds, and the decision of young Kenneth Bligh to stand for election as a Conservative member of Parliament, it was withdrawn at the time."*

With the expectation of an election announcement in the air, *The Power Game*'s regular Monday slot had been filled by imported series on most ITV regions, before ATV's new series *Mrs Thursday* was brought forward on Monday 9th March starring Kathryn Harrison as a charwoman who inherits a fortune. With the 31st March election delivering an increased majority for Harold Wilson's Labour government, *The Power Game* had to wait until 13 June for a two-week slot at the end of *Mrs Thursday's* run.

The postponement from February must have made Caswell Bligh's winter holiday seem a little jarring in the opening scenes. However, a Conservative victory would have made the episode seem even more anachronistic since several plot strands turned on the chances of a Conservative victory at the next election. It's not surprising that Wilfred Greatorex argued against postponement. But ATV and the Independent Television Authority agreed that, *"it would not be right to transmit the programme during the election period."* And it would have seemed odd for ITV to go ahead, when the BBC had even postponed the puppet series *Pinky and Perky* because their next scheduled episode had been *You Too Can Be A Prime Minister.*

Michael Goodliffe (still a few years away from the role of Section chief Hunter in *Callan*) is charming as Geoffrey Packard, a PR man and politician, who prefers to stay behind the scenes. He suggests that Ken Bligh may be adopted as a prospective Conservative MP.

Wilder sees a benefit in Ken's ambitions – *"I know the Minister…but I don't know the shadow Minister."* Ken is quick to perceive that Caswell backs Labour, Ken will back the Conservative's, but Wilder will back the field. *"That,"* Wilder tells him, *"is the privilege of the neutral."*

Jack Watling delivers a nicely judged comic performance as the increasingly frustrated Henderson is sent across the south coast in search of dirt on Caswell. He admits to having misgivings, if not regrets about re-joining Wilder. *"At Scott Furlong, no matter how dirty the game, you could always have the feeling he was*

*responsible for 12,000 men's jobs. Now it's mostly casual labour.
Like people from another planet"*

For those keeping score Packard notes that Caswell Bligh is 58,
Wilder's 49 and Ken is 36.

Thanks to Caswell Drake for the research assist

Monday 20 June 1966   *Confound Their Politics*

Writer Edmund Ward   **Director Rex Firkin**

Patrick Wymark (Sir John Wilder). Clifford Evans   (Caswell
Bligh). Barbara Murray (Lady Pamela Wilder). Rosemary Leach
(Susan Weldon). Jack Watling (Don Henderson). Peter Barkworth
(Kenneth Bligh). Rachel Herbert (Justine Bligh). Ian Holm (Sefton
Kemp). Ralph Michael (Bob Gillingham). Basil Henson (Sandy
Warren). Norma Ronald (Kay Lingard). Norman Tyrrell (Sir
Gordon Revidge). Llewellyn Rees (Minister). Jayne Sofiano (Pat
Henderson). Alan Lawrence (Westland).

*"Wilder's off alright. There's enough leverage under him to shift the
Taj Mahal!"* Sandy Warren (Basil Henson)

Kemp and Gillingham prepare a report calling for an expansion of
the National Export Board but acknowledging that Bligh's are over-
represented on the Board. Kemp leaks the report to a backbench
MP, primed to stir up trouble. Gillingham plans to be out of contact
while the storm breaks and invites Caswell Bligh, journalist Sandy
Warren* and Sir Gordon Revidge to a fishing weekend. Gillingham
also invites Susan Weldon in order to keep her away from Wilder,
unaware that she wants Wilder to be thrown off the NEB so that
their relationship can be more straightforward. Rosemary Leach is
heartbreakingly effective as Susan Weldon in this episode, unwilling
to help Wilder but forced to witness the conspiracy against him.

* Basil Henson had appeared as Sandy Warren in ATV's 1965
series *Front Page Story*, produced by Rex Firkin.

The Friday evening news reports that a group of backbench MP's have tabled a motion protesting the over representation of one firm on the National Export Board, with Wilder being the only one named. Don Henderson overcomes his doubts of the previous episode and offers his resignation to Wilder because, *"If I stay, they'll use me to chop you!"*

Peter Barkworth, as Ken Bligh, has been clumsily insinuating when he tries to win Don Henderson over, but becomes frighteningly callous when the news of the back-bench motion erupts, telling Wilder to forget about his plans for European projects. Wilder is silently rattled after his exchange with Kenneth and we realise how tenuous his future is.

On the Sunday evening, Gillingham tells the fishing party that the Minister has told him to request Sir John Wilder's resignation from the NEB. But Wilder then confronts the Minister with circumstantial evidence that the Government has conspired to 'crucify' Wilder, who has no political affiliations, in order to protect Bligh who has been a Labour Party member for 35 years. Wilder adds that he has given the Shadow Minister the same dossier.

On Monday morning, Sefton Kemp arrives at Wilder's office with a letter of resignation for Wilder to sign. Wilder tells him, *"You're one of the grey men, merging in the bureaucratic wallpaper. You make bullets for people with more guts to fire."*

Back at the NEB offices Gillingham tells Kemp the Minister has phoned to tell him that Wilder is to be seconded from the NEB for 6 months. *"It's to be made clear that he's released temporarily for more valuable services."*

"He's to be offered the post of Britain's special plenipotentiary in Brussels. Made to order, Kemp. One of the ripest plums on the tree. Ambassador status. £15,000 a year [£300,000 in 2022]. Access to the best contact network in the world. You've hashed this one up beautifully."

In his office, Wilder shares a glass of champagne with Kay Lingard. She tells him she's researched the line from the national anthem he wanted, *"Confound their politics, frustrate their knavish tricks."*

It's fitting that Norma Ronald as Kay Lingard gets to share the final scene with Wilder. With the vultures circling, it's Lingard who carries out the pre-digital research (reading through *Who's Who*) to prove a conspiracy against Wilder and comes into the office early on Monday morning to organise the phone lines (before the switchboard girl has arrived) and even brings a flask of her *"most excellent coffee."*

Jayne Sofiano makes her only appearance as Pat Henderson (previously played by Anthea Wyndham in *The Plane Makers*). She would later play Dr Ginny Vickers in the 1969 series of *The Troubleshooters*. Ironically her final screen appearance would be as Richard Greene's secretary in the sequence of *Tales From The Crypt* starring Barbara Murray.

Notes:

1 HANDY, CHARLES. Understanding Organisations, page 124-127

2 MAURER, DAVID.W. The Big Con..Page 93-94

Case Study Six   The Power Game Series Two

Producer Rex Firkin   Script Editor Wilfred Greatorex

Clifford Evans as Bligh   Patrick Wymark as Wilder

It might seem at first that Firkin and Greatorex were departing from their strategy of consistent change with the second series of *The Power Game*. It's very much a continuation of the first, with the same characters and background carried over. But taking into account that the second series of *The Plane Makers* had 29 episodes, it's perhaps not so much a surprise that they were happy to extract more value from the concept.

With the General Election delaying the final two episodes of the first series, there had only been a two-month gap between series one and two of *The Power Game*. But if the first series had run its intended course, it would have been six months since the last series – matching Sir John Wilder's six-month secondment in Brussels.

In the first episode Wilder dismisses Bligh's project as a *"church bazaar"*, Bligh retorts, *"Walk out! Put your two years in the church bazaar to experience"* implying that the first series covered two years.

Probably the biggest shock for returning viewers would be the new "swinging" arrangement of the theme tune. ATV's associate company PYE Records had produced a cover version of Wayne

Hill's theme as a single. The theme was recorded by PYE's A&R Man Cyril Stapleton, who had been leader of the BBC Show Band until 1957. Stapleton opted for a "swinging" arrangement which must have pleased ATV's executives to the extent that the Stapleton version actually accompanied the title sequence of the second series.

Joining the series as Pamela's cousin, Treasury official Charles Grainger was Robin Bailey, who had played Marc Anthony against William Devlin's Brutus in the 1953 Old Vic production of *Julius Caesar* where Wymark and Alan Dobie had made early professional appearances.

The new series was promoted in the 24th September edition of the *TV Times* with an appreciation of Barbara Murray by Stephen Vizinczey, later author of *In Praise of Older Women*.

The only other piece of merchandising for the series was John Burke's novelisation, published in 1966 by Pan Books.

"Wilder looked from father to son with reluctant approval. But he was still calm, and still smiling to himself with that thin, dangerous little smile of his."

John Burke was the 'King' of the novelisers. His career stretched from '*The Entertainer*' in 1960 to '*The Bill*' in the

1980's. Born in 1922, Burke worked as a public relations officer for Shell, and as a story editor for 20th Century Fox, before becoming a freelance writer. Among his novelisations were *Dr Terror's House of Horrors* (1965), and *The Hammer Horror Omnibus* (1967). Under the alias of Robert Miall, Burke also wrote novelisations of ITC film series such as *UFO* and *Kill Jason King*.

As Christopher Fowler observed in The Independent (13 February 2011), Burke rarely made a standard transcript of the film or TV episode. *"Often, his narratives feel more structurally cohesive than the works on which they were based, and have a clearly identifiable style that marks them with the author's imprimatur."*

Burke's novelisation of *The Power Game* demonstrates this approach magnificently. Burke adapts *Point of Balance, Trade Secret* and *Confound Their Politics* but also draws in scenes from other episodes such as *Lady For A Knight*. Burke uses the character of the security officer Hartley (played by Nigel Green in *Point of Balance*) to frame the adaptation. Asked to look into the relationship of Wilder and Susan Weldon, Hartley reviews press reports of Wilder edging himself into Bligh Construction and picks up some office gossip from the ex-technical director who saw himself as rightful Managing Director. Having established the background, Burke relates the televised investigation from *Point of Balance*. But where the TV episode ends with the General deciding to end the investigation of Susan Weldon , Burke has Hartley conclude that, *"There was something in the relationship between Wilder and that girl which needed probing further. There was always something if you were allowed to go far enough, for long enough."* Burke invents a friendship between Hartley and Sefton Kemp , the new Secretary to the National Export Board. While not part of the TV show, the friendship is credible. *"Kemp was much more his kind of man than Townley had been. Kemp would be the first to alert him if there was any promising flicker of a scandal."*

Burke also shows some efficiency in viewing events through the relationship between Susan Weldon and Wilder. Pamela Wilder is glossed over in a couple of sentences. Hartley concludes that, *"She attended various official functions with her husband and they were always civil to each other in public, but little more than that."* Later on, Susan Weldon recalls a magazine photograph, *"Sir John and Lady Wilder arm in arm as they emerged from their hotel (in Switzerland)"*. Burke gives no indication that this marks the aftermath of Pamela's affair with Frank Hagadan. While he lets Susan recall Wilder's comment that the holiday was necessary because, *"there were things he wanted to talk to (Pamela) about,"* Burke leaves Susan oblivious, and only a TV viewer would pick up on the significance.

Perhaps a second novelisation would have focussed on the Wilder/Pamela/Hagadan triangle. However, that was never to be. The decision to eliminate Pamela from the story does lead Burke to creates an alternate view of the scene in *'Confound Their Politics'* where MP's protest about Wilder's membership of the National Export Board. In the TV episode, Wilder and Pamela hear the news at home, but Burke depicts Susan alone in her flat.

"Susan made herself a mug of hot chocolate and threw it away without tasting it. Spinster school-teachers might drink hot chocolate every night before going to bed, but it didn't fit with the image of the wild, abandoned mistress of a tycoon. Susan poured herself a stiff whisky and gagged as she drank it."

"The radio announcer began to summarize the news headlines. Suddenly the words and phrases shaped themselves into significance. 'What they call "gross preference". One of the N.E.B. members concerned was named as Sir John Wilder, a former aviation expert.' Susan stood quite still with the empty glass warming in her hand. She wondered how many of their mutual acquaintances would have heard this announcement. There would be a great rubbing of hands and eager speculation."

Another interesting choice is that Burke makes no attempt to get inside John Wilder's head. His speech may be reported, but Wilder is always shown from the viewpoint of another character. Wilder is initially described by a reporter as having *"the features of an amiable frog, but not as flaccid as a frog's: there was a muscular tightness beneath the skin which could snap the whole face into decisive fury in a split second."*

Later, Hartley meets Wilder and sums up the appeal of the character, *"This might be an opponent, but it was an opponent worthy of respect. It was not just that he brought with him the aura of his reputation.; the man himself exuded an aura of power and of ruthlessness. Hartley found him quite admirable."*

Burke maintains the same approach when Wilder is fighting for his survival. We are shown the scenes where Kemp demands Wilder's resignation, and the Bligh's tell him that has no power within the firm. But of his fight back, nothing is reported directly. Instead, a drunken Kemp meets with Hartley who speculates how Wilder must have researched to prove the conspiracy and then negotiated with the Minister. *"The cut and thrust of the conversation he had with the Minister would probably always be secret...But the general tenor of it could be in no doubt: The results spoke for themselves."*

The Power Game is *indeed "a fascinating novel of the ATV Television Series"*. Thanks to John Burke's ingenuity, it remains worthwhile, even now the series itself is available on DVD.

Sadly, the only other piece of merchandising never reached production: In 1965 Wilfred Greatorex and Peter Draper registered a proposal for a *Power Game* board game and in a January 1966 interview Keith Shackleton of Century 21 Merchandising , *"enthused ... about a variation of Monopoly based on ATV's The Power Game,"* explaining that, *"The good merchandiser exploiter doesn't wait for the games manufacturer to come to him - he goes to the manufacturer with a fully worked out idea of his own."*

A draft proposal survives in Wilfred Greatorex's papers in the BFI Library special collections for a *Power Game Board Game*. The outline begins: *"The object of the game is for a player to take over control of all industry in Great Britain and crush his opponent with cunning, skill and luck together with the backing of political parties, trade unions and merchant banks that he may acquire during the game."*

"The player throwing the highest number with two dice starts, and can nominate the political party in power at the start of the game."

Each player has twelve identity discs. As he moves round the board he can pick up the support of trade unions or politicians with individual markers that he *"piggy backs"* on each of his identity discs. At each edge of the board are *"Press Release"* cards which announce events that can alter the state of play. In the centre of the board is the *"Arena of Power"*. This is divided into red and blue squares, and it is the area *"where the real struggle for power takes place."*

Sadly, it appears that no board game manufacturer was willing to put *The Power Game* into production for Christmas 1967.

The second series would maintain the high audience ratings of the first. An estimated 13,970,00 viewers (in 6,350,000 homes) of the opening episode, *Nothing's Free*, meant it scored joint 14th in the TAM ratings with the BBC's *Steptoe and Son.* In October, the quirks of the ratings system meant *that Grounds for Decision* reached number 10 with 6,300,000 homes. Although the viewing figures dwindled slightly, the final episode, *There's No Such Thing As A Dead Heat*, finished (ironically in view of the title) at joint 10th with ATV's *Mrs Thursday*, winning 11, 990,000 viewers (5,450,0000 homes).

In Australia, film recordings of *The Power Game* were sold to Sydney's TCN-9 by ATV's export arm ITC. Originally scheduled at 10pm on Fridays and then 11pm on Sunday evenings the show had little success. Thanks to a passionate and vocal fan-base, the series was re-scheduled to 9.30pm on Mondays where it quadrupled its audience.

Comparing *The Power Game* with its BBC rival, *The Troubleshooters*, in *The Stage* in October 1966 N.Alice Frick conceded that real-life business people might find both series absurd but, *"to ordinary poor television watchers like me, The Power Game seems more real. Largely because the conflicts between John Wilder and the Bligh's…are always grounded in recognisable action: contracts, tenders, international political situations. You really feel that the Bligh's are out to get Wilder's hide."*

Frick continued that, *" The guiding force of Wilfred Greatorex is evident in all episodes of The Power Game…although each episode is self-contained, there is a continuity that makes it like a serial. No such strong editorial hand is evident in the Troubleshooters."*

In the *Catholic Herald*, crime writer H.R.F Keating noted that, *"Wilder was not the creation of one brain… He was not, as many fictional characters are, at least part of the personality of an author transferred to a communicating medium. (He came) from half a dozen different writers. from a series-editor, from producer and directors, even from the impact of fellow actors. And this enables us perhaps to see that it was no real man we delighted in. What we actually saw was something in the nature of an anthology of a certain type of person. And, like all anthologies, it was more wide spreading than deep."*

Wednesday 26 September 1966.   *Nothing's Free*

Writer Edmund Ward.   Director Peter Moffat.

Patrick Wymark (Sir John Wilder). Clifford Evans (Caswell Bligh). Barbara Murray (Pamela, Lady Wilder). Rosemary Leach (Susan Weldon). Jack Watling (Don Henderson). Peter Barkworth (Kenneth Bligh). Eric Porter (Dr. Vrieling). Robin Bailey (Charles Grainger). Norma Ronald (Kay Lingard). Nita Moyce (Miss Tillingshed). Elma Soiron (Miss Sgier). Michael Reubens (Pageboy).

"I'm not sure I like ambition in women. Bit unnatural – like throwing the discus." Sir John Wilder

Wilder makes a triumphant return, aiming to set up an Anglo-Dutch-Italian consortium for a regional development scheme in Italy. He's already committed Bligh Construction to the project, without Ken and Caswell's knowledge. Wilder also needs to get a credit guarantee from the British Government, and these aren't usually offered to consortia. He asks Pamela to tempt her friend Charles Grainger (Robin Bailey) out of his *"Treasury mousehole"* to get his support.

Pamela (Barbara Murray) warns Wilder that, *"I don't want this Susan Weldon circus starting again. I'm tired of sweet reason and tolerance!"*

Susan Weldon (Rosemary Leach) has heard that Gillingham is resigning as Chair of the National Export Board and Wilder is certain to be offered the post. If that happens, she will be transferred. With Sefton Kemp also leaving, she would prefer to stay at the NEB and offers Caswell Bligh her support. Don Henderson, shunted by Caswell into the "meaningless job" of Director of Personnel Relations, has been quietly researching all Bligh Construction's activities and demands that Wilder give him, *"A golden handshake or a real job. I'm tired of bouncing about in your wake."*

Bligh Construction, meanwhile, has been ticking over with a series of safe, small municipal construction projects arranged by Caswell. Kenneth Bligh is ambitious to run the British end of the consortium but Wilder tells him he's not in the same political league as their collaborators and the Dutch and Italians will eat him alive.

As the episode progresses, Wilder learns from Grainger that there is a long-term plan for the National Export Board to be *"Discretely and quietly absorbed by other bodies."* Knowing that Caswell wants the NEB Chair, Wilder bluffs him by saying he's decided to leave but, *"With control of the consortium plus my present powers I might have an incentive to stay. Plus a share option."*

In the space of an hour, Edmund Ward reasserts everything that viewers had come to expect from "The Power Game". Each of the actors is given a moment to assert themselves. It seems surprising to see Eric Porter in the one-off role of Dutch engineer, Dr Vrieling. Wymark and Porter had both appeared in the Royal Shakespeare Company's production of *The Duchess of Malfi* in 1960, but Porter was still five months away from the role which would make him a household name – Soames in the BBC series *The Forsyte Saga*.

3rd October 1966   *Ambassador Status*

 Writer Peter Draper   Director John Moxey

Patrick Wymark (Sir John Wilder). Clifford Evans (Caswell Bligh). Barbara Murray (Pamela, Lady Wilder). Rosemary Leach (Susan Weldon). Jack Watling (Don Henderson). Peter Barkworth (Kenneth Bligh). Norma Ronald (Kay Lingard). George Sewell (Frank Hagadan). Patrick Allen (David Main). Norman Scace (Peter Bagehot). Bari Johnson (Andre Abwa). Charles Hyatt (Ambassador). David Grey (Edwin).

"If I felt that I owed you a fidelity that you were prepared to give to me, I would probably give it to you. Since, in neither of our cases does that apply, it's a piece of spurious sophistry even to argue about it." Susan Weldon

As new Chair of the National Export Board, Caswell Bligh (Clifford Evans) hosts an evening dinner at which Susan Weldon (Rosemary Leach) catches the eye of Treasury official David Main (Patrick Allen). Meanwhile, Sir John Wilder is having a secret meeting with Peter Bagehot (Norman Scace), another Treasury official who shares his dislike of the Minister.

Although previously opposed to increased powers for the NEB, Bligh now believes that as Chair, *"My job is to make the Board work.* " Bagehot asks how many industrialists like Wilder could be counted on to voice their opposition if there were moves to give the NEB extended powers.

Ken Bligh has been working to establish links with the African state of Magalia. Although Wilder is against it, Bagehot encourages Ken telling him that, *"There are people who think it important that your company go into Africa as soon as possible. Diplomacy nowadays if frequently done behind a spearhead of commerce."*

Meanwhile, at the Italian Embassy, Pamela Wilder (Barbara Murray) encounters Frank Hagadan (George Sewell).

"Where's John?" Hagadan asks. *"As always, with his back to me,"* Pamela replies.

"Old friends should never meet when they're serving free drinks" she says, before prompting him to ask her to lunch.

Rosemary Leach is similarly assertive after an evening stroll along the Thames with David Main. She wonders if he will invite her back to his flat for coffee and Main replies that, *"We passed my flat ages ago. I can't stand that awful silence after the girl says no."*

"It's probably what holds most Englishmen back, "Susan replies, *"Still, I'm glad that's what it was. Otherwise, I'd have been worried why I hadn't been asked."*

Draper also amusingly sketches a scene at the Mogalian Embassy where the Charge d'Affairs Andre Abina (Bari Johnson) tells Ken that the Ambassador has been recalled. *"I'm surprised he lasted this long. He's a peasant. That's the trouble with us emergent countries, Mr Bligh. The right sort of diplomats don't always emerge at the same rate."* If there is a patronising overtone to this portrayal, Draper at least acknowledges as much by having Abina compare the Ambassador to John Bird's then-popular portrayal of Jomo Kenyatta.

Norman Scace, who had appeared with Wymark in the BBC's *Malatesta*, offers a twee interpretation of Draper's lines as Treasury man Bagehot although he becomes remarkably sinister during the scenes with Ken Bligh filmed at Heathrow Airport.

Patrick Wymark once more shows a relatively softer side to Wilder - thrown off-balance, distracted from business by Susan Weldon's show of independence. But in typical Wilder fashion he offers little weakness. When Rosemary Leach angrily cuts short their lunch date at the waiter's arrival, Wymark shows a millisecond of distress before matter-of-factly turning to the waiter and ordering avocado.

As Andre Abina says, quoting Harold McMillan, *"Power is like the Dead Sea Fruit. When you achieve it, there is nothing there."*

Edmund Ward would re-use the name of Patrick Allen's character, David Main for his 1969 TV series *The Main Chance*, starring John Stride.

10 October 1966   *Grounds For Decision*

Writer Raymond Bowers   Director David Reid.

Patrick Wymark   (Sir John Wilder). Clifford Evans (Caswell Bligh). Barbara Murray (Pamela, Lady Wilder). Rosemary Leach (Susan Weldon). Jack Watling (Don Henderson). Peter Barkworth (Kenneth Bligh). Rachel Herbert (Justine Bligh). Norma Ronald (Kay Lingard). George Sewell (Frank Hagadan). Michael Lees (Basil Simpson). Jocelyn Birdsall (Stewardess).

"To a civil engineer, tumult is music." Caswell Bligh

Another dyspeptic script from Raymond Bowers sees an unlikely series of events leading Wilder to believe that even Don Henderson is betraying him. Returning home to hear Pamela listening to Japanese music, Wilder peers at the record player and calculates that there *are "Eight inches left out of twelve. Fifteen plinking minutes."*

Turning off the record he's confronted by the noise from the M27 motorway construction works. *"We'll have that day and night now"* Pamela tells him, *"Until they've knocked the village down and replaced it with a polygonally foliated clover leaf apparently modelled on Hampton Court Maze."*

Despite being barred from involvement in Bligh's due to his NEB Chairmanship, Caswell Bligh reminds Don that he's also chair of the National Motorways Council. *"Britain today is stifled by an out-of-date transport system. Every national vision must take this into account."* Bligh believes that the Americans will want to build new airbases and also sponsor a NATO contract for *"a communications complex to integrate logistics"* (aka a highway). Bligh attempts to woo Don with the promise of his patronage within the company. He wants Don to ensure that Bligh's are not over committed abroad, so that the company will be in a position to tender for the new American project.

Meanwhile, Justine Bligh (Rachel Herbert) triggers a farcical series of events when she tries to broker a reconciliation between Don Henderson and Frank Hagadan, whose new employers Infell's are prospective partners in a Greek NATO harbour contract. Henderson is looking for a London flat to escape the road construction, and Justine has agreed to show him one. She offers Hagadan the key, so that he can meet Henderson, but Don then asks Pamela Wilder to check out the flat when he is detained by Wilder.

The M27 mentioned in this script is a fictional contract crossing from Hertfordshire to Oxfordshire. The real M27, begun in 1972, spread across Hampshire. It's likely that the construction works attributed to Billy Straker in this episode were actually the M1 extension east to Scratchwood.

After some sign of ambition and determination in the opening episodes, Jack Watling's face evokes pure horror when Wilder finally puts Henderson on the spot. Recalling the scene in *The Plane Makers* where Wilder demanded unconditional support from James

Cameron-Grant, Wilder tells Henderson that he wants his vote – *"No explanations"*. As Wilder tells Ken Bligh, *"When you buy a share in Bligh's you take a risk – ON ME!"*

17 October 1966   ***The Front Men***

Writer Wilfred Greatorex.   Director Dennis Vance

Patrick Wymark   (Sir John Wilder). Clifford Evans (Caswell Bligh). Barbara Murray (Pamela, Lady Wilder). Rosemary Leach (Susan Weldon). Jack Watling (Don Henderson). Peter Barkworth (Kenneth Bligh). Norma Ronald (Kay Lingard). George Sewell (Frank Hagadan). Roger Delgado (Farid Salem). Fred McNaughton (Bissett). Denis Holmes (Frank Howarth). Brian Haines (Bruce Murray).

"That's his victory roll! Who's he shot down today?" Pamela Wilder (Barbara Murray)

Both Bligh Construction and Infells are competing for an oil-money-backed construction project in Beirut. As the episode opens Frank Hagadan (George Sewell) is celebrating with champagne, while Ken Bligh (Peter Barkworth) is surprisingly laid back about Infells' victory. Back in London, Ken gleefully informs Wilder that, *"We missed out because we are now on the Arab blacklist."* For once Wilder is shocked. Don tells him that, *"they raked up something about your selling aircraft spare parts to the Israelis while we were at Scott Furlong."*

Ken suggests that Caswell calls Wilder as a witness to a National Export Board investigation into the Arab blacklist. If Wilder testifies, his name on the blacklist becomes public knowledge and the Board of Bligh's will sack him as a liability. If Wilder refuses to testify, Caswell will have the proof he needs that the NEB needs greater powers for the NEB. And the board will still fire Wilder.

Caswell orders Susan to rush through the set-up of the Arab Blacklist committee. She knows that if she warns Wilder, the leak will clearly come to her, and believes Caswell half expects her to breach confidentiality. Meanwhile, Salem (Roger Delgado) suggests to Wilder that Bligh Construction buys up a firm called Rashid Amara. The company's board is made up of respectable deadwood, and with Salem appointed at a handsome salary, he would be able to ensure that the firm wins the construction contract.

Roger Delgado gives an assured single episode performance as the self-serving Salem. He is business-like in his opening with Wilder, knowing he only has seconds to catch his attention, but relaxes into cod-Arabianism when he needs to reassure Wilder (the *"empty blanket"* of a company, Rashid Amara *"could be your overcoat, Sir John, and the desert is cold."*).

Wilder appears to play along, buying up shares in Rashid Amara. Salem also buys-in, hoping for a windfall when Wilder orders Bligh Construction to acquire the firm. But after some advice from Susan, Wilder instructs his stock-broker to sell and orders the press officer to put out a release saying there is no truth to the rumours that Bligh Construction is interested in the company. Jack Watling gives an amusing performance as he listens to Wilder's phone call and takes in the implications, before rushing off to sell the *"thousand or so"* he's bought in Rashid Amara.

Salem's mask only slips when Wilder reveals that Bligh's are setting up *"the sort of company whose Board carries more weight than your greediest dreams."* It won't matter that Wilder's behind it. *"They only ever see the men in front!"*

Dennis Vance allows a much broader theatrical approach throughout this episode, with Patrick Wymark strutting in Shakespearean style as he instructs Don Henderson in his plotting, and delivers roaring rebukes to Ken and Salem in turn.

Monday 24 October 1966   *A Matter For Speculation*

Writer Edmund Ward   **Director John Cooper**

Patrick Wymark (Sir John Wilder). Clifford Evans (Caswell Bligh).
Barbara Murray (Pamela, Lady Wilder). Rosemary Leach (Susan
Weldon). Jack Watling (Don Henderson). Peter Barkworth (Kenneth
Bligh). Robin Bailey (Charles Grainger). Norma Ronald (Kay
Lingard). Alan MacNaughtan (Hendrik Van Meeren). Kevin Stoney
(Eduardo Contini). Lloyd Lamble (Edward Luke). Donald Pickering
(Bennett). Douglas Muir (credited as the Professor, but does not
appear in recording).

*"I have no intention of letting Contini crack his feudal whip over
me!"* Sir John Wilder

Van Meeren (Alan MacNaughtan), Dutch financial controller of the
consortium (see *Nothing's Free*) tells Wilder that a speculator is
threatening the project. A British company called Land Enterprises
has bought up the property earmarked for the first development
stage and is demanding a high price. Land Enterprises share a bank
and solicitors with Bligh Construction. *"If this speculation is not
yours, a lot of trouble has been taken to link you with it."*

Wilder deduces that Bennett (Donald Pickering), the planner to the
consortium is behind Land Enterprises and fires him. As Bennett is
also son-in-law to Contini (Kevin Stoney) the politician behind the
Italian side of the consortium, Van Meeren says this won't be the
end of the matter. Wilder tasks former Fraud Squad officer Edward
Luke (Lloyd Lamble) with investigating Land Enterprises

Meanwhile, Caswell Bligh (Clifford Evans) wants Bligh
Construction to fund a Chair in Civil Engineering at Garford
University. He says this will establish "an attitude" which will be
helpful in his political work. It will "put something back" into the
industry. Ken Bligh (Peter Barkworth) is opposed, saying the
company can't afford it.

Contini meets with Treasury officer Grainger (Robin Bailey)
threatening to break up the consortium unless Bennett is reinstated.
However, Wilder refuses threatening to publicise the reason for

Bennett's sacking and let the Italian press speculate whether his father-in-law was involved in the scheme.

But although Luke proves that Bennett was involved in Land Enterprises, he uncovers two other property companies in Liechtenstein and Switzerland with links to Don Henderson and Pamela Wilder!

Using the construction industry expertise that would culminate in *The Hanged Man (*1976), Edmund Ward delivers a satisfying mystery for Wilder to solve. Like all good thrillers it has a 'ticking clock'; Van Meeren will cut Bligh Construction out of the consortium if it can be proved that Wilder is behind the speculative buying of land.

Director John Cooper oversees a spectacular argument between Patrick Wymark and Barbara Murray, circling around their living room as Wilder demands to know how Pamela has got involved in a land-grabbing company with Charles Grainger. Telling him she's made a profit on her own capital which Wilder himself has relied upon in past ventures, she says, *"I'm not a Victorian chattel – a mindless warming pan. Yes, I've made money! You don't have the monopoly on profit. And with your record of risks you may be very glad of a cushion to land on when they kick the ladder away from under you!"* Stabbing her cigarette like a lethal weapon she adds, *"And with your penchant for affairs, I may be glad of a nest egg for my solitary old age!"*

Regarding the land scam, Edmund Ward reflects a mood of occupational hazard. Wilder initially tells Van Meeren he suspects the architect Bennett because, *"It isn't me and it isn't you. We would have taken a quiet profit. This is a greedy amateur profit. It must be Bennett."* And when Edward Luke finds proof of Bennett's involvement, he confirms the amateurishness saying, *"it didn't need much digging to find Bennett as principle."*

Ward's script firmly reflects the year in which it was transmitted, with Pamela saying Wilder has a machine in the bathroom to measure his blood pressure and calling him The Complete 20th Century Executive with a touch of *Batman* (the Adam West TV show was a big hit that year, with a mass of merchandising already swelling shop shelves for Christmas). More telling, the economic situation was reflected in an exchange between Ken Bligh (Peter Barkworth) and his father Caswell (Clifford Evans).

"Your Promised Land's arrived," Ken tells his socialist father, *"The indolent society. Where there's no incentive to work 14 hours a day because the rewards are the same and we can all live like bus drivers."*

"Better than the old days, "replies Caswell, *"When 10% of the country skimmed the cream and the rest starved."*

The class war also raises its head when the aristocratic Contini refers to Wilder as. *"Like a peasant in the market, bargaining for the best price for his pig!"*

Jack Watling, as Don Henderson, demonstrates some independent thought, supporting Caswell's plan to found a Civil Engineering chair at University by citing the brain drain saying, *"We're losing professional men at the rate of one a month. They've had this country."* When Wilder demands to know who is backing the land-grab company he's set up in Switzerland, Henderson refuses to tell. *"I intend to find out Don."* Wilder says. Reflecting back to *the "Hoopla of Haloes"* episode of *"The Plane Makers"*, Henderson replies, *"I remember Corbett telling me that, more than once."*

Curiously, the cast list includes Douglas Muir (Tom Bancroft in *"The Plane Makers"*) as a Professor. But although Wilder makes reference to being late for an NEB meeting where, *"Caswell has found a tame professor"*, Muir does not appear.

Monday 31 October 1966   *The Big View*

Writer Peter Draper   **Director Dennis Vance**

Patrick Wymark (Sir John Wilder). Clifford Evans (Caswell Bligh). Barbara Murray (Pamela, Lady Wilder). Rosemary Leach (Susan Weldon). Jack Watling (Don Henderson). Peter Barkworth (Kenneth Bligh). Robin Bailey (Charles Grainger). Norma Ronald (Kay Lingard). George Sewell (Frank Hagadan). Norman Scace (Peter Bagehot). George Pravda (Bacciardi). Bill Horsley (Freddy Cutter). Fred McNaughton (Bissett). Heather Kyd (Typist).

"I would hate to think of you going to the Treasury just because of this Main chap. I should miss you." Sir John Wilder

Caswell Bligh (Clifford Evans) works behind-the-scenes to get Susan Weldon (Rosemary Leach) promoted to deputy secretary of the National Export Board, reasoning that she won't "jeopardise the plum she's been reaching for," by giving Wilder further help.

Ken Bligh (Peter Barkworth) and Don Henderson (Jack Watling) discover that the Bligh Construction specification for the Italian project has no provision for the housing of construction workers. Wilder shrugs it off saying that part of the project has been sub-contracted to Bacciardi, an Italian company. But Ken discovers that Bacciardi is a fish merchant. *"How, if you're a fish merchant, can you fulfil a contract to erect houses?"*

After the high-pressure of *A Matter For Speculation*, Peter Draper delivers a relatively laid-back episode. George Pravda plays Bacciardi, who spends much of the episode misleading Ken and Don with his cheery tourist act as they try to discern what Wilder has agreed with the fish merchant – *"If it's a good scheme we have to be on John's side against father,"* Ken tells Don, *"If not we have to be with father against John."*

Wilder regards it all with amusement, eventually agreeing to take Don and Ken into his confidence. *"Bacciardi is not a fish merchant;*

At least not in your rather unimaginative sense. He delivers food in lorries insulated by plastic he produces, which can be moulded to any wagon or any size. If it keeps cold in, it can keep cold out."

Bacciardi has agreed to share the cost of constructing the worker's village because he needs to demonstrate the viability of plastic dwellings.

"You only have to stop thinking of a house as a conventional structure. This will be a plastic house and it will have a plastic shape. It doesn't have to please anybody aesthetically because it's completely utilitarian."

This slightly science fictional revelation (you can imagine a sequel appearing five year's later in the BBC *Doomwatch* series) inspires Ken. When Caswell opposes the idea, Ken berates him. *"You only ever think of your image. You never think 'is it a workable idea? Is it suitable for requirements'? Only 'has it ever been done before? Nasty new idea! How's Bligh's going to look?'"*

Ken and Wilder take "the big view". But Caswell also has his own "big view" planned. Don has been trying to discover why Freddy Cutter (Bill Horsley) of Architects Malpet and Keen is measuring up the top floor store-room. The answer is that Caswell has decided to install a penthouse flat to give himself an excuse for dropping into the office.

After the slight disconnect of previous episodes, *"The Big View"* .sees an attempt to link back to previous stories. After his previous arrogance, Wilder is now shown waiting at Susan's flat hoping to see her. Wymark gives quiet sincerity to his enquiry after David Main (from *Ambassador Status*) and his question as to whether she is moving to the Treasury.

Pamela is shown dining with Charles Grainger on behalf of Wilder (*"I'm really just a runner with a message on a cleft stick"*) but then meets with Frank Hagadan for an afternoon at the zoo.

There are some interesting views about Susan Weldon's suitability for promotion. Charles Grainger says, *"the ghost of John Knox still haunts the corridors of power."* There's an implication that a woman needs a sponsor to get though.

In retrospect, this is a perfectly "good" episode – there are no massive revelations or confrontations, which makes it seem slower-paced, but the "big idea" in this episode is easier to grasp than some of the previous stock manipulations. Considered in isolation this is an enjoyable story.

Monday 7 November 1966   *The Dead Sea Fruit*

Writer Peter Draper. Directors Dennis Vance & John Cooper

Patrick Wymark (Sir John Wilder). Clifford Evans (Caswell Bligh). Barbara Murray (Pamela, Lady Wilder). Rosemary Leach (Susan Weldon). Jack Watling (Don Henderson). Peter Barkworth (Kenneth Bligh). Rachel Herbert (Justine Bligh). Elizabeth Sellers (Esther Kelp). George Sewell (Frank Hagadan). Ray Brooks (Andrew). Robin Bailey (Charles Grainger). Norma Ronald (Kay Lingard) . Norman Tyrrell (Sir Gordon Revidge). Jeanne Le Bars (Charlotte).

"I've decided to do something more intelligent with my money than underwrite my husband's ambition." Pamela Wilder

After the laid-back amusement of *The Big View*, Peter Draper follows up with the sucker punch of *The Dead Sea Fruit*. Pamela Wilder (Barbara Murray) tires of her husband's indifference and withdraws her capital from Elberdson's Merchant Bank.

While waiting for Wilder to arrive home one evening, Pamela is challenged by old friend Esther Keir (Elizabeth Sellers) over her unrealised ambitions. She asks when was the last time Pamela visited an art gallery or the theatre. *"When you were 18 you told me you wanted to marry a man who was intellectually your superior and who wanted to leave some small part of the world different from how he found it. Whose hair fell over his eyes. Who had crinkled and bewildered eyes like Henry Fonda. Who was creative. Gentle. Fond of children. Sexy and six foot ten."*

As if acknowledging that only the first quality could describe Wilder, Pamela resignedly tells her that, *"Men who are your intellectual superior soon get tired of having to slow down to speak to one."*

After a preoccupied Wilder returns home and barely acknowledges her, Pamela spends the next day at an art gallery where artist Andrew (Ray Brooks) chats her up. Inspired, with the thought of opening an art gallery, Pamela visits Sir Gordon Revidge and tells him she wants to withdraw her money from Elberdson's Merchant Bank. This money supports Wilder's position at Bligh Construction and the Merchant Bank. The fact that Wilder rushes home at mid-day after previously ignoring her only increases her distress. *"You neither love me nor want me. What brought you home just now was the money."* But Pamela is still uncertain whether to leave him, and she only decides to walk out when a coincidence makes it seem that Wilder is still seeing Susan Weldon.

The Plane Makers episode *Loved He Not Honours More* established that Pamela Wilder had given John Wilder the £3000 deposit on their house in exchange for shares in Scott Furlong. Over the next ten years, the shares had increased in value to a quarter of a million (1964) pounds. Following the work of her financial advisor Mr Telliter (John Wentworth) in that episode, Pamela had become the largest shareholder in Scott Furlong (Elberdson's Merchant Bank had previously held a 27% controlling interest). In this episode we see the unexercised power it gives Pamela.

This episode also revisits *The Plane Makers* episode *Sauce For The Goose* by David Weir. Then it was Georgina Cookson as a "man-hungry" friend who introduced Pamela to young American Al Bonner (Murray Hayne). That episode concludes with Pamela telling Wilder that *"I wanted to pay you back – but couldn't… if he had been any less of a nice person I would have slept with him."* To which Wilder replies, *"Then you might as well have done."* In *"The Dead Sea Fruit"* Pamela refuses the overtures of young artist Andrew. She also tells Frank Hagadan (George Sewell) that if she does leave Wilder, *"I won't be leaving him...just to go away with someone else. I want to find out what happened to me."*

The centrepiece of this episode is a massive confrontation between Pamela and Wilder when Sir Gordon tells him that Pam has decided to remove her capital from the bank. Barbara Murray is in her bedroom emptying the contents of her day handbag into her evening handbag when Patrick Wymark enters, still wearing his overcoat. Fixing her with a narrow-eyed glare, he closes the bedroom door behind him and advances slipping his hands into his pocket ("the Wilder walk".)

As they start the conversation about the money he walks around the bed and then explodes in exasperation, *"For God's sake Pamela, this is a business matter! Why do you have to drag your stupid emotions in?"*

A raft of emotions pass over Barbara Murray's face; *"Why the hell do you think I'm taking my money out if it isn't because of emotions? Do you think they're any less important than money? Oh God, John, I'm sick of you believing that the only important problems are those to do with money!"*

Wymark adopts a calmer, rhetorical stance and asks, *"WHY?"*

Barbara Murray smiles in a challenging manner, as if listing reasons she's gone over a hundred times in her head. *"Not just because we had a 'silly row' the other night. Not just because I hardly ever see you. Not just because the only time you ever do come home is when you want me to do something for you."*

Wymark turns away, pacing to the side as if trying to avoid the accusations. He wags his finger in exasperation as if telling off a child. *"Do you realise the incredible trouble this is going to cause?"*

Barbara laughs, eyes narrowed, squaring up to him. *"Yes, I do. I realise exactly what incredible trouble this is going to cause. I can do ANY SILLY THING I LIKE. I've decided that I can't go on like this."*

Deflated, Wymark sits on the bed as her realises she is talking about leaving. For the first time he looks scared. Barbara Murray stands with her back to her immaculate fitted wardrobe. *"You neither love me nor want me. What brought you home just now was the money."*

Wymark closes his eyes regretfully. He gets up and walks round to put a hand on Barbara's shoulder. She flinches away *("No, John please don't touch me.")* but he continues putting his other hand on her right shoulder and trying to draw her towards him *("Let's forget about it. Let's go..").* Barbara pushes him off shouting, *"Leave me alone! I'm sick of being a possession of yours!"* She begins crying.

"I'm sick of you coming home from another woman's bed. I lie there and I know where you've been. You stink of her scent. The smell of it's all over you. I lie there and I say to myself, what am I for?"

Unable to suppress his nature, Wilder says, *"We've got to talk about this seriously some time...if only about the money."* His self-defeating response finally reduces Pamela to hysterical laughter. At the end of the episode when Pamela is packing to leave, Wilder stands bereft in the bedroom, fingering her powder compact like it's a precious thing. Pamela she's not taking the compacts and Wilder says hopefully that she can always come back to collect it later. And then Wilder says, *"Pamela – what are you going to do about the money."*

The episode title is justified by Ken Bligh (Peter Barkworth) who recalls Andre Abina telling him in "Ambassador Status" that, *"Power is like the Dead Sea Fruit. When you achieve it, there is nothing there."* Although the loss of Pamela's capital would destabilise Wilder's position at Bligh Construction, Ken is wary of his father coming back to take control of the company. He acknowledges that Wilder has built the firm up and is willing to support him against Caswell (at least until his own position is more secure).

"The Dead Sea Fruit" benefits from two strong guest performances. Elizabeth Sellars as the three-times married, three-times divorced Esther Keil is a plausible catalyst for Pamela's frustration although the "terrifying" young girls at Esther's boutique *("Like a race of barbarians. And all so confident")* remind her that starting again would be a challenge. And Elizabeth Sellars' wheedling phone call to her younger boyfriend conveys the insecurity of her freewheeling life. The Glasgow-born actress had appeared in the Royal Shakespeare Company production of *The Taming of The Shrew* with Patrick Wymark, Peter Jeffrey and Ian Holm. She also appeared in *The Barefoot Contessa* (1954) and had just completed filming on Hammer's last production at Bray, *The Mummy's Shroud* (1967).

Ray Brooks had recently starred as womanising Tolan in Richard Lester's *The Knack* (1965). Trendy young artist Andrew is arrogant and written to show up Pamela's strengths. Andrew compliments her on the fact that she was actually looking at the paintings, while the other viewers have their backs to the paintings. *"They're telling each other how lovely they are and how cleverly their minds work. Later on, they'll buy a painting because they love art and because they hope to god the value goes up."*

When Pamela calls at Andrew's flat to discuss setting up a gallery, he assumes she has other motives and decides to cut out the small talk. *"You're not the first long married lady who's been round here. You know, suddenly in the middle of the evening, nothing to do. Why not phone up the bohemian young man. Have a look at a few pictures and who knows, have a little adventure. Very strange. It's always around 9'O'Clock at night, maybe that's when their own hubbies are whooping it up."*

Ironically, although she told Wilder she would have slept with Al Bonner if he had been less of a nice person, it's Andrew's obnoxiousness that seems to earn him a slap round the face. Bearing in mind her earlier aversion to the "confident...barbarian" girls in Esther's boutique, it's probably not surprising that when Andrew says *"I shouldn't think a woman's done that to a man since your generation",* Pamela gives him another slap saying, *"it's an awful pity that your generation's had to cop the lot."*

Although Ray Brooks is appropriately condescending and arrogant in this role, the following week, would see a totally different role in the ground-breaking BBC Wednesday Play *Cathy Come Home* – Jeremy Sandford & Ken Loach's expose of homelessness in Britain.

Monday 14 November 1966   *The Chicken Run*

Writer Wilfred Greatorex   Director David Reid

Patrick Wymark (Sir John Wilder). Clifford Evans (Caswell Bligh). Rosemary Leach (Susan Weldon). Jack Watling (Don Henderson). Peter Barkworth (Kenneth Bligh). Norma Ronald (Kay Lingard). George Sewell (Frank Hagadan). Calvin Lockhart (Kofe Lokwe) .John Barron (Sir Trevor Hoylake). Earl Cameron (Jordan Kobola). Ray Lonnen (Chris Roney). Frank Cousins (Bobo Naranda). Kenneth Gardnier (Desk Clerk) . Fred McNaughton (Bissett).

"Our High Dam is like a bone with two dogs fighting over it – East and West." Jordan Kobola

In the African state of Magalia, a new dam is behind schedule and the Government is looking for a contractor to take it over. Ken Bligh made connections at Magalia's embassy in *"Ambassador Status"* and has already flown out. So has Frank Hagadan (George Sewell) now working for the rival firm of Infells.

Wilder takes charge of the project telling Kay Lingard to book three tickets for himself, Don and Susan Weldon. Wilder knows that

Susan was at the London School of Economics with Jordan Kobola (Earl Cameron), premier of Magalia and asks Caswell Bligh to release her from the National Export Board. Susan objects to what can be seen as a misuse of Government resources to benefit a private firm but Caswell warns her that if Wilder went over his head to the Minister, it could bring her previous relationship with Wilder to attention.

In Magalia, the communist Chinese and Soviet Union have sent representatives to compete for the contract. Local agitators have slowed down the work, stealing equipment and running trucks off the road. The current contractors will be happy to lose the job. At the British High Commission, Sir Trevor Hoylake (John Barron) introduces Wilder to Bobo Naranda (Frank Cousins) the Minister of Public Works. His signature is needed to win the contract, and Naranda is curious as to why Bligh Construction would want to take on a troubled project.

Also at the High Commission is Chris Roney MP, played by Ray Lonnen (later Willie Kane in *The Sandbaggers*). Roney is supposedly writing a series of articles about Magalia, but is observing on behalf of the National Export Board (and Caswell Bligh).

During a site visit to the dam, Hagadan dares Wilder *to "ride the bucket"* – observe the construction from a large cement bucket suspended from a cable over the yawning chasm. Ken had recalled the previous night that Wilder, *"can't stand static heights...refused to meet somebody for lunch in the Post Office tower restaurant."* In front of his hosts, Wilder has no choice but to take part in *"the chicken run"*. Henderson offers to take Wilder's place but Sir John tells him, *"only two can play at this game, Don."*

When Kofe Lokwe asks if *"the chicken run"* is something to do with the public school system, Ken Bligh laughs and explains (harking back to *"A Hoopla of Haloes"* in *The Plane Makers*) that,

"Hagadan never went to one – and Sir John's was minor...borderline"

Meanwhile, Susan meets Jordan Kobola who has fond memories of his studies in London but questions why the Export Board should send Susan to support a European consortium when Hagadan *"represents an all-British consortium."*

Despite Ken's suspicions as to why Hagadan should give them a lead *("my inherent sense of fair play. We're all British here."* Hagadan explains) Wilder says Lokwe is *"obviously on the make"* and tells Ken to *"offer him a nice juicy personal kickback"*. Knowing that Ministers' bank accounts are under scrutiny, Ken meets Lokwe in the hotel lobby and offers a £50,000 villa in the south of France. Lokwe indignantly rejects his offer. Wilder tells Kobola that, Ken's actions were *"Ill-judged and quite disgraceful. Mr Kenneth Bligh acted without the authorisation of the European Consortium which I represent. He had no authority whatsoever."*

Wilder returns to the hotel to find Caswell Bligh waiting, obviously having been alerted by Chris Roney to his son's plight. *To Be Continued. Same Power Time, Same Power Channel.*

Earl Cameron (1917-2020), playing Jordan Kobola, had made his film debut in Basil Dearden's 1951 *Pool of London*, playing seaman Johnny Lambert. Ashley Clark, writing in Sight And Sound (November 2016) said, *"handsome, ever-composed Cameron was the closest Britain had to an authentic black film idol, despite not being marketed as such."* Cameron was made a CBE in 2009 and appeared in Christopher Nolan's *Inception* the following year.

Fellow Bermudan Calvin Lockhart (playing Kofe Lokwe) would go on to appear in the 1970 film version of *Cotton Goes To Harlem* as the Reverend Deke O'Malley although fans of Amicus horror films will also remember him as Werewolf-hunter Tom Newcliffe in *The Beast Must Die* (1974).

Monday 21 November 1966   *Safe Conduct*

Writer Wilfred Greatorex   **Director John Nelson Burton**

Patrick Wymark   (Sir John Wilder). Clifford Evans (Caswell
Bligh). Rosemary Leach (Susan Weldon). Jack Watling (Don
Henderson). Peter Barkworth (Kenneth Bligh). Rachel Herbert
(Justine Bligh). Norma Ronald (Kay Lingard). George Sewell
(Frank Hagadan). Calvin Lockhart (Kofe Lokwe). John Barron (Sir
Trevor Hoylake). Earl Cameron (Jordan Kobola). Kenneth Gardnier
(Desk Clerk). Danny Daniels (Immigration Officer). Willie Jonah
(Army Officer). Louise Nelson (Stewardess).

*"I'm throwing myself on your better judgement Sir Trevor. I'm a
distressed British female abroad in temporary need of funds."* Susan
Weldon.

Ken is served a deportation order while Wilder meets with prime
minister Jordan Kobola to secure the contract for the Dam. Caswell
tells Hagadan that he knows Ken fell into a trap set for Wilder, but
this convinces him that they need Hagadan leading Bligh
Construction and offers to top whatever salary Infells are paying.

With Wilder holding her return air ticket, Susan pleads with the
High Commissioner (John Barron) to help her get back to England.
But when a military coup topples Jordan Kobola's government, it's
Hagadan who is offering an escape route with a safe conduct pass
signed by Kofe Lokwe.

The coup is economically played out on a couple of interior sets
with some newsreel footage inserts as Caswell and Don Henderson
(Jack Watling) peer out of the hotel windows. Despite the machine
gun bullets raking the hotel lobby, the coup is played mainly for
laughs. Jack Watling gets to do the old reaching-up-to-the-bar-for-a-
drink-only-to-have-the glass-shot-at gag. Susan Weldon is at the
High Commissioner's residence when the shooting starts. Sir
Trevor tells Susan *"theres some civil disturbance involving the
military"* and offers her a particularly fine whisky (this episode was

filmed two years before *Carry On Up The Khyber* but John Barron's performance anticipates Sid James in the climactic dinner party scene). The *Carry On* similarities continue towards the end of part two as everyone dashes onto the plane and then, as it takes off from Magalia, Wilder looks around the seats and says, *"Wait a minute. Where IS Hagadan?"* Cut to George Sewell grinning as he watches the plane take off.

Part three deals with the consequences, as Wilder returns to London and finds his enemies massing against him. Ken reveals that he and Hagadan agreed that whoever won the contract would take the other in with them. But Wilder says there is no way they are sharing a contract with Hagadan. The resolution of the story seems a little lazy. We expect Wilder to do something clever, but in this case he relies upon the vagaries of African politics.

The fictional state of Magalia is portrayed with a relatively even hand. The presence of a High Commissioner suggests this is a British protectorate, rather than a former colony. The competition from communist China and the Soviet Union against British and American interests to complete the Dam indicates that it is one of the many small states which attempted to preserve their economic independence by remaining non-aligned. Viewed from a 1960's perspective, the two episodes provide a challenging view of an emerging nation. Kobola and Lokwe aren't played for laughs – nor are they sanctified. They're regarded with the same cynical eye as Sir Gerald Merle and James Cameron-Grant in *The Plane Makers*.

Monday 28 November 1966   *The Side of the Angels*

Writer Edmund Ward   Director David Reid.

Patrick Wymark   (Sir John Wilder). Clifford Evans (Caswell Bligh). Barbara Murray (Pamela, Lady Wilder). Rosemary Leach (Susan Weldon). Jack Watling (Don Henderson). Peter Barkworth (Kenneth Bligh). Rachel Herbert (Justine Bligh). Robin Bailey (Charles Grainger). Norma Ronald (Kay Lingard). George Sewell (Frank Hagadan). John Tate (Billy Straker). Peter Howell (William

Metcalfe). John Scott (Gilbert Tremayne). Douglas Muir (Minister). James Cossins (Henry Outram). Richard Hampton (Alan Cleeve). Tom Kempinski (Joe Maguire). Chistine Pilgrim (Waitress).

"You're not God, Mr Tremayne. Just a Consulting Engineer."
Kenneth Bligh.

Following the loss of the Magalian High Dam, Wilder looks for compensation. Bligh Construction was urged to seek the contract by the Treasury (specifically Bagehot in *"Ambassador Status"*) and the Department of Transport is urged to give Bligh's the Coalmouth Bridge contract to make up for their losses. Caswell is determined that Ken and Wilder won't "botch it" . He tells Ken and Wilder that the design is 20 years out of date and that they will lose money on the job, but neither is willing to jeopardise the contract. So Caswell pressures the directors of Bligh Construction to request a new design for the bridge.

Edmund Ward once more brings his knowledge of the construction industry (which would form the background of his 1976 series *The Hanged Man*) to deliver an entertaining story with a mixture of drama and humour.

Early on Don Henderson (Jack Watling) attends the Department of Transport to receive the Tender details from the director of contracts William Metcalfe (Peter Howell). Consulting Engineer Gilbert Tremayne (John Scott) is also at the meeting. As Metcalfe pointedly tells Henderson Tremayne's firm has worked for the Ministry since just after the First World War. *"He's a very able man. Almost one of us."*

Tremayne stands in front of Don and says he's dealt with Bligh's before, *"They built a harbour for me. Nevertheless, I shall deliver my usual short homily, as I do with all contractors..."* Jack Watling performs the visual equivalent of a P.G.Wodehouse paragraph as he listens aghast to Tremayne's lecture. *"A contractor is only as good as his professional supervision. You'll find that I require an orderly site, working to a strict programme which I must approve –*

adequate material storage, weekly meetings, a daily progress report in five copies…and proper sanitary accommodation."

After the meeting we learn that other firms have made losses on Ministry contracts designed by Tremayne. Caswell Bligh confirms that Tremayne's work is 20 years out of date. He shows the plans to Alan Cleeve (Richard Hampton) an award-winning engineer who works in Europe because he's tried and failed to break into the British closed-shop. Cleeve suggests some improvements and Caswell begins to lobby for change.

Wilder doesn't want to rock the boat. He's in it for profit, not aesthetics. But Caswell tells him there will be no profit, *"The job will be late. It'll be overspent. There'll be questions in the House and they'll all blame the poor stupid contractor, not the design."*

Ken Bligh (Peter Barkworth) agrees with Wilder that until they're awarded the contract there should be no challenge to the design. But Caswell phones his hand-picked directors and bullies them into sending a letter requesting a design review. He also approaches Treasury man Charles Grainger (Robin Bailey) on behalf of the National Export Board saying that Britain exports skills and the present system stifles skills.

Though Caswell's motivations are questioned, everyone – even the feline Grainger- agrees that his argument is justified, if doomed. *"We know the system is Victorian,"* Billy Straker says, *"They make the rules. Play the game their way or stay on the outside and go bust."*

Ward manages to make the abstract drama personal, by bringing Pamela Wilder back to London. In an earlier scene, Miss Lingard (Norma Ronald) had passed on a message from Wilder's gardener, told him about a repair bill for his London flat and reminded him that, *"Eggs and grapefruit go in the normal refrigerator – not in the deep freeze."* As Wilder keeps a dinner date with Caswell, Pamela has also asked Charles Grainger to accompany her to lunch with her cousin Henry Outram (James Cossins) who just happens to be a senior civil servant at the Ministry of Transport. Pamela confides to Grainger that the rest of her family , *"are smug because I've left John and they've been proved right about him."* Henry greets Pamela by saying she's lost weight, and when she thanks him, he replies*, "I didn't mean it as a compliment."*

Further humour is provided by Wilder's visit to a Health Farm, where he knows the Minister of Transport (Douglas Muir) is a frequent guest. It's part of a charm offensive which also entails an hour's socialising with Gilbert Tremayne (*"As a relative new boy to the industry I appreciate your advice"*) although as soon as the engineer is out of the door, Wilder tells Miss Lingard, *"Remind me to get a snuff box and some mezzotints of the Great Brunel."*

Caswell's meddling finally pushes Ken too far. He tells Justine (Rachel Herbert) that, *"Strong tea. Bacon soaked in lard. All the old stories. It's easy to be charmed. But you don't see the bullying. The refusal to listen. The humiliations. "*

Ken threatens to resign and sell his stock in Bligh Construction and also make his reasons public. For interfering in business matters, Bligh will lose the National Export Board.

Wilder resolves to settle matters by leaking news of the dispute to Sandy Warren of *The Globe* (from *Confound Their Politics*). Now, instead of something that can be swept under the carpet with another company winning the contract, both sides of the argument are in the public domain. *"I've no objection to you and Caswell organising a family shipwreck,"* he tells Ken, *" but I'll make damned sure I'm not on board when it happens."*

David Reid stages the final confrontation at the Ministry of Transport like an Elizabethan court. Wilder dominates the scene perched on the contract director's desk as Grainger, Cousin Henry, Ken and the Minister sit.

"I think the time has come for what the current jargon calls a full and frank discussion," Wilder tells the Minister, *"We were*

promised the Coalmouth Bridge as a reward for sticking our neck out in Africa." Wilder implies he'll publicise the deal if the Minister goes back on it.

When Metcalfe objects that Bligh's call for a re-design calls the whole mechanism of the Department into question, Wilder replies, *"I don't care if we put the bridge up in marzipan – as long as we get a fair business return with a handsome contingency clause, of course. If we're working to donkey cart principles, I want some form of insurance."* In return, Wilder promises, *"Rationalised Management, Critical Path Job Analysis… use enough syllables to suggest good faith and you're home and dry."*

The episode ends with Caswell aware that it's Wilder, not Bligh Construction that has won the contract. While obviously simplified for the purposes of a one hour TV show, Ward's script touches on some of the issues relating to construction contracts. It's not clear whether Norman Scace's character of Bagehot was a substitution for Grainger but Grainger accepts responsibility for the now absent Bagehot's actions in urging Ken to pursue the Magalian contract.

Ward delivers a fair degree of humour with Wilder's devious pursuit of the Minister at the Health Farm (when we first see Wilder packing tobacco into a pipe it's not clear whether he's assuming the guise of a Labour supporter ala Harold Wilson, but subsequent scenes imply that pipe tobacco was viewed as a healthy alternative to cigarettes in the sixties).

The Minister is played by Douglas Muir (below), who had appeared in the semi-regular role of Tom Bancroft in *The Plane Makers*. As noted, Muir appeared in the cast list of *A Matter For Speculation* as a Professor although he was not seen in the transmitted episode. Whatever the reason, it's interesting to see Muir playing a Minister in this episode – although fairly benign in his early scenes, the Minister is capable of slapping Wilder down in the final confrontation – certainly something that Tom Bancroft would never have done.

In a nod to continuity, John Tate returns from the first season as Bligh's pal and competitor Billy Straker. Since John Tate is a similar physical type to Douglas Muir, this increases speculation as to whether Muir was originally intended to play the Minister in this episode.

Tuesday 29 November 1966   A Royal Gala

Patrick Wymark, Barbara Murray and Jack Watling appeared in character in a short sketch set in a hospital in front of the Queen and the Duke of Edinburgh. The charitable show featured several ITV characters such as Mr Rose (William Mervyn) and the cast of Coronation Street.

Monday 5 December 1966 *Tax Return*

Writer Raymond Bowers   Director John Cooper.

Patrick Wymark (Sir John Wilder). Clifford Evans (Caswell Bligh). Barbara Murray (Pamela, Lady Wilder). Rosemary Leach (Susan Weldon). Jack Watling (Don Henderson). Peter Barkworth (Kenneth Bligh). Robin Bailey (Charles Grainger). Norma Ronald (Kay Lingard). George Sewell (Frank Hagadan).

"Lord Wilder, newly ermined, couldn't be bounced out of Bligh's within a year." Caswell Bligh.

Wilder sends Henderson to Rome to invite Pamela to confirm their tax arrangements at Wilder's London office. However, Wilder is surprised to find that Pamela has asked her friend, Treasury officer Charles Grainger to attend the meeting. In the closest *The Power Game* has ever come to an "action sequence", Patrick Wymark pushes Robin Bailey out of the office, slamming his weight against the door to stop him getting back in. It's Wilder's fury at Grainger's interjections which finally makes it clear to Pamela (and perhaps to Wilder himself) that he was missing her.

Bowers retreads ideas from his Plane *Makers* script, *Loved He Not Honours More*, only this time the Bligh's believe a scandal about

Wilder's marriage will stop Wilder being ennobled, and manipulates both Susan Weldon and Pamela Wilder in an attempt to draw attention to it. Ken, and Caswell try to engineer a scandal by inviting Susan and Wilder to separate evening meetings in the Bligh building. They calculate that Susan will call in to see Wilder after their meetings. Wilder tells her that gossips would naturally conclude that as an impartial Civil Servant, her only reason to be in the Bligh building would be to visit Wilder.

Bowers raises the interesting proposition that Wilder put his trust in advisors to allot his and Pamela's assets in the most tax efficient way (as he reminds Treasury official Grainger, *"Tax evasion is illegal, tax avoidance is not"*) for a marriage, but neither of them is clear on who owns what.

The late evening meeting also serves to illustrate Wilder's relationship with Kay Lingard (Norma Ronald) – distracted by personal worries, Wilder only tells her about the meeting as she's packing up to go home. Barely missing a beat, Lingard's only question is how long the meeting will take as she's *"got a man"* and is attending a party with him. Lingard is sanguine about keeping the man waiting, obviously no stranger to sexual politics. Later on, Wilder notices that Miss Lingard has been sewing a button on his coat. He tells her that Lady Wilder wasn't in the habit of sewing buttons and bluffs that he still has domestic staff. In the closest she comes to a rebuke; Miss Lingard tells him to see that his staff brush beneath his coat collar (*"It's a dirty winter"*). When Wilder later checks beneath his coat collar and says it is clean, Miss Lingard coolly concurs, telling him that's because she brushed it. There's a great moment where Wilder –with a mixture of sheepishness and off-handedness – thanks Miss Lingard and she responds with a brief smile. Lingard is no hero-worshiper, but she still values a difficult acknowledgement at the same time as Wilder suddenly realises what Pamela used to organise without him noticing.

During the end titles, as the reconciled Wilders leave the office, we see Pamela help Wilder on with his coat.

As we've noted before, *The Plane Makers* and *The Power Game* were never repeated in the 1960's, so the production may have felt justified in repeating old themes. Despite the echoes of previous episodes, this is still a satisfying conclusion to the "story arc" concerning the Wilder marriage.

Monday 12 December 1966   *Where Do I Want to Go?*

Writer Peter Draper.   Director David Reid.

Patrick Wymark (Sir John Wilder). Clifford Evans (Caswell Bligh). Barbara Murray (Pamela, Lady Wilder). Rosemary Leach (Susan Weldon). Jack Watling (Don Henderson). Peter Barkworth (Kenneth Bligh). Norma Ronald (Kay Lingard). Guy Doleman (Stephen Gray). Arthur Pentelow (Christopher Matcher). Reginald Barrett (Pickthorne) Gilly McIver (Lucy). Peter Evans (Waiter).

" This time you really could get the chop!" Caswell Bligh.

Bligh Construction has made a massive profit on the M23 Motorway Construction venture*. A profit so large that the Public Accounts Committee will ask if Bligh's overstated the tender. As Wilder prepares his defence, Stephen Gray (Guy Doleman) is recalled to London to investigate on behalf of the Auditor General's office, and to ask Susan Weldon (Rosemary Leach) to decide between him and Wilder. Meanwhile, Don Henderson (Jack Watling) is nowhere to be found.

*One anomaly is that in earlier episodes Frank Hagadan's machine was built to construct the fictional M27 motorway (the real-life M27 was not built until 1972) . This episode refers to the equally fictional M23 - the M23 from Surrey to Sussex was not begun until 1972.

" Where do I want to go?" is the question a drunken Don Henderson asks as he sits in the back of a taxi. The question also applies to Susan Weldon's relationship with Sir John Wilder. The

resentment which Don Henderson has shown throughout this second series, now flares up into a full-scale depression. Susan Weldon, on the other hand, is forced to take control of her life and make a decision about her future.

Peter Draper had introduced the character of David Main (Patrick Allen) as a romantic interest for Susan in the second episode, *Ambassador Status.* Unfortunately, Allen was playing government minister Roger Quaife in the BBC's adaptation of C.P. Snow's *Corridors of Power* (22 November 1966) and the new character of Gray had to be substituted. Nevertheless, the sardonic Guy Doleman (Colonel Ross in the Harry Palmer films) provides a credible opponent to Wymark.

Ken Bligh is outraged that a firm could be criticised for making a profit but his father tells him their competitors would be the first to complain that Bligh's took an unfair advantage in the bid. Wilder tells Ken that *"the image that we present is that we **failed**. Oh, we may have made a million pounds profit, but in this instance as far as public morality is concerned, we failed."*

Wilder's explanation for the profit is Frank Hagadan's invention. He says, *"We spent £70,000 on developing a machine to do the job more effectively. We took a chance that it would work. If it hadn't, we'd have had to foot the bill. It did work. So, the Government has to foot it. So now you're trying to wriggle out of it."*

Wilder gets the auditors in to examine the project, *"I want the figures that got lost because accounts came in late and when they did come in, they were slipped into another budget to save doing it again. Cash flows that covered two projects at once. Any item of expenditure that might have possibly slipped over to another balance. You might also try to get a figure for the materials the men half-inched on the job."*

Don Henderson is increasingly irritated by Wilder's behaviour. He tells Ken Bligh that there was a time when Wilder, *"was about the best boss possible to have. He was fair. He was direct, and he was honest. Now all he cares about is success."*

Susan Weldon tells Wilder: *"While your wife was away, you hardly ever came near me. Now that she's back you start asking me out to lunch."* Rosemary Leach is totally convincing, whatever conflicting emotion she displays. When Stephen Gray appears at her flat she greets him joyfully but is also apprehensive. As if on cue, Wilder appears, walks into the flat and quickly sizes up the situation. With excessive politeness, Wilder says, *"I'm terribly sorry, I didn't realise you were having a party."* Calling Susan *"Darling"* he tells Gray he's glad to meet him as he's heard so much about him and smarmily asks, *"How do you like the flat? I'll warn you it's a hell of a high rent in this area."* As Wilder departs, Susan furiously tells Gray that Wilder doesn't pay the rent and never has done, *"I just can't get the key back off him."* Gray coolly observes that she could always change the lock.

Wilder tries to sink any investigation into the M23 project by telling an opposition MP that Gray and he *"share a mistress"* and that Gray is motivated by malice. He also primes Don to let Susan know what he's done. But when Wilder arrives at Susan's flat, Gray tells him that there will be no scandal. He and Susan are to be married. Like a pantomime demon king, Wymark frustratedly raises his fist holding the key to the flat and Dolman purrs, *"yes, you can return the key or throw it away. The lock is being changed in the morning."* Wymark and Leach share one brief parting look before he walks out.

Writing in *The Catholic Herald*, H.R.F. Keating said, *"We are lucky to get playwrights of the calibre of Peter Draper and Edmund Ward writing for a series such as this. They are capable of doing what is one of the writer's prime tasks: illuminating areas of human experience."*

As an example, he cited Draper's line for Stephen Gray, after the defeated Wilder has left Susan's flat. *"Oddly enough, you know, at times you have to prevent yourself feeling sorry for him."* Keating says, *"This is a good and true piece of insight. Oddly enough, and quite unfairly, it is the toughies, the biters and barkers, who rouse more pity in defeat than the ones who invite squashing all along the line."* *

**The Catholic Herald 23rd December 1966*

19 December 1966   ***There's No Such Thing as a Dead Heat***

Writer Edmund Ward   Director Rex Firkin.

Patrick Wymark (Sir John Wilder). Clifford Evans (Caswell Bligh). Barbara Murray (Pamela, Lady Wilder). Rosemary Leach (Susan Weldon). Jack Watling (Don Henderson). Peter Barkworth (Kenneth Bligh). Rachel Herbert (Justine Bligh). Robin Bailey (Charles Grainger). Norma Ronald (Kay Lingard). Norman Tyrrell (Sir Gordon Revidge). Lindsay Campbell (Joe Ryan). Gerald Case (Minister). Bruce Beeby (Minister's Aide). Leslie Anderson (TUC Representative). Michael Hall (CBI representative).

"You don't warn people like me, Caswell. I've had two days" Sir John Wilder.

Bligh and Susan learn that the National Export Board is being wound up, and Charles Grainger (Robin Bailey) tells them that Wilder has known for a year that they were wasting their time at the NEB.

Grainger offers Susan an escape route, telling her they represent *"Four centuries of unostentatious power. We can squash the .freebooters – the Wilders and the Bligh's – without ever moving from our drab chairs... We hold the strings. You have a chance to tighten your grip."*

Ward provides a comic coda to Wilder's relationship with Susan. Invited to Susan's flat, where an iced bucket of champagne waits, Wilder condescendingly assumes that she's finished with her *"lackey in the Auditor General's Department"*. Rosemary Leach seethes quietly before letting rip about the way he's used her over the NEB. The scene ends with Leach throwing a glass of champagne over Wymark, who does an Oliver Hardy slow burn while reaching out and drinking down the second glass.

Caswell returns to Bligh Construction, taking over Ken's office and cancelling several sub-contracts arranged by Ken and Don Henderson. Furious, Ken decides to sell the 15% shares in Bligh Construction left to him by his mother and use it to fund the purchase of a redriven piling company in partnership with Don. With his vision of a family dynasty threatened, Caswell visits Sir Gordon Revidge (Norman Tyrrell) offering to sell his 55% stake in Bligh Construction to Elbertson's Merchant Bank on condition that Wilder is sacked from both Bligh's and the bank..

As Wilder returns from Rome,. Don Henderson (Jack Watling) demonstrates one final act of loyalty, meeting him at the airport to warn him that Bligh is reorganising the company. Don says he's written a letter of resignation. *"Caswell's playing Hitler and I'm a sort of voluntary Sudetenland."* Wilder reads the implication that he's next and quietly, sincerely thanks Don before watching him walk away.

Wilder meets Bligh and Revidge and tells them he's warned the Consortium that Caswell is taking control. The Consortium has invoked a "Change of Management" clause in the contract, and Bligh's is out. Wilder has negotiated a new partnership for the Consortium with a German company earning a £100,000 fee. This ensures revenge on two fronts because with Bligh's now out of the project, Grainger will have to explain the waste of foreign capital the Treasury committed to the Italian venture.

Wilder also has a seven-day option on Ken's shares (in exchange, Ken and Don's new company gets two year's back-dated contracts with Bligh Construction). If Sir Gordon won't buy the option for £150,000, Wilder threatens to sell it to Infells, giving 15% of Bligh's to its biggest competitor.

Revidge sees it's not a bluff and agrees to buy. In return, Wilder resigns from both Bligh's and the bank. *"You're an arrogant, destructive old man, Caswell"* Wilder says in farewell. *"Wrap it up how you like*," Caswell replies, *"You lost"*

" But with enough money to soak up most of the blood."

As in the final episode of *The Plane Makers,* Wilder perceives that the situation is against him. His original strategy of exploiting the tension between the Bligh's to take control of the company has failed dismally. But he uses his greater knowledge (the Change of Management clause) , his ability to read the likes of Ken Bligh and his skill at putting a deal together on the run, to profit from the situation.

With Patrick Wymark committed to a West End run in John Mortimer's The Judge, together with more film and TV work, the question of how Wilder and co might be reassembled for a third series would have to wait.

Case Study Seven - Playhouse: The Curtis Affair.

Monday 15 January 1968

Writer Wilfred Greatorex. Director David Reid

Michael Jayston as Gerry Hackett MP

This one-off play, directed by David Reid, (who would produce series three of *The Power Game*) is almost the missing link between series two and three.

In *Where Do I Want To Go?* the penultimate episode of the second series, Bligh Construction is threatened with an investigation after it makes a massive profit on the M23 motorway project. In the end, the issue of the Public Accounts Committee was left hanging, but in *The Curtis Affair*, Wilfred Greatorex shows how it might have played out.

Electronics tycoon Ramsden Curtis (Andrew Keir) is called to Committee Room 13 of the Houses of Parliament for an inquiry into alleged excessive profit made by one of his firms on a government contract. The Select Committee chairman Austin Withers (Geoffrey Bayldon) is a Tory MP, who has journeyed from Public School to the Army to Parliament. Labour MP Gerry Hackett (Michael Jayston) is a *"political whizz kid"* who can be *"indignant with conviction...assured, able and unscrupulous (covering) intense personal ambition with the glove of social justice."* Fellow Labour MP Audrey Moate (Rowena Cooper) is *"attractive, ambitious but unsure of the ways of Westminster"*. Tory MP Mrs Cliveden, (Annette Kerr), loathes Mrs Moate.

Andrew Keir at 42 was substantially younger than the scripted Curtis, who was described as, *"a self-made tycoon of 54."* In a prolific career he had recently starred as Professor Quatermass in the Hammer Films adaptation of *Quatermass and the Pit*.

Michael Jayston was 33 at the time (also younger than Hackett, who was scripted as 40 years of age). A member of the Royal Shakespeare Company, Jayston had appeared on TV before, but this was his most substantial role to date.

The actresses playing the female members of the committee both had a connection with Patrick Wymark. In 1962, Rowena Cooper had played Eliza Tharm, mistress to the Rugeley poisoner William Palmer (Wymark) in the BBC's *They Hanged My Saintly Billy*. Annette Kerr played the nurse of Patrick Wymark's Jason Webb in the final scene of *Doppelganger* (1969) and would also play a nurse in *Identified*, the first episode of *UFO*.

Greatorex describes Chairman and Managing Director, Ranny Curtis, as having built his empire in *"another age, when the freebooter could express himself. Today some of the foundations of his throne have been eroded by successive governments. He has never come to terms with the politicians and is lost in the Westminster maze of rules and regulations and red tape and grey men."* His wife and two daughters have left him and he is living with a much younger woman.

Curtis' electronics firm agreed a fixed price contract to provide the Government with a radar system. Hackett believes that price should have been lower because Curtis had a report showing that modifications to the system would bring the overall production costs down. Curtis retorts that, *"The modifications only promised economies. They were theoretical. Like politicians' ideas they could have been half-baked."*

Curtis fights back, showing Hackett was on the board of a development company which made a 68% profit on land resold by the government after a compulsory purchase. Hackett has previously agreed that a profit of 60% on a public contract is *"wildly excessive"* but protests that he voted against the sale of the property. Curtis counters, *"but you didn't resign!"*

Curtis has also learnt that Withers' father ensured his firm avoided death duties by taking out a loan equal to the book value of the company, and buying works of art. When he died, his estate showed a firm with debts equal to its assets. *"Death duty nil. Death duty not a penny."* The art was sold by the man's heirs within a week and the bank was repaid. "And that's how our noble and honourable chairman today kept his father's firm."

Examining the detail of the contract, Hackett says the firm had produced a report showing modifications to the radar equipment would produce economies of scale. Curtis' deputy managing-director, *"shrewd and calculating "* Eric Sheldon (Jeremy Longhurst), testifies that Curtis proposed certain other costs be set against the radar job to make it seem less profitable. Curtis prepared the final accounts with the financial controller but Sheldon agreed the contract because Curtis wasn't available.

Hackett reveals why: *"You were in a nursing home. An alcoholics' retreat. Drying out."*

A furious Curtis comes across the committee room and grabs Hackett by the lapels. *"Did anyone ever give birth to you, Hackett? Or did you claw your way out of the slime clutching a handful of filth to throw? You destroy and never create. You burn people with your envy."*

Curtis suddenly clutches his chest. From Curtis' POV we see the circle of onlookers, faces closing in. The sound is a blur of words from the onlookers. Suddenly sound and vision go black. Curtis crashes to the stone floor. Efforts to revive him are futile.

Withers tells the shaken Hackett that it's not his fault, but *"Mrs Moate says everything with her eyes. She is blaming Hackett."*

The final irony comes as Withers tells Hackett that, *"Only royalty can die in a royal palace. And this is the Palace of Westminster. He can't die here."*

"He has done," Hackett argues.

Withers knows better, *"I suppose the Queen's coroner has been sent for. They'll meet the ambulance outside the gates and pronounce that he died in the street."*

The final film sequence shows the Houses of Parliament and an ambulance leaving the palace yard. It stops outside the gates and a doctor and coroner get in the back. Hackett's car is prevented from leaving by the ambulance and he sees Withers' prediction come true. Finally, the ambulance and car move off in different directions.

Rehearsals for *The Curtis Affair* began on 6 December 1967, with recording on 2 January 1968 and transmission on 15 January 1968.

In *Called To Account* Margaret Hodge, former chair of the Public Accounts Committee, reminds us that, *"Members of Parliament prefer to dissect new policy proposals rather than current budgets. The departmental select committees of the House of Commons spend their time exploring the challenges for the future. They rarely use the reports on past and present departmental expenditure produced by the National Audit Office for the basis of an enquiry."* The modern-day Curtis is safe.

Many thanks to Victoria Bennett of the British Film Institute Special Collections for her help in viewing Wilfred Greatorex's rehearsal script for *The Curtis Affair*.

Case Study Eight:
The Power Game - Series Three

Producer David Reid   Script Editor Wilfred Greatorex

Michael Jayston as Dowling   Patrick Wymark as Wilder

The question of whether *The Power Game* would return for a third
series may have been postponed, not just by Patrick Wymark's need
to explore other roles, but more importantly because of the
Independent Television Authority's controversial June 1967
reallocation of the ITV franchises. ATV's original franchise had
seen it provide weekday programmes for the Midlands and weekend
programmes for London. The ITA decided that from July 1968,
ATV would provide 7 days of programmes to the Midlands with the
weekend output being provided by a new company, London
Weekend Television. The loss of the key London audience was a
blow to ATV, as indeed was the necessary reorganisation. ITV as a
whole was in a state of flux during 1968, with the franchise losers
seeing no reason to put in much effort, and the new entrants trying
to get their resources together (Yorkshire TV, for instance, had to
build new studios, with its first drama series being made in hired
London studios).

However, Patrick Wymark and *The Power Game* were still in the public consciousness. Singer Matt Munro had included an impersonation of Patrick Wymark in his show at London's Talk of the Town (Wymark was also allegedly accosted in a theatre bar by an autograph hunter who insisted he was Matt Munro). This led, on 23 June 1968, to Munro playing Wilder in a *Power Game* sketch on the BBC's *Dave Allen* show which also featured *The Troubleshoooters'* Ray Barrett.

By the time a decision was made to go ahead with a third series, original producer Rex Firkin had left ATV to work as a freelance director on the Hammer TV series *Journey to the Unknown* (*The Madison Equation*). He subsequently joined London Weekend as their head of drama. David Reid, director of *The Curtis Affair* was made producer of the third series (Reid had previously produced an ATV anthology series called *Trapped*).

Wilfred Greatorex had written treatments for two new series in late 1967. One, about an Arms Dealer would become *Hine* in 1971. *"Ambassador At Large (Special Envoy)"* became the basis of the third series of *The Power Game*.

The *Special Envoy* format was first been announced as a standalone series before a clarification was issued that this would be the third series of *The Power Game*. Whether this points to some behind-the-scenes negotiation on Greatorex's part, or uncertainty over whether the now highly-paid Wymark would return is unknown. But each episode would be billed with the *Special Envoy* strapline.

Lew Grade supposedly insisted on the slightly implausible return of Clifford Evans. Bligh and Wilder now working inside Government; Wilder as Roving Ambassador for Special Situations and Trade. Bligh as his Minister. Michael Jayston joined the cast as Lincoln Dowling, Wilder's civil service private secretary.

With Edmund Ward now writing *The Main Chance* for Yorkshire TV, this would be the first time that the opening episode was written by Greatorex.

Wilfred Greatorex had technical advice on this series from Ronald Higgins, a former Foreign Office diplomat who had been Edward Heath's private secretary in 1960 during Britain's first, failed attempt to join the Common Market. Advice on parliamentary procedure came from Sir Peter Kirk MP, a former Under-Secretary of State for War in the Douglas-Home government, and a strong supporter of Britain's entry to the Common Market.

The BBC's oil industry drama, *The Troubleshooters* had built consistent audiences during *The Power Game*'s absence and would start a new series on 9 January, so the new globe-trotting focus of *The Power Game* may have been a response to the success of *The Troubleshooters*.

The new series was promoted by an article by Ken Martin in the January 4th edition of *TV Times* written during filming of *Private Treaty* (4 February). Martin recorded that the production began taping at 4.50, and ending at 8pm and made no secret of the fact that Wymark fluffed his lines but got it right on the second take. During an interview, Patrick Wymark dropped a remark that would have interested anyone who recalled his first episode of *The Plane Makers* or *The Chicken Run* episode of *The Power Game*. *"Wymark admits he is terrified of heights. Wilder is a physical coward."*

Martin revealed that, *"the new character everyone on the series is talking about is Lincoln Dowling, played by Michael Jayston, a Royal Shakespeare Company actor getting his big television break. Dowling becomes Wilder's secretary, although as the series progresses it becomes clear his loyalties are divided."*

Nottingham-born Jayston, trained as an accountant with the National Coal Board, before winning a scholarship to the Guildhall School of Drama. Initial recordings of *The Power Game* had to work around performances as Tom Fashion in Vanbrugh's *The Relapse* at the RSC Aldwych opposite Barrie Ingham as Lord Foppington.

Reviewing the episode *Standard Practice*, theatre critic Michael Billington wrote in *The Times* on 26 February 1969 that ATV should consider quitting while they were still ahead. Despite the move from industry to diplomacy, it was still the mixture as before. *"Admittedly Caswell Bligh is now visibly ailing, but he and Wilder still glare at each other over polished desk tops in their perennial game of one-up-manship. Henderson is still the nice guy fallen among machinators and the storyline is still the kind one would recommend to fresh, rather than tired businessmen."*

Writing in *The Times* for 11 January 1969, Julian Critchley opined that Wilder's *" virtues are the contemporary ones. He is a bully and a boor. He is forgiven only if he gets results....no doubt businessmen view the series with contempt. As a class they suffer from too many interviews by bright young men with more brains but who are less successful. The public, however laps it up."*

Despite the misgivings, The Power Game soared back into the JICTAR ratings for the week ending January 12th at number 11 with an estimated audience of 14,630,000 (6,650,000 homes). Despite the figures from the Yorkshire TV area being excluded due to the collapse of the Emley Moor mast in March 1969, The Power Game held its viewing figures of around 14,410,000 viewers (6,550,000 homes) until the end.

Tuesday 7 January 1969   *One Via Zurich*

  Writer Wilfred Greatorex   **Director David Reid.**

Patrick Wymark (Sir John Wilder). Clifford Evans   (Caswell Bligh). Barbara Murray (Pamela, Lady Wilder). Jack Watling (Don Henderson). Michael Jayston (Lincoln Dowling). Richard Hurndall (Sir Jason Fowler). Bari Jonson (Narada). Geoffrey Lumsden (Sir Trevelyan Stamp). Geoffrey Chater (Arthur Stilton). Jonathan Elsom (John Lacey). Preston Lockwood (Reisling). Elizabeth Weaver (Janie Kent). Keith Grenville (Franklyn). Huw Thomas (Newsreader). Richard Aylen (Peter Sinclair).

"If Whitehall had run Dunkirk, we'd never have got a boat out!" Sir John Wilder.

Sir John Wilder is recruited by the Government as a Special Envoy – the Ambassador for Special Situations and Trade - with the newly ennobled Lord Bligh as his Minister. In his first mission, Wilder has to return to the African state of Malia where a British copper mine has been seized and its engineers imprisoned.

At the end of series two, Bligh was promised recognition to compensate for the National Export Board being wound up. In this episode, the recognition only comes after Wilder's appointment as Ambassador when Bligh is announced as the new Minister for Special Situations and Trade; a position which brings with it a life peerage.

The frankly implausible pairing of Wilder and Bligh (allegedly at the request of ATV managing director Lew Grade) calls for Reid and Greatorex to use misdirection worthy of stage magicians by calling attention to the implausibility of it. Foreign Secretary Arthur Stilton (Geoffrey Chater) reminds Bligh that he and Wilder, *"practically hacked one another into a communal grave,"* and questions why he should suggest Wilder as his Special Envoy. In a similar vein, the need to bring Jack Watling back means Don Henderson's partnership with Ken Bligh has to be in (plausible) trouble. Wilder can guarantee a year's work for the company if Don agrees to come on board as his Personal Assistant. And Ken Bligh just happens to have the secret information that will help Wilder resolve his first mission.

The first and second series of *The Power Game* had taken place against the background of Harold Wilson's Labour administration. The third is set firmly within the Government arena. Thankfully the "tired and emotional" George Brown had resigned as Foreign Secretary in March 1968, replaced by the more anonymous Fulham MP, Michael Stewart. Writing in *The Times* , former Conservative MP Julian Critchley found the first episode, *"a victory of competence over content,"* with the situations, *"sufficiently authentic to deceive all save those who have actually taken part in them."*

Returning to London airport after winning an £80 million Hydroelectric contract for a French company Sir John Wilder cheerfully agrees to an impromptu press conference at the airport. Writing in The Times, Julian Critchley commented that, *"the opening sequences of a jet landing at Heathrow (with the camera tracking) Wilder as he heads triumphantly for the press room could not fail to win the viewer's attention."* Reporters ask if Wilder should have helped the British firms competing for the contract, and whether he thinks what he has done is patriotic. Wilder replies: *"Put that to the four-hour-a-day national heroes who represent us abroad; Who don't know the difference between a contract and the Boys Own paper. The deadbeats who think work is cocktails at sundown. The pension seekers. The time servers. The civil servants living it up on the gravy train. "*

Foreign Secretary, Arthur Stilton asks Bligh why he's recruited a *"Little Napoleon"* as his Ambassador for Special Situations and Trade. Bligh replies that Wilder will *"put bombs under those featherbedded nonentities we've got around the world."*

Bligh introduces Wilder to Lincoln Dowling (Michael Jayston) who will be Wilder's Private Secretary. Dowling is a cool young civil servant who will show him how Whitehall and the Diplomatic Service works.

Although Permanent Under Secretary, Jason Fowler (Richard Hurndall) tells Dowling that, *"Our service has no place for men like Wilder. They're motivated by greed. Security risks all of them."* Dowling counters that Wilder *"has all the money he'll ever need. His kick is Power."*

"I smell scandal" Fowler insists. *"You never did with Philby"* Dowling replies, setting up a running gag for the series. Hurndall looks hurt. *"That was rather below the belt."*

Wilde's first Special Situation is in the African state of Malia which has turned to China, after Britain cut back international aid. A

British copper mine has been confiscated by the Government and the engineers arrested. Wilder's job is to get them out.

Wilder sends Don Henderson to Malia, and then ruthlessly blows Don's cover, so that he's intercepted at the airport by Malian Special Branch officers. A deeper level of deceit is unveiled which allows Wilder to negotiate the release of the hostages.

The state of Malia represents the biggest sleight of hand in this episode. Caswell Bligh tells Wilder, *"I remember how much it cost Bligh Construction the last time you went there"* and part of the plot turns on Ken Bligh divulging the route by which he bribed Government minister Naranda (Bari Jonson). But in the second series, Bligh Construction went to MaGalia and Ken Bligh was tricked into offering a bribe to another Minister (played by Calvin Lockhart). The bribe was refused and Ken was expelled. Bari Jonson played Abina, the Charge d'Affairs at the Magalian embassy, while the Minister Bobo Naranda was played by Frank Cousins. It's likely that with *The Power Game* never being repeated in the 1960's, Wilfred Greatorex gambled on the audience only having a hazy memory that Bligh Construction had visited an African state two years before, and recast the facts to resolve the new story. Nevertheless, on top of the implausibility of Bligh and Wilder teaming up, it does add another uncertain note to the opening episode.

Monday 14 January 1969   *The Big Nothing*

Writer Roy Clarke   **Director Cyril Coke.**

Patrick Wymark (Sir John Wilder). Clifford Evans   (Caswell Bligh). Barbara Murray (Pamela, Lady Wilder). Michael Jayston (Lincoln Dowling). Richard Hurndall (Sir Jason Fowler). Joanna Rigby (Helen Ferguson). Geoffrey Chater (Arthur Stilton). John Gabriel (Lister). William Job (Alan Harwood). Geoffrey Wincott (Frost).

"I'm afraid your overdeveloped sense of individualism has affected others in the Department. I had a very unpleasant scene with Dowling." Lord Bligh.

Muito De Nada – "The Big Nothing" – is a barren stretch of land in South America. Helen Ferguson, a PR consultant for the new president of Andarovia tries to persuade Caswell Bligh that Britain should invest in mining the minerals below "the Big Nothing". Bligh rejects the idea, but Sir John Wilder tries to raise the private funding that will be needed to set the plan in motion.

Wilder is disillusioned when he discovers that business executives are as risk-averse as Bligh. *"They moan about Government interference, but give them a chance to go it on their own and they start trembling."*

Wilder proposes to invest his and Pamela's money in the scheme and Dowling warns him that, *"You and your wife can't dabble for private gain in something you're promoting as a public servant."* But Wilder's apparent recklessness is revealed as a cunning strategy. The "clean hands" of public service compel Wilder to promote the scheme without risking his own cash. Mrs Ferguson later congratulates him on having manoeuvred himself out of investing his own money. Bligh too finds that Government intentions are harder to read than he imagined. The Foreign Secretary (Geoffrey Chater) was concerned about Wilder's methods but would hate to see the British taxpayer lose out to France or Germany in exploiting Andarovia. *"As long as you're certain that Wilder will behave himself, I think we can proceed."*

Joanna Rigby, playing confident, astute and flirtatious Helen Ferguson, had recently appeared as Honoria Glossop in the BBC series *The World of Wooster*. Ferguson is similar to Laura Challis in *The Plane Makers* but where Challis had warned Wilder that she made it a rule never to have an affair with a man in the same industry as her, Mrs Ferguson is affronted that Wilder turns down her offer of sex. Wilder apologises, *"I just can't afford the time...Affairs are very easy to start but hell to end. All that covering up of tracks..."*

This is a fast-moving episode with several changes of locale and a conversation between Bligh and Wilder spread (movie-style) over unrelated scenes such as Bligh and Wilder shaking hands with a line of foreign dignitaries. It sometimes becomes hard to follow just where the plot is going – perhaps because the ultimate prize is an ambiguous right to prospect for minerals. However, this second episode of the series does succeed in further defining the relationships between the characters in this new situation.

While Roy Clarke now has several long-running BBC comedies to his credit (*"Still Open All Hours", "Keeping Up Appearances" and "Last Of The Summer Wine"*) in 1969 he was at the start of his career. Clarke had written *The Dispossessed*, the 5 April 1968 episode of *The Troubleshooters* featuring Ronald Fraser as "Wallace Nicholls", a washed-up relic of the British Empire. ATV producer Dennis Vance would later develop this format into *The Misfit*, a TV series which would win Clarke his first award. Clarke would also script several episodes of ATV's darkly humorous spy thriller *Spyder's Web*.

21 January 1969   *The Outsider*

Writer Wilfred Greatorex   **Director Peter Moffat**

Patrick Wymark (Sir John Wilder). Clifford Evans (Caswell Bligh). Barbara Murray (Pamela, Lady Wilder). Michael Jayston (Lincoln Dowling). Jack Watling (Don Henderson). Richard Hurndall (Sir Jason Fowler). Donald Burton (Jan Novak).Anthony Nicholls (Sir Holford Bagenal). Ralph Nossek (Minister Koziel). Coral Fairweather (Lady Bagenal). Frank Duncan (Conyers).

"When I was building pipelines across the Syrian desert, I played poker every night with a man like you. He always developed an imperative air when he had nothing in his hand!" Lord Bligh.

Polish fixer Jan Novak (Donald Burton) tells Sir John Wilder he wants British firms to supply plant for a new road building contract in communist Poland. Novak is reputed to be the top Polish intelligence agent working in the UK, but Conyers (Frank Duncan) of MI5 tells Wilder to *"string Novak along."* Wilder, Dowling and Henderson fly to Warsaw but are hindered by British Embassy staff who think it's a waste of time. Ambassador Sir Holford Bagenall (Anthony Nichols), intercepts a telegram showing that Wilder has been investing in the firm most likely to win the contract, and sends Fowler the evidence he needs to finish Wilder.

Greatorex's script reflects the contradiction of Britain trading with communist-controlled Eastern Europe. It reiterates the theme from the opening episode (as Julian Critchley put it in The Times), *"the belief, implicit in the series that the 'players' in the shape of Wilder are frustrated not by their infelicities but by the machinations of the gentleman amateur."*

As in the second series episode *Point of Balance,* Wilder has been misdirecting his enemies and takes great pleasure in proving that he recommended all three firms to the Polish Trade Minister and didn't buy shares in any. The telegram was sent for Bagenall's eyes to demonstrate the naiveté of the Foreign Service professionals. Lord Bligh tells Fowler that he fell into Wilder's trap and warns him at the risk of his career to leave any future Wilder-baiting to Bligh himself.

Don Henderson (Jack Watling) is allowed to demonstrate his original sales expertise, briefing Wilder on the specifications from the three rival firms. Recommendations which Wilder later repeats to the Polish Trade Minister: *"Listons will give you three meters per hour more road, Steadley's appear to need less maintenance. Bolton's have the best after-service."* However, even though Wilder exploit's Henderson's expertise, he relies on his own personal touch for the deal-breaker. When the Minister asks about the most important criterion of delivery time, Wilder says, *"I'll personally put a bomb under whichever management you offer the contract to."*

Whether or not Wilder could have won the Polish Trade Minister over, we learn at the end of the episode that the Americans have invoked a NATO agreement barring sales of strategic equipment to the Eastern Bloc. Road-making can be considered strategic, Bligh explains, *"as it could lead to increased mobility of Soviet forces."*

One of the most entertaining scenes comes when the Wilder's party arrives in formal dress for what Novak had promised would be, *"a very personal and private dinner with the Minister of Trade."* Instead, they are confronted by a massive affair with informal dress. Dowling quickly discerns that the Wilder's have been placed at insignificant seats on the table and this must have been with the agreement of the British Embassy's protocol officer. Noting that Lady Wilder is not due to receive one of the bouquets being presented to prominent female guests, he desperately tries to organise one for her, but in the face of a language barrier it's Novak who comes to the rescue with a wink. Barbara Murray continues to sparkle as Lady Wilder. The wife of the British Ambassador tries to put down the Wilder's for wearing black tie. *"Diplomacy is full of ironies,"* she tells Pamela, *"I suppose you imagine these people, being communists, might try and impress and dress for dinner."* Pamela assures her that, *"I think all the communists look quite delightful,"*

28 January 1969   *The Goose Chase*

Writer Peter Draper   Director Cyril Coke.

Patrick Wymark (Sir John Wilder). Clifford Evans(Caswell Bligh). Barbara Murray (Pamela, Lady Wilder). Michael Jayston (Lincoln Dowling). Richard Hurndall (Sir Jason Fowler). Michael Aldridge (Heathcoat Mobbs). Caroline Blakiston (Margot Fellowship).

Terence Rigby (Nightingale). Martin Wyldeck (Langcrost). John Line (Stephen Wales)

"I must say intellectually I'm not wholly enthusiastic about some of my country's pursuits. But it's the only country I have." Professor Mobbs.

Professor Heathcote Mobbs (Michael Aldridge) is vetting Lincoln Dowling (Michael Jayston) as a potential recruit for MI6. Dowling is unaware of this, or that Nightingale (Terence Rigby) has him under surveillance. Pamela Wilder (Barbara Murray) is set to make her debut as a diplomatic hostess, but Margot Fellowship (Caroline Blakiston) is planning to host a society party on the same night. As part of Mobbs' scheme, Lord Bligh agrees to send Sir John Wilder to Vienna with a film crew making a documentary about refugees. The poet Vaclav Vitek from the Czech Ministry of Foreign Affairs is expected to cross the border and this has been deemed a "Special Situation".

The casting of this episode now seems prescient because ten years later in 1979, Michael Aldridge and Terence Rigby would play two of the title characters in the Alec Guinness version of *Tinker, Tailor, Soldier Spy,* while Michael Jayston would be cast as "scalp hunter" Peter Guillam.*

John Le Carre's novel was not even written at the time this episode was broadcast and Michael Aldridge was then best known as Ian Dimmock, one of the university-based criminologists in Granada *TV's The Man In Room 17.* However, the character of Mobbs is much less robust and vigorous than Dimmock. With his wild hair and camp, distracted manner he comes across as a blend of Tom Baker and Jon Pertwee, or perhaps a visualisation of Edmund Crispin's academic detective Gervase Fen.

Extending the irony, Rex Firkin the original producer of the "The Power Game" was involved in abortive attempt in the mid-1970's to adapt the Le Carre novel for London Weekend Television.

Not surprisingly, the treachery that would form the basis of *Tinker, Tailor, Soldier, Spy* is referenced in this episode. The running joke about Jason Fowler (Richard Hurndall) failing to spot real-life double agent Kim Philby (much as Aldridge's Percy Alleline would be fooled in the Le Carre adaptation) is brought to the fore. Mobbs takes great pleasure in telling Dowling that Fowler worked for MI6 before the war and "has one blazing star of achievement – he recruited Kim Philby!"

Earlier, when Fowler complains that he finds Mobbs' continual recruiting drive rather tedious, Mobbs apologises that, *"We've had to have a re-think since that tiresome business with Mr Philby. We're not so keen old Old Etonians as we were."* And when Fowler persists that he's unhappy having agents recruited from his department, Mobbs comforts him with the thought that, *"At least, my dear, you'll have the satisfaction of knowing this one's working for us."*

We learn that Dowling won a scholarship to Manchester Grammar School. As in "The Outsider" when Wilder was said to have *"gone to the wrong school for treachery"*, Dowling's downmarket education is seen as a plus. *"Since that business with Philby,"* MI6 is *"not so keen on old Etonians as we were."*

After three years at Kings College, Cambridge, he emerged with an interest in cybernetics. Dowling tells Lady Wilder that he sees the point of machines as being *"to free people to do more, not less."* In tune with the whole "White Heat of Technology" of the Wilson Government, we learn that Dowling took a Civil Service position because a lot of the change people are talking about has already happened. *"The job of people like me is to help absorb the changes into society."*

When Mobbs lunches with Dowling, he is taken aback by the younger man's directness. *"You have a most penetrating way of making conversation, dear boy. Don't you have any small talk?"*

Mobbs asks. *"No,"* Dowling replies, *"I'm not very good at it."* It's noticeable that, although Jayston is the newcomer to the series, director Cyril Coke keeps the attention on him, alert and calculating when listening to Fowler, direct and satirical when responding to Mobbs.

Writing in *The Stage*, Angela Moreton observed that the series, *"could with greater logic be called Son of The Power Game,"* but acknowledged that, Peter Draper's script, *"was honed like the finest steel, finely and sharply. Every word counted, there was not a surplus one, ad when the episode ended one felt like a gourmet after a five-star meal."*

Dowling is delegated by Wilder to help Pamela with her debut as a society hostess *("I gather for the good of the country it's essential that its leader's meet and drink champagne.")* and this leads to a lunch where Dowling once again finds his loyalty to Wilder tested.

The episode features a striking cameo by Caroline Blakiston as Margot Fellowship, an admirer of Wilder's who is organising a party for the same day as Pamela's. Blakiston was well established as a femme fatale in ITC shows like *The Champions* (*The Experiment*) and *The Saint* (*The Convenient Monster*) and it's unfortunate that the battered export kinescopes used for the Series 3 DVD produce such a washed out image that diminishes her blonde glamour.

Even so, she has a devastating impact as she charges into the restaurant like a huntress, laying a proprietary hand on Dowling and exchanging insincere pleasantries with Pamela Wilde. When she later learns that they're both holding their parties on the 28th, Margo drawls, *"Isn't it awful? Two marvellous parties at the same time – everyone's wildly excited.!"* As Dowling points out, Margo's guest lists run to over 150 prominent people. Including those Pamela needs at her party. *"Why can't she stick to adultery?"* Pamela asks, *"At least it doesn't tie up half of London!"* Dowling is not so sure, but comes up with a plan to nobble the five or six most prominent guests, ensuring that Margo cancels her party.

Angela Moreton observed that Barbara Murray, *"filled Mr Drapers pauses with inflections, glances, smiles and coy looks that were an inestimable complement to the script. In fact, as The Power Game slides gently down, Miss Murray is creating something substantial both for herself and Lady Wilder, a part that was once just an appendage to prove that Sir John was married."*

(Page 12, The Stage February 6 1969).

In fact, Wilder is shunted out of the way for most of the episode by the "goose chase" of the title. Alluding to the Soviet invasion of Czechoslovakia in August 1968, Caswell Bligh (Clifford Evans) tells Wilder that after, *"those bumpkins in the Kremlin sent their tanks into Czechoslovakia, some of the Warsaw Pact countries thought they could control it but now are beginning to have their doubts."*

As Envoy for "Special Situations" Wilder is sent to welcome poet Vaclav Vitek to the West. In fact, Vitek has been invented by Professor Mobbs so that Wilder can decoy the Americans from the refugees MI6 are really interested in. But when Wilder returns to London he tells Bligh that the Americans had scooped up the refugees the previous day. He takes pleasure in telling Bligh that there was no-one called Vitek at the frontier, although he mentions in passing that there was *"someone called Mobbs wandering about looking very worried."*

Draper's script gives Jason Fowler a concluding speech which sums up the mood of disillusion. Previously depicted as a petty opponent of Wilder, Fowler is shown in this episode to be a good manager, protective of Dowling's interests and determined to make him aware of the implications of the approach from MI6. Fowler reflects that, *"We seem to be pursued into necessity. One does something because it seems right – because it seems to be the things one stands for - humanity -'the country' – only to find one has done it for quite the opposite reason. I suppose the decay of religion took away our sense of moral absolutes."*

Tuesday 4 February 1969   ***Private Treaty***

Writer Raymond Bowers   **Director Robert Tronson.**

Patrick Wymark (Sir John Wilder). Clifford Evans (Caswell Bligh). Barbara Murray (Pamela, Lady Wilder). Jack Watling (Don Henderson) . Michael Jayston (Lincoln Dowling). Richard Hurndall (Sir Jason Fowler). David Savile (Peter Hindlesham). Gay Hamilton (Fredalina). Bari Johnson (Naranda). George Howe (Minister Kidrich). Robin John (workman).

"For Sale by Private Treaty: Tudor Manor House, Park, formal garden, Home Farm, Lodge, 2 Cottages. In all 120 acres!" .

This and the following episode *Without Prejudice* make up a two-part story that could arguably have been told as one. Perhaps the producers "owed" Raymond Bowers an episode. Unfortunately, this first episode is played as a farce with comic comings and goings and misunderstandings.

In 1966 Yugoslavia was a non-aligned communist nation. Its leader Marshal Tito played NATO off against the Warsaw Pact and also cultivated the emerging powers of China and India. Believing that Bligh intends to steal credit for a deal with Yugoslavia, Wilder brings First Minister Kidrich (George Howe) to Hackton Hall, the Wilder's country house to keep him out of Bligh's clutches.

Wilder and Henderson learn that the house is up for sale, with the caretaker in hospital and the electricity cut off. As they go to the village to try and get the electricity reinstated, Pamela arrives with Hindlesham (David Savile), Lord Bligh's private secretary. Wilder has told Pamela to 'cultivate' Hindlesham so that he can learn Bligh's plans.

In the kitchen, Pamela meets Yugoslavian secretary "Fredalina" Vanek (Gay Hamilton). Pamela assumes she is Wilder's latest conquest after she thinks she hears the girl call out "Darling". She doesn't know that Fredalina was calling out to Dowling (Michael Jayston) who has been out scouring the copse for wood to burn in the range. Pamela roars back to London before Wilder can prove his innocence.

Lord Bligh has suggested that Pamela sell the family home now to avoid Capital Gains Tax. But Bligh is meeting Naranda (Bari Jonson), the African Minister who was forced to flee his country after Wilder exposed his bribery in *One From Zurich*. The British Government has allowed Naranda to enter the country via a loophole and he is now looking to buy Wilder's country house to bring his family into the country.

Jack Watling is brought back to do very little. Both Henderson and Dowling are there to type up a report for Wilder and the hapless Hindlesham (David Savile) carries out their usual function of Pamela Wilder's purse carrier through this episode.

There is a lot of Noel Coward style bickering between the Wilder's which produces one good speech from Patrick Wymark: *"We have to behave in public – to hell with private – in such a way that will not send shivers of delight down the grubby backs of the clean-mouthed, clean-living, dirty minded tax payers who are lusting to chop us down when we show the first sign of the common humanity that they're too narrow-minded, jealous, or incapable of enjoying for themselves except by proxy through their Sunday newspaper!"*

Wilder is surprised when Pamela introduces him to the prospective buyer of their house, but Naranda explains that he cannot return to Malia; *"My job as Minister of Home Security was to cultivate the Chinese publicly so that the left would not notice my Brother-in-law the Prime Minister was adhering to the British secretly. The right don't want me because they think I'm pro-Chinese, and the left think I failed them."* Patrick Wymark's non-verbal reaction is polite enough to signal that he accepts what Naranda says without altogether believing it.

Nevertheless, Naranda says he needs a home because he's entered Britain as an alien dependent. His father, a bus conductor, has been a British resident for 17 years. While this gives him an "in", we also know that the Immigration Service consulted Lord Bligh over Naranda's application.

Once again, this 1969 episode has relevance for post-Brexit Britain with the simmering fear of non-white immigration. Only a year before, in 1968, the newly independent Kenyan Government had begun forcing Asians out, creating fears of an "influx" of immigrants. In March 1968, the Labour Government capitulated to those fears by invalidating their British passports. A strict quota was imposed, with a loophole left for those Kenyans whose parents had been born in Britain (who would invariably be white).

Unfortunately, for any audience members who had stayed with this flaccid episode expecting a clever resolution, the story ends on a cliff-hanger.

Tuesday 11 February 1969   *Without Prejudice*

Writer Raymond Bowers   Director Peter Moffatt.

Patrick Wymark (Sir John Wilder). Clifford Evans   (Caswell Bligh). Barbara Murray (Pamela, Lady Wilder). Jack Watling (Don Henderson) . Michael Jayston (Lincoln Dowling). Richard Hurndall (Sir Jason Fowler). David Savile (Peter Hindlesham). Louiza Flamma-Sherman (Trina). Deborah Grant (Jill). Bari Johnson (Naranda). Robin John (workman). Nicholas Grimshaw (older workman).

While Naranda flies to Switzerland to collect the money he needs to buy the Wilder's house, he leaves his 18-year-old daughter Trina (Louiza Flamma-Sherman) in the Wilder's care.

This episode sees the introduction of Deborah Grant as Jill Tenby, Sir John's Personal Assistant. Her role appears to be restricted to helping Wilder off with his coat as he enters the office and bringing in a cooked breakfast for Wilder and Henderson.

As an odd piece of social history, Wilder is astonished to see Hindlesham in the corridor with his Civil Service issue towel tucked under his arm and asks what he's doing. Hindlesham says he's going in the bathroom and Wilder pokes his head in before declaring, *"It's insanitary in there. A grubby, communal loo!"*

Reminding us that there is a wafer-thin piece of public service negotiation at the heart of the story, Wilder explains to Henderson that the deal he's trying to negotiate with Yugoslav minister Kidrich involves trying *"to winkle British capital into a Yugoslav combinat that is openly using Russian technicians. Russians won't like it because it capitalises communism. British hardliners won't like it because it communises capitalism."* Bligh, who wants to take credit for the deal, tells the Prime Minister that it will mean an increase of £15 million in trade.

Wilder learns that Bligh has set him up. Naranda plans to use the Hall as a refuge for rich Africans, who have entered under diplomatic visas because they couldn't get through the normal immigration controls. Wilder realises he will be implicated in an immigration scandal, and puts the Hall back on the market. When Bligh finds out, he instructs Dowling to look at sacking Wilder under the Race Relations Act for refusing to sell his house to a minority.

With no staff at the hall, Wilder takes Naranda's daughter to the local pub for dinner. Still under 21, 18 year-old Trina is legally a minor in 1969. But when she changes out of her school uniform into an expensive gown, she seems older. Despite this being the pre-digital age, word of Wilder dining with a glamorous young girl makes its way to London and by the next morning, Hindlesham tells Dowling that Pamela is suing Wilder for divorce. *"Got it from a solicitor – Charlie Grainger – used to be in the Treasury."* This refers to the character of Pamela's cousin played by Robin Bailey (So now we know that the *"large smelly pigeon"* Wilder dumped in Grainger's in-box at the end of the last series resulted in Grainger leaving the Treasury and going back to private practice).

Bligh concludes that a prosecution under the Race Relations Act will fail if Wilder is being accused of sleeping with a black girl. Pamela is finally convinced to withdraw the divorce proceedings. Naranda returns from Switzerland with his suitcase full of money. And they all lived happily ever after.

The 1968 Race Relations Bill prohibited racial discrimination in employment, commercial services and housing. It was set against a background in which landlords had signs on their doors reading, "No blacks, no Irish". It was also passed weeks after the British Government passed a bill to invalidate the passports of Kenyan Asian refugees. The Race Relations Bill met strong opposition, not least from Conservative MP Enoch Powell who spoke for "ordinary English" people who had a "sense of being a persecuted minority."

In this episode, the Race Relations Bill is seen as a weapon to be used by the wealthy elite for private malice. As Dominic Sandbrook points out in '*White Heat :A History of Britain in the Swinging Sixties"*, racial prejudice has elements of class resentment; "*liberal politicians and commentators usually lived in areas far too expensive for most immigrants whereas poorer working class voters had to compete with them."* Bowers script arguably includes an element of wish-fulfilment for viewers who felt this way, when Naranda purposely targets the heart of upper middle-class privilege.

It's notable also that while the Commonwealth Immigrants Act of 1962 specifically restricted incomers to those with specific skills or contracts or the dependants of those with residency, the socialist Lord Bligh is shown supporting the rich Naranda's exploitation of a loophole, claiming to be a dependant of his bus driver father.

While the 1960's arts and media are often characterised as being part of a left wing conspiracy, it is notable that this episode depicts a right wing point of view. It's argued by some that the success of legislation such as the Race Relations Bill led to the eradication of casual racism and the gradual repositioning of the threatening "other" on Europe and the EU. Poor as it is, this episode does speak to the Britain of the 21st Century and the Brexit view that the fears of the ordinary disenfranchised Briton are not just ignored but devalued by a patronising, self-serving elite.

18 February 1969   *Cat is You, Bird is Me*

Writer Peter Draper   Director Robert Tronson.

Patrick Wymark (Sir John Wilder). Clifford Evans (Caswell Bligh). Barbara Murray (Pamela, Lady Wilder). Jack Watling (Don Henderson) . Michael Jayston (Lincoln Dowling). Richard Hurndall (Sir Jason Fowler). Felicity Gibson (Perpetua Cataline). David Gooderson (Armaton). Eric Dodson (Mr Handle). Jeffrey Segal (Wisselman). Marcia Ashton (Mrs Waters). Clyde Pollitt (Customs Officer). Antony Brown (Higher Officer). Liz Digby-Smith (Anita Lett). Robin Scott (Goodall).

"Much as I disapprove of Wilder – O, There Are Times When I Could Wish I Were He!". Jason Fowler

The Power Game captures the *zeitgeist* of the middle-aged breadhead chasing a wild, free spirit (two months later, Tigon Films would release *What's Good for The Goose* unbelievably casting Norman Wisdom as a bank manager bedhopping with hippy Sally Geeson). The back story identifies a pivotal moment in the post-war economy as the international exchange mechanism shudders towards self-destruction.

Jason Fowler urges Wilder to meet Herr Wisselman (Jeffrey Segal) who is due to speak at a world bank seminar in Geneva. Fowler thinks Wisselman could change the whole concept of modern finance.

Wisselman has published an article which states that South Africa and Russia control 30% of the world's free gold. Fowler enthusiastically endorses the proposition that the world will divide into two power blocs – with South Africa, the Soviet Union and China in one bloc, Britain, Europe, North America and Australia/New Zealand in the other.

This episode was made at a time when the system of fixed exchange rates agreed at Bretton Woods in 1944 was coming under increasing pressure. Under the Bretton Woods agreement, the International Monetary Fund managed a system in which each country set an exchange rate for its own currency relative to an ounce of gold valued at 35 US dollars. While the system had produced stability for 20 years, it was an "adjustable peg" system which allowed members to adjust their exchange rate.

A financial crisis in 1967 had seen the UK pound devalued by 14% and while the international system held, the resultant price rises and cuts in imports produced a sombre mood within Britain. Other nations, with conflicting aims, began to exploit the relief mechanism by which central banks could exchange their dollar holdings for gold bullion; France demanded to "cash in" its gold from the New York Federal Reserve. With the Bretton Woods system struggling to service rapidly expanding world trade, an alternative was needed.

Fowler says that Wisselman, *"made the point that unless we move away from gold in the next 50 years, we could be subject to intolerable blackmail."* The banker has suggested a system of *"paper gold"* (which is the name often given to the "Special Drawing Rights" actually created by the International Monetary Fund later in 1969). Fowler says a lot of people want to silence Wisselman because his "original and unorthodox thinking." threatens the established order. Fowler thinks Wilder could persuade him to make his theories public.

Wilder is unenthusiastic until he meets 20-year-old interpreter Perpetua Cataline (Felicity Gibson) and hears her views on the hedonistic life-style. Wilder decides to drive with Perpetua to Geneva, while Don Henderson (Jack Watling) is sent ahead to make contact with Wisselman.

Wilder and Perpetua sit sipping champagne in the back of his Departmental Rolls Royce, as the Beatles' *Fool On The Hill* plays over the radio.

Wilder's initial seduction technique – connecting rooms in a St Moritz hotel, candlelit champagne dinner served in their suite by waiters, Wilder in smoking jacket and cravat – falls flat when Perpetua asks, *"Did you see a lot of Ronald Colman movies when you were young?"*

Abandoning their suite for mod dancing in the restaurant downstairs, Wilder is gradually won over. Perpetua observes that everything about Wilder is neat as if he thought he could tidy up life. *"Shall I tell you how to do the dances today? You do them how you want to do them! Just let yourself go. The thing about dancing nowadays is that if you're enjoying it, you're doing it right!"*

When Wilder confesses that he doesn't even understand the language, Perpetua translates that, *"Cat is you, bird is me"* and Wilder asks wistfully, *"Will this cat get the bird?"* Finally, he wins her over by reciting from Andrew Marvell's *"To His Coy Mistress"* and *"The Definition of Love"*. She concludes that, *"Underneath the neat shirt there's a poet."* And tells him it's time for bed.

Jack Watling as Don Henderson serves as a comic foil to Wilder, warning him that he's *"overdrawn at the fun bank."* When Wilder asks, *"If you saw me in a bar with that girl and I said I was 49, what would you think?"* Henderson replies, *"Oh come now, John. 49's young – for a dirty old man!"*

(Wilder's date of birth had been given as 1917 in the 1965 *TV Times* article, which would have made him 51 in 1969. This ties in with the first series episode *The Man With Two Hats*, where Packard says Wilder is 49 in 1966.)

But when Wilder finally meets Herr Wisselman (Jeffrey Segal) the banker explains that his article was a joke written for a Swiss satirical magazine. Wisselman says he thinks they're the only ones who have taken his article seriously. He says of Fowler, *"he struck me as a man who needed an idea – perhaps because for years an idea has been expected of him and he has never been able to deliver."*

Wilder and Perpetua return by the new *Seaspeed* Hovercraft to Dover where Wilder tries to claim diplomatic immunity at Customs. Patrick Wymark signals an underlying unease when he tries to pull the *"do you know who I am"* routine, and the unease is justified. After the Surveyor (Anthony Brown) insists that Wilder and Perpetua get out of the Rolls and submit to a search, Fowler confirms that Wilder does not have diplomatic immunity. He's *"not actually accredited – not to any country."* A furious Wilder return to find a rummage crew taking the Rolls apart. One of the Waterguard officers (Clyde Pollitt) confirms that all they've found is Perpetua's expensive shopping, which needs the duty paying.

"I could have told you that," Wilder replies *"If this is the gateway to England, the country would be far better off if they put you back in your laboratory jar in which you obviously spent half your life"*

"We get a great many diplomats through here, Sir John," the Surveyor replies, *"If they all paid their duty, perhaps the country could afford the formaldehyde."*

As a parting shot they tell Wilder that, *"Although we have the right to take the car apart if we think it necessary, it is not incumbent on us to put it together again."*

Furious, Wilder tells Perpetua to pay the duty on her shopping and also orders his driver to give her a screwdriver to help put the car back together again.

While Wilder and Perpetua are talking in the discotheque, the background music is a mod electric organ piece used in the 1968 Central Office of Information film for *"Keep Britain Tidy"* featuring Roy Hudd as a litterbug.

22-year-old Felicity Gibson (Perpetua) had previously appeared as Kando in the 1968 Patrick Troughton *Doctor Who* story *The Dominators.* She would later appear with Barbara Murray in *The Duchess of Wiltshire's Diamonds,* an episode of *"The Rivals of Sherlock Holmes* starring Roy Dotrice as Klimo. Although Clifford Evans is absent from this episode, he would star in John MacKenzie's 1971 film *"One Brief Summer" ("A young wife who didn't love him enough, a daughter who loved him too much"*), which earned Felicity Gibson an "introducing" credit.

As noted above, while the paranoid racial scenario endorsed by Fowler has not come into play, the Bretton Woods system was threatened by speculators and other self-interests exploiting gold's status as a commodity with a rising value. "Paper Gold" - was introduced by the International Monetary Fund in 1969 in the form of "Special Drawing Rights" that had no value other than as a medium of exchange for member currencies. It was never a lasting solution and in 1971 the United States abandoned dollar convertability to gold. In 1973 the world moved to floating exchange rates.

Tuesday 25 February 1969   *Standard Practice*

Writer Raymond Bowers   Director Robert Tronson.

Patrick Wymark (Sir John Wilder). Clifford Evans (Caswell Bligh). Barbara Murray (Pamela, Lady Wilder). Jack Watling (Don Henderson) . Michael Jayston (Lincoln Dowling). Richard Hurndall (Sir Jason Fowler). Deborah Grant (Jill). Peter Barkworth (Kenneth Bligh). Peter Hawkins (Interpreter). Wolfe Morris (Mejulik). Preston Lockwood (Swiss Banker).

"It doesn't suit me to have a fading Minister ready to blow up…and blowing me up with him!" Sir John Wilder.

At the end of the last series of *The Power Game*, Kenneth Bligh (Peter Barkworth) resigned from Bligh Construction, setting up a sub-contracting firm with Don Henderson (Jack Watling). At the beginning of this series, Wilder tempted Henderson to join him at the Foreign Office, with the offer of two years' worth of contracts for his struggling company.

In this episode, Lincoln Dowling ensures that Bligh sees a large expense claim which Henderson has left for Wilder to sign. Don and Ken Bligh have been trying to set up a road-building contract with the Albanian government, and Caswell takes charge of the negotiations, determined to cut both Ken and Wilder out of the deal .

There are tragic undertones to the story. His health failing, Caswell Bligh shows regret. After sarcastically asking whether Wilder is signing Henderson's expense claim as a birthday present Bligh thinks of Ken, musing, *" Last Tuesday was his birthday.. And Wednesday was mine..In happier days I agreed that it was the one thing he'd always be ahead of me"*. But he still can't resist trying to cut his son out of the building consortium he's spent months setting up. As Wilder tells Bligh*, "To see him standing on his own two feet would knock you off your own!"*

During an argument with Wilder over Don's expense claim, Bligh falters as the sound of a beating heart is laid over the soundtrack. Clifford Evans is disturbingly effective as the disorientated Bligh, struggling to retain his composure. Wilder watches intently, no longer in a mood to argue. When Wilder later meets with Kenneth Bligh, he counsels him to seek advice from the family Doctor about Caswell's health, warning him not to push his father too far. Just in case it seems that Wilder has suddenly become charitable, he makes it clear that he doesn't want to be dragged down by a *"fading Minister"*.

But Ken is more interested in getting Wilder to sign off Don's expense claim. They have spent three months of travel and negotiation with the Albanians and Ken needs to cash in. Normally, Bligh would have to know, but Ken suggests that *"My father cannot express a Ministerial opinion about an enterprise in which his son is privately engaged, so he's left the matter entirely to you."* Wilder, more realistically replies that his father would say Ken's firm is too small, unsuccessful and badly managed to take part in such a risky enterprise. For Ken, the importance of the expense claim is to convince potential partners that he has the blessing of the Foreign Office.

In the real world, the People's Socialist Republic of Albania had been in dispute with the United Kingdom since a British ship was sunk by Albanian mines in the Channel of Corfu in 1946. Albania had failed to pay the £844,000 awarded by the International Court of Justice and the UK cut off diplomatic relations. However, Albania had become isolated from post-Stalinist Russia and had withdrawn from the Warsaw Pact following the Russian invasion of Czechoslovakia in August 1968. Too hard-line communist to cosy up to the West, Albania had looked to Communist China for support. In the story, Wilder believes that China might pay off the fine on behalf of Albania. And that would make it possible for a British consortium to build roads in Albania, backed by the British Government. Wilder foresaw the need for a road after the Soviet invasion of Czechoslovakia. With Albania isolated from Russia they might need to call on Yugoslavian tanks "the next time the Kremlin went crazy!".

Ken's firm is too small to fulfil the contract on its own, but Don is putting together a consortium led by Bewdley and Son. Ken has arranged a meeting between Wilder and Mejulik (Wolfe Morris) the Albanian commercial envoy in Paris, who has entered the country on false papers.

Wilder instructs Dowling to get him all figures on Britain's trade dealings with Albania before 1946. Wilder has told Ken that

Dowling, *"is in some ways my most valuable instrument here,"* and is not surprised when Lord Bligh asks him questions about Albania and a road building consortium,

Scenting success, Bligh tells Wilder he's already asked for a government guarantee for the consortium and will take over the negotiation with Mejuilk. Wilder warns Bligh that Mejulik may be a *"primitive hardline Marxist"* but allows himself a sly smile when Bligh says they're the easiest type to deal with. Later on, he advises Don who is hosting the negotiations, *"telephone me immediately when Caswell louses up the deal."*

Ken is shocked when he walks into the Balkan Star restaurant to see Dowling and Caswell already waiting. When Sir James Bewdley (Anthony Woodruff) enters Caswell immediately lays the ground for cutting Ken out by telling him Government backing is out of the question if the consortium wants *"to carry sprats"*. Bligh continues to dominate when Mejulik and his interpreter (Peter Hawkins) arrive but when Ken interjects that Bligh has never been to Albania and should *"have the brains to leave it to people who have,"* a furious Bligh grabs Ken to throw him out and suddenly has a seizure.

The effect is economic but effective – a close-up of Bligh's shocked face – a pounding heartbeat – the picture blurring into a montage of reflected light and out of focus faces as snatches of conversation blend together.

Finally, Bligh recovers, watched closely by Dowling and Henderson as he tells the interpreter. *"There will be no agents' fees, and no form of commission to any individuals. "*

The interpreter (Peter Hawkins) tells Bligh that the meeting is over and relays Mejulik's response that Bligh has *"accurately reflected Karl Marx's theory. "*. As Wilder explains to Bligh later, *"Their communism is no different from any other of their systems of government. It's just something to make the peasants suffer. And the reward for people in positions of state hasn't changed either.*

Mejulik wanted a bribe. An honourable, unexceptionable bribe. Not Marxist practice. Standard practice!"

Wilder suggests that Bligh tells the Prime Minister he has decided to hand negotiations back to the initiator. However, Dowling brings in an intelligence briefing which concludes that the Chinese have been steering the road-building initiative in order to sour British relations with America. *"Henderson was nobbled by the Chinese – not they by him – he is of course an amateur."*

As Wilder peers at the briefing, fruitlessly trying to find something that will rescue the deal, Bligh triumphantly tells him he should have taken Dowling into his confidence sooner.

A tightly written episode by Raymond Bowers ensures that the series remains unpredictable by ensuring that Wilder doesn't win every time. The episode is most memorable for the disturbing scenes where Caswell Bligh's heart begins to falter.

At the heart of the episode is a memorandum which Wilder sent the Foreign Secretary, the day after the Soviet invasion of Czechoslovakia. Bligh says that under Civil Service procedure, the memo was diverted to Bligh as Minister. This may seem anachronistic since the first episode was broadcast in January 1969. However, *The Power Game* had started production in August 1968 and this makes it clear that Wilder's appointment as Special Envoy took place at some time before 20 August 1968 when the invasion began.

Although Wilfred Greatorex enjoyed lengthy script conferences and used technical advisers to get the political details right, Raymond Bowers appears to have prided himself on getting the language and customs correct. Wolfe Morris doesn't speak a word of English in this episode, and Peter Hawkins (the original voice of The Daleks in *Doctor Who* and of *Captain Pugwash*) translates Bligh's comments back to him. Apparently, Hawkins attended the England V Rumania football match on 15 January 1969 and rehearsed his lines, confusing the "away" supporters by shouting *"I would like to introduce Lord Bligh"* in Albanian at them.

To show that Wilder honours his promises, he ensures that Don and Ken's expenses are well-covered. He engages in some tricky business with a Swiss banker (played by Preston Lockwood, who was also the banker involved with the pay off to Naranda in the first episode). Earlier, Wilder had instructed his stockbroker to buy up shares in Bligh Development Limited, in the name of Don Henderson. Before the news of the failed deal gets out he instructs the Swiss banker (Preston Lockwood) to sell a fraction of the shares and deposit the proceeds in the name of Don Henderson, while the rest can be deposited in a Swiss bank account.

Lord Bligh's assertion that his department is expected to make budget cuts, reflects the legacy of Chancellor Roy Jenkins 1967 attempt to rescue the pound by cutting £800 million from public spending and his 1968 budget raising taxation by £900 million. The desperation to improve balance of trade payments is also reflected in this episode's "prize" of winning an overseas construction contract.

Tuesday 4 March 1969   *The Heart Market*

Writer Wilfred Greatorex   Director James Omerod.

Patrick Wymark (Sir John Wilder). Clifford Evans   (Caswell Bligh). Barbara Murray (Pamela, Lady Wilder). Jack Watling (Don Henderson) . Michael Jayston (Lincoln Dowling). Richard Hurndall (Sir Jason Fowler). David Saville (Hindlesham). Peter Barkworth (Ken Bligh). Colette O'Neil (Mrs Taylor). Kendrick Owen (surgeon). Tutte Lemkow (Prime Minister). Frank Olegario (Pastore).

"Less than 15 months ago, the world was staggered by the news that a South African surgeon, Dr Christiaan Barnard, had replaced the failing heart of a 56-year-old man with that of a young woman. Tonight, in The Power Game, Sir John Wilder's long-standing rival, Caswell Bligh goes under the knife to receive a new heart. What are

his chances? According to Dr Barnard, about three-to-one against. Since that historic operation in December 1967, 109 heart transplant operations have been carried out. More than 30 of the patients are still alive. The operations have been shrouded in controversy; their cost is tremendous.... The Power Game raises other questions. The inevitable one being – could men of power and wealth be first in the queue for new hearts?" TV Times.

The ailing Caswell Bligh (Clifford Evans) attaches himself to Sir John Wilder's mission to Somalia in the hope of claiming credit for Wilder's success. In the middle of an argument with Wilder, Bligh collapses and is flown back to London. He is told that his heart is failing and that he could die at any moment. Although Bligh initially rejects the idea of a heart transplant, Wilder taunts him into accepting.

Don Henderson (Jack Watling) sends for Bligh's estranged son Ken (Peter Barkworth) and tells him that Caswell is dying. Ken refuses to see his father, blaming him for the breakdown of his marriage. However, Ken demands that Wilder give him a contract for building the hospitals in Somalia.

Script Editor Wilfred Greatorex delivers a powerful episode which brings the conflict between Wilder and Bligh to a climax. After a meeting in Somalia, Bligh and Wilder return to the hotel. Hindlesham (David Saville), Bligh's private secretary brings him a tablet. He leaves Bligh with Wilder who says, *"I never thought to see you prostrate – but it doesn't please me."*

Bligh refuses Wilder's advice to go home, saying he's going to see the contract's agreed. Wilder reminds Bligh that he'd tried to send Wilder to a conference in Geneva. The Foreign Secretary told Bligh to release him, after Wilder told the Foreign Secretary about the Somalia deal. *"He knows you had nothing to do with it. Everyone knows."*

Director James Ormerod ramps up the tension within the hotel room - lowering the lighting, with Wilder facing one wall, while Caswell looks towards the other. *"All I know,"* says Caswell, *"Is if it hadn't been for you I wouldn't have sold my firm. Then you interfered and smashed up my relationship with my son. Now you sit there gloating...you don't care about Britain. All you care about is your own glory!"*

Bligh tries to continue as the pain sweeps over him and suddenly collapses into Wilder's arms. Shocked, Wilder tells the hotel switchboard to call the Prime Minister's doctor, and then gets Henderson and Dowling to organise flights back to London via Nairobi and a private clinic in London.

Back in London Don sends for Ken Bligh (Peter Barkworth) who comes to the office thinking he's going to be offered a contract. Ken is drunk and embittered about the break-up of his marriage for which he blames Caswell. Even when Don tells him Caswell is dying, Ken refuses to see him.

At the clinic, Bligh's surgeon Graham Harrison (Kendrick Owen) tells him *"With luck and care you could live a year. Without...tomorrow – today if you insist on charging off."*

Harrison proposes a heart transplant. Bligh initially refuses. *"I'm against all this spare part surgery. I'm not going to be made a guinea pig. If my heart isn't good enough, neither is anybody elses!"*

Wilder is infuriated. *"You sound more and more like a 20th century Roundhead. I've always doubted this progressive streak you've claimed"*. Bligh persists that, *"They'll put nobody else's heart in me!"* and Wilder leans over the bed, challenging Bligh, *"Or is it that you're scared? It's not the principle that worries you – the philosophy. You haven't got the guts!"*

Chastened, Caswell tells Harrison he's decided to go ahead with the surgery and then characteristically demands that they start right away. Harrison warns him that it's not so easy. First they need a heart.

As Wilder returns to his office, he is visited by Ken who demands a contract for the work in Somalia. *"When you took Don as your PA, you robbed me of a loyal partner and promised me enough work for two years."* Wilder tells him he gave him two contracts. *"You fell flat on your face with the first and under-priced the second. You haven't learned anything."*

Wilder placates Ken with the possibility of other jobs in the pipeline, on condition that he makes up with Caswell who is *"like an aging Sheepdog."*

Back at the hospital, Bligh's surgeon has located a heart. The potential donor is a young husband and father smashed up in a motorbike crash. *"He's got a heart in what you may call mint condition"* His surgeon tells him there's no need for sentimentality *"When you were a civil engineer you needed ballast and tarmac to build your roads. We need spare parts to rebuild people."*

The surgeon estimates that the man has 72 hours to live. *"The most difficult problem of all (is) the permission of the next of kin."*. Bligh gets Hindlesham to find out the man's identity and then asks Ken to visit Mrs Taylor (Colette O'Neil) and offer financial help. *"This is buying a heart"* Ken challenges, but Caswell denies it. The exhausted wife and mother asks to see Caswell. Before she goes into his room, she tells Ken she will give permission. She just wants to what his father's like. But Caswell assumes Ken hasn't sealed and genially starts making financial offers. Horrified, Mrs Taylor flees the room. Ken follows saying Caswell doesn't deserve a heart, but she softly chides him saying Caswell's his father. She asks him to put £20,000* in a trust fund for her children. *"I wouldn't touch a penny but the children might need it – I hope they won't - but they may do."*

*About £300,000 in 2022.

The next day, Hindlesham is dispatched to deliver a wreath to Mrs Taylor, while Bligh is prepared for the operation. Wilder visits, lying to Bligh that Ken is on his way. As Caswell is wheeled out of the room, he tells Wilder *"If I don't come out of this bury me standing. Facing you."*

Ken arrives, in time to see his father being taken down to the Operating Theatre. He has nothing to say.

The final scene is in Wilder's office. Hindlesham, Dowling, Don and Ken follow Wilder, all dressed in mourning. Wilder apologises to Ken saying he can't help with the contract. That will be the new Minister's decision. When Don protests that it's only an hour since they buried Bligh, A tearful Ken says, *"You always wanted him out of the way"* but Wilder snaps back, *"It wasn't me that hated him."*

A powerful episode that ensures the conflict between Bligh and Wilder goes out with a bang. Greatorex deals forcefully with the issues, particularly the difficult question of gaining consent. Despite the publicity, this was still a high-risk procedure. The listing in the *TV Times* had warned that 30 out of 109 heart transplant patients were still alive. By 1970, the figure was 10 out of 160 live transplants.

Peter Barkworth's farewell performance as Ken Bligh is sad but convincing. We see him looking wistfully at the family photo of accident victim Mr Taylor with his children, and his drunken recital to Don over the breakdown of his marriage show a broken man. Even Caswell finally regrets what he's done to Ken advising him not to waste his inheritance. *"Pay off your debts and get out of it. You were never cut out for business. You should have been a parson or a schoolmaster."*

Since the last series of *The Power Game*, Barkworth had been incredibly busy, appearing in Peter Draper's *A Roof Over Our Mouths* (1967), with Wendy Gifford in the Doctor Who story *The Ice Warriors* (1967), and in *Where Eagles Dare* (1968) with Patrick Wymark. In January 1970 he would star as French resistance leader Vincent in former *Power Game* producer Rex Firkin's London Weekend TV series *Manhunt*.

Clifford Evans delivered a typically robust final performance as Caswell Bligh. Evans would go on to star in the August 1969 BBC play *Codename Portcullis* as former Government Minister Sir Ian Carfax, now a master of a Cambridge University college who was secretly working for British intelligence. This would spin off into the 1970 series *Codename* starring Evans, Alexandra Bastedo and Anthony Valentine.

Tuesday 11 March 1969   *The New Minister*

Writer Wilfred Greatorex   Director Cyril Coke.

Patrick Wymark (Sir John Wilder). Barrie Ingham (Garfield Kane). Barbara Murray (Pamela, Lady Wilder). Jack Watling (Don Henderson) . Michael Jayston (Lincoln Dowling). Richard Hurndall (Sir Jason Fowler). Deborah Grant (Jill). Jean Harvey (Mrs Bunty Lovell).Caroline John (Maggie). Peter Cellier (Frank Archer). Hamilton Dyce (Prescott). Robert McBain (Simon Davey).

In the race to succeed the late Lord Bligh as Minister for Special Situations and Trade, Wilder supports Mrs Bunty Lovell MP (Jean Harvey) because he thinks she's the only contender he can control. But self-made millionaire Garfield Kane (Barrie Ingham) has spent too long on the Labour back bench and is eager for promotion.

Barrie Ingham had played smarmy David Fleet in *The Plane Makers* episode *A Bunch of Fives* and recently starred in Hammer's *A Challenge for Robin Hood* (1967) with John Arnett (Peter Humphreys in *The Plane Makers*) as Sheriff of Nottingham. In July 1968, Ingham had starred at the Aldwych as Buffalo Bill in Arthur Kopit's *Indians* (opposite Michael Jayston as Custer), but he was more familiar to TV viewers as Sejanus in Philip Mackie's *The Caesars* (Granada September 1968). While this episode is about the contest for the Minister's job, pre-publicity, plus the fact that Ingham's name occupied Clifford Evans' spot in the title sequence, may have given viewers a clue to the outcome.

Lincoln Dowling alludes to former Foreign Secretary George Brown when he says, *"We've had enough of Ministers with big lungs, sharp tempers and outsize thirsts."* Wilder congratulates him on *"learning to speak out instead of wrapping everything up like so much diplomatic fish and chips.".* Dowling suspects Wilder is backing Mrs Bunty Lovell in the hope that she will be a short-term appointment, allowing Wilder to replace her. Wilder reiterates his philosophy, *"Let's get this straight. I never join any political party. Certainly, never for however brief and dazzling power in government. I have to remain independent."*

Dowling backs *"Someone pacing himself from the back like a quality miler."* Garfield Kane MP "Mr Instant Success" a Francophile gourmet and industrial consultant who started life in an orphanage. Lincoln manages to surprise Wilder by telling him. *"he's at this moment dining at Le Gourmet Francais – lunching with your wife.".*

Kane charms Pamela Wilder (Barbara Murray) relating his background, and telling a story about a former union official and government minister which reflects on the British attitude to French cuisine (salt and vinegar with everything, even snails). Kane has invited Pamela to work on a charity fund-raising committee, but quickly drops in that he wants to work with Wilder "as his Minister"

Jason Fowler (Richard Hurndall) and Dowling agree that Prescott (Hamilton Dyce), the acting Minister, should not succeed Bligh as he intends to merge their department with his own and bring in his own staff.

Wilder favours Mrs Bunty Lovell MP (Jean Harvey) as minister. Dowling's assessment of her *("She's a pusher. She has talent she's tough. She has one drawback – she's a woman.")* is relatively moderate for the time: Barbara Castle, the then Minister of Transport was only the fourth woman Cabinet Minister in history. Don's assessment is more predictable*:" She's the hottest politician since Eva Peron."*

Wilder's view of Mrs Lovell is similarly sexist. She has been a Parliamentary Private Secretary (an MP acting as a Minister's PA) but Wilder says he hears, *"you had half your civil servants over the moon after you."* Jean Harvey, who had played magazine editor Joanne Minster in the BBC's *Compact* (1962) and was nominated for a Bafta as Sally in *A Man of Our Times* (1968) pushes back.

Bunty refuses to be flattered and warns Wilder she'll fight him all the way. She reminds Wilder, *"You wouldn't take that woman who was such an expert in swing wing geometry onto your board at Scott Furlong."* He responds in a reflection of 1960's boardroom mentality, *"It was her own geometry that bothered me – I didn't want distracted directors playing footsie"*

Jean Harvey plays Mrs Lovell with a touch of light operetta, but would still have made an intriguing opponent for Wilder as Minister. Unfortunately, Wilfred Greatorex's script reflects the level at which women were generally regarded in the 1960's. Deborah Grant, as Wilder's secretary turns the tables by sexually taunting Jason Fowler when they're alone in Wilder's office, while a 60-year-old French aviation industry expert proposes a night on the town to Kane's secretary (Caroline John, who would soon be assisting the new *Doctor Who*, Jon Pertwee).

Pamela Wilder indulges in some mild flirtation with Lincoln Dowling when he reveals his jealousy over her lunch date with Kane. In publicity for the series, Wilfred Greatorex acknowledged that Dowling and Pamela's romance had originally been intended as a passing affair. However, once he saw how the actors played it, the decision had been made to take the romance further. A struggle to see if Dowling's fingers are *"pudgy"* while drawing up her social diary nearly turns into a kiss before Wilder walks into the room with Mrs Lovell.

Pamela tells Kane that Wilder *"Wouldn't join your party if you gave him the powers of Cromwell."* Kane replies, *"Hasn't he caught the Oliver C virus? Spreading worse than Hong Kong Flu?"* (Patrick

Wymark had, of course, played Cromwell in *The Cruel Necessity* (1962*), Royalist and Roundhead* (1966) and *Witchfinder General* (1968) while both Wymark and Michael Jayston would appear in Ken Hughes' *Cromwell* (1970) filmed soon after *The Power Game*).

Patrick Wymark seems to play a lot of this episode in "quotation marks" overemphasising his reactions for comic effect. But this is one of the two episodes of this series to make reference to Wilder's previous life in *The Plane Makers*. Wymark conveys a rare enthusiasm as he and Henderson meet up with Simon Davey (Robert McBain) a previously unseen executive at Scott Furlong who is developing a new executive jet.

As Wilder admires the aircraft blueprints, Simon Davey asks him if he'd ever go back to the airline industry. Wilder says only when he has a European set up that can smash in on the Americans. *"I think that's what you've missed John all these years. The challenge of keeping 20,000 people in work."* It's certainly the most engrossed Wilder has appeared for a long time.

Although Scott Furlong is almost tied up in a German co-production, Wilder suggests showing the plans to the French, using them as bait to force the German's hand while Wilder takes care of any anti-German prejudice on our side. *"You sure that's all John? Nothing more to it?"* Wilder looks him frankly in the eye. *"What else could there be?"*

Wilder subtly initiates negotiations with the French, ensuring that Kane's finds out on the grapevine, so that it is Kane who brings up the subject with Wilder, telling him he could hasten a deal with France."

As Prescott and Kane entertain the French to drinks, Dowling drafts a letter of complaint from Scott Furlong about this French interference which Simon Davey signs. This is sent to the Foreign Secretary with an accompanying memo from Wilder (also drafted by Dowling).

Prescott gets a phone call from the Foreign Secretary telling him they're potentially botching a big deal with the Germans that could be signed today. For Prescott it's a fatal blow, but Kane has been helping the Whips hold off *"a half dozen recalcitrants"* from attacking the Government.

Meeting with the Chief Whip, Kane shows grudging respect for Wilder's trap, but learns that his persuasive manner with the rebels has won him the post of Minister."

Kane calls on Wilder at home and tells him he might well offer him a drink. *"After all, I did come here. As your new Minister I could have well sent for you."*

Tuesday 18 March 1969   ***Drinks On Sunday***

Writer Peter Draper   **Director Robert Tronson.**

Patrick Wymark (Sir John Wilder). Barrie Ingham (Garfield Kane). Barbara Murray (Pamela, Lady Wilder). Jack Watling (Don Henderson) . Michael Jayston (Lincoln Dowling). Richard Hurndall (Sir Jason Fowler). Deborah Grant (Jill). John Sterland (Littlejohn). George Roubicek (Papajay). Juliet Kempson (Suky). Anne Jameson (Mirabelle Wentworth).

"I've been a civil servant far too long to commit myself to anything so bold as a judgement." Jason Fowler.

Sir John Wilder is entertaining Littlejohn (John Sterland) and Papajay (George Roubicek), two American Treasury officials who have arrived ahead of next week's negotiations on solar energy. As Minister for Special Situations and Trade, Garfield Kane (Barrie Ingham) should know what they are doing, but he and Deputy Under Secretary Jason Fowler (Richard Hurndall) are equally in the dark. They hope to learn something when Wilder brings the Americans to a Sunday lunchtime drinks party organised by Mirabelle Wentworth (Anne James). But Don Henderson (Jack Watling) and Lincoln

Dowling (Michael Jayston) are under orders to keep make sure Kane doesn't catch the Americans alone.

When Wilder takes the Americans to lunch, Lincoln Dowling invites Lady Wilder (Barbara Murray) back to his flat to watch an old film on TV. But a sleepy Sunday afternoon suddenly becomes compromising

Peter Draper delivers an entertaining script, which probably owes its plot to the input of script editor Wilfred Greatorex. Previous episodes had touched upon the decline of the American-led Bretton Woods financial exchange system, and this episode picks up on the resultant strained relations between Washington and Paris. In the world of *The Power Game* though, nothing is ever as straightforward as it seems. A British scientist has developed a new photovoltaic cell and motor array which can cut the costs of solar energy by a fifth. There are only two factories capable of developing the system – one in France, the other in Germany. Wilder supports the German bid, while Francophile Kane supports the other. The question is, which way will the Americans go?

Now established as Minister for Special Situations and Trade, Garfield Kane is finding it as difficult as his predecessor did to determine just what Wilder is playing at. Unlike Caswell Bligh, Kane is an experienced back-bencher, respectful of the civil servant's power to obstruct a Minister's ambitions and willing to make use of their intelligence. Jason Fowler warns him that, *"Wilder doesn't really care, you know, whether the contract goes to the French or the Germans. What he wants, as always is that he shall be on the winning horse and you, preferably, will be on the loser".*

Dowling learns that the two Americans are not from the American Treasury, but from the foreign economics department of Central Intelligence. Littlejohn (John Sterland) and Papajay (George Roubicek) are depicted as an amusing double act. Their surnames sound like codenames and it's never clear how sincere their exchanges are. Littlejohn describes Papajay as a chauvinist, and Papajay retorts that *"Mr Littlejohn wishes he'd been born European."* Littlejohn admits to admiring European culture, which Papajay finds *"Admirable but dead".* Littlejohn closes the conversation by saying, *"I never think it's polite to tell people their culture is dead. Especially when it's an admirable culture."*

Dowling tries and fails to get advice from Professor Mobbs (*from The Goose Chase*) but Littlejohn signals that he's aware of Dowling's connection, asking after Mobbs and saying, *"I hear there's been quite a few changes at MI6. I hear they even considered installing a computer. But only if it makes tea."*

While Dowling takes Pamela Wilder (Barbara Murray) out for lunch, Jason Fowler and Don Henderson are stranded in Whitehall with post drinks gloom. Henderson refers to Barbara Castle's 1967 introduction of the breathalyser saying he's *"too slightly sloshed to risk the breathalyser on the M4"* (the Motorway only extended as far as Maidenhead at this time) and invites Fowler to lunch at a nice little restaurant in Pimlico that he knows. Unfortunately, there is no mention of his wife (Jane Sofiano having gone over to the BBC to play a regular character *in The Power Game's* main competitor, *The Troubleshooters*) and Don only expresses a quiet wistfulness that he doesn't get to take Pamela for lunch.

The most significant development comes after lunch when Dowling invites Pamela back to his flat to watch an old film on TV. Although they kiss, things don't go much further because Pamela answers Dowling's phone and hears Wilder's voice. He's back at the office and asks to speak with Dowling, wanting to know where Dowling keeps a security file. Unsure whether Wilder has recognised her voice, Pamela returns home to prepare for another party in honour of the Americans. Unknown to the guilty couple, Kane had driven to Dowling's flat with the intention of questioning him about the Americans and has spotted Pamela's car with her distinctive hat slung on the rear window.

Dowling is summoned to the party and both he and Pamela are in a state of tension as to whether Wilder knows it was Pamela. Wilder doesn't ease the tension when he tells Pamela, *"Did you know Lincoln has a Sunday secretary? I rang him this afternoon and a girl answered."* He turns to Dowling and asks *"Who was she Lincoln?"*. Dowling bluffs that it was just a friend, but Wilder's behaviour suggests he knows or suspects. Even if he doesn't, Garfield Kane has already told Dowling that he was passing his flat earlier, *"Did Lady Wilder lend you her car? I noticed it outside."*

The issue is left hanging, as Wilder answers Kane and Dowling's curiosity about the reason for the American's visit. Their system appears quite rational – chauvinistic Papajay and Europhile Littlejohn prepare two separate reports and then a third party prepares a *"Readers Digest"* version for the decision-makers. However, Fowler has warned Kane that *"A very great deal of American foreign policy is based on emotionalism."*

When Wilder and Papajay had discussed the merits of the French and German factories, Wilder gave an economic argument for German reliability – *"Germany is set on a clear road for ten years."* Interestingly, even though there is American investment in the German factory, when Wilder argues that the French communist party is strong (and therefore may interfere with productivity), Papajay counters that the communists *"are conservative – their part in the student riots showed this."* (the communists supported the wildcat strikes but denounced the student leaders.)

Eventually Wilder discerns that the American interest is much more focussed. The new solar motor can be used to drive a tank and will be particularly useful in developing nations with more than four hours sunshine a day. The Americans would really prefer that the British scientist takes his invention to the United States. But if he insists on staying in Europe, they are concerned that the owner of the French factory has a son in the communist party. As in *The Plane Makers* episodes *It's A Free Country Isn't It?* and *A Question of Sources* the economic concerns are outweighed by the political.

The security file of Dowling's which Wilder was so anxious to consult highlights the French factory owner as a risk. As Wilder tells Kane, *"If your great grandmother waved at Karl Marx out of a bus they'd underline your name in red."*

Kane realises that Wilder has backed the winning horse – if the scientist can't be persuaded to go to America, the British Government will support the German bid.

For Pamela and Dowling, the consequences of the afternoon are left unspoken. As Pamela says, *"It was quite an innocent afternoon really – all things considered."*

The establishing scenes of this episode are set against the opening of the long-running BBC Radio show *Family Favourites* (credited at the end *"by permission of BBC Radio"*). This episode will probably have extra nostalgic value for anyone who is old enough to remember sitting down to Sunday lunch as *Family Favourites* was playing. Although often remembered as *"Two Way Family Favourites"* with requests played for service men stationed in Germany, by 1969 it had expanded to *"Worldwide Family Favourites"*. Michael Aspel gives the introduction *"In Britain it's twelve noon, in Canada it's 6am, in Australia it's 9pm. Time once again for Worldwide Family Favourites"*. The excerpt plays James Last's 1966 cover version of *Lara's Theme* and Manfred Mann's 1967 hit *"Ha Ha Said the Clown"*. Bill Paull from Canadian Broadcasting is also heard and the soundtrack does create a very strong sense of time and place. It would probably have had an even greater effect at the time of transmission when it was still part of the Sunday lunchtime ritual.

It would probably also be too much to read anything into the fact that Littlejohn is sitting in one of the Eero Aarnio designed ball chairs used in *The Prisoner* when he questions Dowling. Having said that, John Sterland and Patrick Wymark previously worked together in the BBC production of *Brand* starring Patrick McGoohan.

George Roubicek, who voiced *The Count of Monte Cristo* in the Halas and Batchelor cartoon series, also appeared as the space captain in the classic *Dr Who* serial, *"The Tomb of the Cybermen"*.

Garfield Kane is shown hanging on original Mondrian on his office wall. In contrast to Caswell Bligh for whom paintings were an investment to hold his wealth in his bank vaults and pass on to his grandsons, Kane is an enthusiast. He tells Fowler he's traded up from a small watercolour in the same way as a car owner starting with a clapped-out old Ford. When Fowler suggests he *"get a man"* in to hang the painting, Kane says he prefers to do it himself, saying it's the only chance you get to touch the painting.

Party guest Suky looks remarkably like Sally Geeson (who would play Sid James' daughter in *Bless This House*) but is actually Juliet Kempson who later played Sid James' daughter in the one-off special *All This And Christmas Too* (1971).

Tuesday 25 March 1969   *Triangles*

Writer Peter Draper   **Director Cyril Coke.**

Patrick Wymark (Sir John Wilder). Barrie Ingham (Garfield Kane). Barbara Murray (Pamela, Lady Wilder). Jack Watling (Don Henderson) . Michael Jayston (Lincoln Dowling). Richard Hurndall (Sir Jason Fowler). Deborah Grant (Jill). James Cossins (Candleford). Arthur Brough (Walter Hallam). David Healy (Edmans). John Ringham (Leehouse). Yvonne Mayal (Stripper). Barry Wilsher (agent).

"John, if you don't get out of my hair, I may well break your back." *Garfield Kane.*

When Fowler informs Dowling that he's been promoted to the Embassy in Jakarta, Dowling is unsure whether Kane or Wilder is trying to move him out of the way.

Wilder convinces Dowling that they have a common cause in undermining Kane. Dowling's security contacts follow Kane to Paris, where he meets a French Maoist and the owner of a Chinese binocular factory at a safe house run by French counter intelligence. When Dowling has to justify that use of resources to MI6 officer Leehouse (John Ringham) he explicitly suggests that Kane is conspiring with communist agents. Draper shows that power can be misused, not for any grand malign purpose but for a combination of small bad decisions.

The plot centres on the "strategic list" which prevents trade with communist nations in goods that may be of military use. The list has featured in previous episodes - Caswell Bligh was undermining it *in Trade Secret* and it scuppers Wilder's plans in *Standard Practice*. American envoy Edmans (David Healey) defends the list, saying America could not send men into action in Vietnam while undermining them in trade. But Garfield Kane says, *"You could draw up a strategic list that prohibits the export of chewing gum."* Kane reveals that he was *"asked or told"* at the highest levels to get the "strategic list" amended. Britain is trying to be both a commercial and political power – but if you don't have commercial power you lose political power.

As we have seen, Britain in 1969 was under intense economic pressure. The American commitment to sustain Europe's exchange range mechanism was in doubt. Two attempts to join the Common Market had been vetoed by France. Kane's meeting Chinese with the knowledge of French security services indicates an attempt – not just to open up trade – but also win favour with a belligerent European neighbour.

However, Wilder tells Kane that, *"this absurd scheme had no chance of ever getting off the ground (because the Americans are) not only a military power. They're a commercial power."* In Wilder's view America is protecting its commercial interests and must be dealt with like any other competitor. In the end, both Kane and Wilder agree with America that optical equipment will stay on the "strategic list" in return for opening up other items.

The most shocking scene in this episode comes when Dowling tries to enlist Jason Fowler's aid in stopping Wilder and Kane from "tearing the Department apart." Dowling locates Fowler in a strip club *(" a minor lunchtime sin").* The Deputy Under Secretary is surprised to see Dowling *("I didn't know you were a drinker of darkness, Lincoln.")* He's then unsettled when he realises that people know he frequents the club. Fowler is momentarily aggravated when Dowling tries to talk about Wilder and Kane's squabbles and then reveals to Dowling that he is *"incurably not well,* "with *a condition that is, "irreversible – rather like politics."*

Fowler tells Lincoln that while the condition is not immediate, he's been advised to *"put his house in order"* and summarises his house as, *"Eight leather-bound first editions of the Waverley Novels, 100 minor editions, and the good lady Mrs Hatley, who prepares my food, my bed and cleans my bath every morning.* "He says that when he gets home, *"It always seems to be dark. I have to switch on all the lights. It's as if she's saving up all the electricity somewhere in a box for some great, bright day when all the lights of the world go on."*

Throughout the scene, dreamlike music accompanies the stripper (Yvonne Mayol) creating an otherworldly mood. Fowler gazes at the girl and questions the attempts to make the performance erotic. *"I don't know what I want – a wife, a mistress, or a daughter. So stupid to have missed all three."*

Fowler's final scene in the episode shows him returning home after Dowling has refused his invitation to dinner – stood in the vast, quiet hallway of a Georgian townhouse, Fowler calls out to his housekeeper. Getting no answer, he switches on the lights and slowly climbs the stairs.

In the first half of the show, Dowling has to decide whether to accept Ken Bligh's offer of a directorship in one of his companies.

When he tells Pamela that it will mean spending two years in Canada she agrees that, *"We are coming rapidly to a decision."* The threat of the Foreign Office posting to Jakarta adds further pressure. Pamela agrees to uproot her whole life, leave Wilder and join Dowling in Canada. But when the threat of the posting is removed, Dowling is less inclined to jump into the private sector. Pamela is disillusioned to find that Dowling is as self-centred as her husband.

The song which the disappointed Pamela listens to in her car journey with Wilder during the final scene is *Scarborough Fair* by English folk singer Deena Webster. The cover-version of the tradition folk song about impossible demands of a love (popularised by Simon and Garfunkel) was arranged by Barbara Moore and released on Parlaphone on 18 October 1968.

James Cossins had played a cousin of Pamela's in the second series, but here is disguised by an outrageous pair of sideboards as the absurd MP Candleford. A self-satisfied buffoon, Candleford is used to raise questions in the House about the strategic list so that Kane can be seen as responding to the will of Parliament. Rhodes Boyson, an extravagantly side boarded MP of the Thatcher government was still a headmaster at the time this made, but it is possible that Candleford was inspired by the exotically-moustached Sir Gerald Nabarro. Berating *"long-haired layabouts"* he is challenged about his own hair and tells Wilder, *"I always say you should earn your whiskers."* He is contrasted with Walter Hallam (Arthur Brough), chair of the Aviation Engineers Association who says he calls one long-haired employees *"Lady Godiva",* but says there's no-one better to do air frame analysis. Looking after Candleford at an Association dinner, Hallam confides to Wilder that, *"He makes me want to grow my hair down to my blasted boots if I could!*

There are hints in this episode that Wilder is beginning to tire of the diplomatic world. At first it seems Wilder is challenging Dowling when he observes how much time the younger man spends with his wife. But then Wilder allows –*"One meets too few people who seem absorbed in the things that interest oneself. When one does one tends to cling on to them. I always wished I could have met more such people."*

After dining with Walter Hallam, he tells Pamela that, *"I think it's the most pleasant thing that's happened to me this week. It made me want to go back into Aircraft.*

Tuesday 1 April 1969   *Mergers*

Writer Wilfred Greatorex   **Director David Reid.**

Patrick Wymark (Sir John Wilder). Barrie Ingham (Garfield Kane). Barbara Murray (Pamela, Lady Wilder). Jack Watling (Don Henderson) . Michael Jayston (Lincoln Dowling). Richard Hurndall (Sir Jason Fowler). Ernest Clark (Frank Orwell). Andre Maranne (Cartier). John Serret (Masson). Richard Aylen (Carey). Paul Bacon (Wendall). George Belbin (Norton) Helen Dorward (Jane).

"Wilder's about as capable of being inactive as Vesuvius." Garfield Kane.

Garfield Kane (Barrie Ingham) the Minister for Special Situations and Trade, has isolated his Ambassador Sir John Wilder, leaving him with no work to do. Kane knows Wilder has too many friends in Cabinet to sack him, but hopes enforced idleness will trigger some indiscretion. Kane pressures Wilder's assistant Don Henderson (Jack Watling) to keep him advised of Wilder's actions.

Kane also offers Wilder's official secretary Lincoln Dowling (Michael Jayston) a contract to leave the Civil Service and join an Anglo-French consortium he's setting up with Frank Orwell (Ernest Clark) of National Electric to win contracts in developing countries. Kane is aware of Dowling's relationship with Pamela Wilder (Barbara Murray) and suggests she's more likely to leave Wilder if Dowling is on an inflated salary with the consortium.

It's either ironic, or another instance of the loose script editing in *One Via Zurich* that Don Henderson criticises Kane's treatment of Wilder saying, *"I suppose you learned that when you were a business consultant – leaving someone so far out on a limb that they resign out of boredom.*" Ironic because this was a strategy of Wilder's at Scott Furlong. It was so well-known that it even had a name – Wilder's Island Game.

Kane attempts to subvert Don Henderson just as the Bligh's had done in previous series. Once again Jack Watling plays along so guilelessly that he credibly raises doubts as to whether Henderson has betrayed Wilder. Watling has been an exceptional "non-verbal" performer throughout *The Plane Makers* and *The Power Game*. His reactions in this final episode as Kane forces him to endure a meeting in a sauna are amusing, although it's questionable whether Don is affecting his discomfort in the same way that he overplayed his drunken-ness in Magalia. Certainly, Don manages to drop the false information Wilder wanted before making his hurried exit from the steam bath.

Kane's proposed joint venture between National Electric and Electroniques Francaise is conceived as a strategy for co-operating in bids for contracts in developing markets, rather than competing. With the Anglo-French Concorde having just completed its first flight, co-operation between the two countries was firmly in the public mind, but Kane's proposed consortium would have been aimed firmly at the vital export market. Unfortunately, at the end of part one, Wilder tells Lincoln Dowling, *"That consortium is not going to happen. I have a better idea."*

Wilder's "better idea" is to organise a merger between National Electric and a rival firm owned by Norton (George Belbin). Carey (Richard Aylen) of the Commercial Reconstruction Board supports the idea as a *"natural marriage"*. Wilder says it promises cost reduction and vastly increased exports. Wendell (Paul Bacon) of National Electric worries that his fellow board members will, *"see their muddled old heads rolling in the City of London."* He says Orwell will fight, three of the younger Board members will agree immediately, and *"others are open to persuasion, provided they can be promised places on the new combined Board."*

Wilder ironically asks Dowling to pass the Armagnac as he negotiates the deal that will sink the Anglo-French consortium.

The deal is reminiscent of the 1967 takeover of Associated Electrical Industries by Arnold Weinstock's General Electric Corporation. The takeover had financial support from the Industrial Reorganisation Commission under Tony Benn, who had been charged by Harold Wilson with creating "national champions" capable of competing on world markets.

Dowling is wary of both Kane and Wilder's offers. He questions whether Kane will honour the offer of a job with the consortium once he's resigned from the Foreign Office, and knows Wilder has dealt vindictively with his wife's lovers before. When Wilder warns Dowling that the tightrope he's walking between himself and Kane could be yanked away, Dowling replies that he's got a safety net. In the end, MI6 provides a Deus Ex Machina to resolve Dowling's dilemma. A voiceover tells Dowling that, *"Whether we get the British merger or the Anglo-French Consortium is academic. But it is important that we penetrate an organisation of that size selling military equipment and electronics to other foreign powers."*

Wilder is confirmed as Managing Director of the merged company, but Dowling is imposed on him as a director. Earlier in the episode, Wilder had told Dowling that, *"with a little bit of practice, you may not look out of place behind a cigar."* At the episode end, Wilder offers Dowling a cigar and tells him he'll find a cutter on the drinks table. *"That's all right, "* Dowling says, *"I have my own now."* The episode ends with the hysterical laughter of Pamela Wilder, who realises that her chance to redeem Dowling has passed, and he has become another Wilder.

Afterword:

Writing in the *TV Times* the following week, Anthony Davies observed that ATV had tempted fate with *The Power Game*. There was the danger of a flop, but although the ratings varied, it had reached number one at times, being viewed in seven million homes.

At the end it had an estimated 6.5 million homes in its closing weeks, maintaining a loyal audience that kept it in the Top 20.

Davis noted that, *"the stage is set for another series, with a new antagonist for Wilder in his erstwhile assistant. And with the triangle of the two men and Pamela unresolved."*

Speaking in the *TV Times* Wymark said that, *"I shall miss John Wilder. It's a wonderful part and I have really enjoyed it. After all this time I have got to know him pretty well. There are rumours of another Power Game, but nothing has been decided. In the right circumstances I'd do another series and I'm certainly not fed up with Wilder."*

While popular with the viewers, Patrick Wymark's fondness for a liquid lunch made the logistics of building a series around him increasingly difficult. Rex Firkin admitted that, *"Pat didn't know why he was now adored...He didn't know how he did it every week and every week we were asking him to do it again."*

Speaking at a convention, Michael Jayston recalled that while there were plans for another series of *The Power Game*, it would probably have been reworked to star Barrie Ingham. Out-manoeuvred by Wilder, Garfield Kane had calmly resigned as Minister, but was unlikely to have settled for defeat. Barrie Ingham had delivered a controlled, charismatic performance throughout the final few episodes of the series, and at the time of Wymark's death in October 1970 was starting rehearsals as a ruthless arms dealer in Wilfred Greatorex's 1971 series *Hine*.

If *The Power Game* had returned, the next series would have been in colour, which might have ensured repeat screenings and even the retention of the tapes by ATV. Sadly, it was not to be. But *The Power Game* did go out on a high with a strong final episode looking forward to the dominance of professional managers.

David Reid would go on to produce prestige productions such as *The Strauss Family* and become ATV's head of drama.

In November 1970, the *TV Times* published a letter from Ronald Eddowes of Guildford, Surrey, *"Normally, I am against repeats...but I and many of my friends are baffled why ITV has not commemorated the late Patrick Wymark by a repeat showing of The Plane Makers and The Power Game. It would be a fitting tribute to one of the biggest stars ever made by TV."*

In response, the *TV Times* said, *"The same suggestion has come from many sources but ATV say, 'Most of the tapes of The Power oGame have been wiped. Not enough are left to do justice to the original series.'"*.

Happily, this was not entirely correct. On Saturday 10 January 1987 Channel Four began a repeat screening of the first series of *The Power Game*.

In 2005, Network DVD released box sets of the first two series of *The Power Game*. At the time, the third series was thought to be lost but in 2007, fair quality ITC export prints were discovered and released. In 2010 and 2011, the second series of *The Plane Makers* was put out on DVD in two box sets. As with *The Power Game*, the previously "lost" third series was rediscovered and released in 2013.

As of writing, the legacy continues with the retro-Supermarionation series *Nebula 75* paying homage to Wilder and Scott Furlong in the episode, *For the Ashes of His Fathers* .

Why were *The Plane Makers* and *The Power Game* so successful? It's impossible to say for sure. There was nothing new about the ingredients. Patrick Wymark had already played a press baron for the BBC. ITV had run plays with a business background. Books and films about the executive suite were already established enough for some critics to call *The Plane Makers* 'old hat'.

Arguably the success was due to Firkin's long-range planning, Greatorex's all-day script conferences with the writers and the extensive rehearsal period given the actors and director. This was only possible because Lew Grade and Bill Ward let Firkin go into production without a clear idea of the finished product. Their decision to continue with *The Plane Makers*, even though the first series had fallen short of expectations, was also bold.

If Grade and Ward's attitude anticipates the 'Agile' philosophy of *"fail fast, fail often"* it may also seem remarkably uneconomic to 21st Century eyes. But, if it is true that Grade regarded domestic tv shows as "turnover product" – something to fill the schedules in order to bring in the advertising revenue – it makes more sense. And Bill Ward's legendary verbal harangues for the producer at the end of transmission hardly suggests an air of complacency.

And if the 1960's approach seems uneconomic, it can hardly be less so than the 21st Century approach to TV described by David Graeber in *Bullshit Jobs* (1), where projects are endlessly stalled. *"The longer the process takes, the greater the excuse for the endless multiplication of intermediary positions, and the more money is siphoned off before it has any chance to get to those doing the actual work."*

The fact is that millions of viewers tuned in to the World of Wilder, and like the critics, they loved it. When all's said and done, it was a magic trick.

Notes:

1 GRAEBER, DAVID. Bullshit Jobs (2018) Penguin, page 187

Wilder as a Manager or a Leader

"There was a time when John was about the best boss possible to have." **Don Henderson**

The preceding pages cover the two distinct phases of Sir John Wilder's career. In *The Plane Makers* he was established at Scott Furlong, making a product that people wanted to buy. Even his enemies acknowledged his positive contribution to the aviation industry. He was also keenly conscious of 20,000 men depending on him for their living.

In *The Power Game*, he moved into new worlds of banking, construction and politics. Wilder has less expertise, other than transferable skills (he is able to put together a tender document in one night, when it should take days). With more emphasis on personal gain, the projects Wilder champions are interchangeable means to an end. There is an assumption of corruption and inefficiency and it's not clear if anything that he works on benefits anyone but himself.

In attempting to walk in Wilder's footsteps, it's important to see the link between the two phases of his career.

As Charles Handy noted, the period from 1950 to 1976 saw, *"the emergence of 'the manager' as a recognised occupational role in society."* (1) One of the biggest questions that emerged was whether the best managers were those who had an expertise within an industry and were promoted to management, or those who had no occupational expertise but possessed a set of skills which could be applied to any situation.

In, *I Think I'll Manage* (1997) Dr George Sik looked at the specialist manager whose success or failure is manifestly evident every Saturday: the football manager. The question of whether former star players made better managers than 'backroom boys' seemed to be answered by the results. *"The two most successful managers in this season...came from the older tradition of working their way up through coaching and assisting existing managers, rather than being thrown in at the deep end."* (2)

But that wasn't the end of the story. Along with deep tactical understanding, the managers also needed, *"strong self-belief and optimism (and) the need to win at all costs!"*

For Wilder, his technical knowledge in the airline industry gave him an edge, but once he was cast out of that industry, it was his self-belief and need to win which carried him through.

"I want that production contract; the Minister's slip of paper. The £40 million ticket. And I want it now!" John Wilder, The Island Game.

In The Myth of the Strong Leader (2014), Archie Brown points out that, *"the more power is accumulated in just one leader's hands, the more that leader comes to believe in his own unrivalled judgement."* (3) Abraham observed that many managers *"prefer to reply on their own intuition – euphemistically known as 'common sense,"* (4) As an avid reader of C.P. Snow, Wilder would have been well aware of Snow's *Science and Government* (1960), in which the potentially disastrous consequences of one single scientist gaining Churchill's confidence and over-ruling opposing opinion were outlined. *"He believed that he could solve any problem by his own thought. This is the commonest delusion of clever men with bad judgement. For anything like reasonable judgement, a man has to know when to rely on others.*" (5)

But Brown, Abraham and Snow are writing about what is best for their country and best for their fellow-men. Wilder's only concern is what is best for Wilder.

If you are going to follow in the footsteps of Wilder, you must put aside any considerations of public service or philanthropy. It's all for one and one for one.

NOTES:

1 HANDY, CHARLES. Understanding Organisations, page 92

2 SIK, GEORGE. I Think I'll Manage, page 244

3 BROWN, ARCHIE. The Myth of the Strong Leader, page 9

4 ABRAHAM, NEVILLE. Big Business and Government, page 91

5 SNOW, C.P. Science and Government, page 125

The Indispensable Miss Lingard

*"More women in high places can only be good for organizations
can only be good for organizations as well as in line with natural
justice, but the stage has not yet been reached where I could
credibly write 'she' and ask the reader to assume 'he or she'."*
Charles Handy, Understanding Organizations, 3rd Edition (1985).

In the 1960's the world of management was overwhelmingly male.
Even Laura Challis is a kind of exalted personal assistant *("Sir
Gordon uses her like a spoon to stir up trouble, "* says one
character). An organisation of Scott Furlong's size maintained a
large pool of typist/secretaries of varying levels of skill. The duties
of a secretary were varied, but in the 1960's they could be summed
up as *"keeping the boss happy."*

In *The Plane* Makers episode, *The Flying Frigates*, Raymond
Bowers uses the secretaries to reflect the characters of their bosses.
Don Henderson's secretary Trilby (Chip Coveney) laughs at his
flustered reaction to Wilder's unannounced return. Elizabeth
Wallace as Harriet Evans grows increasingly annoyed as the
fastidious Corbett makes several false starts dictating a letter. And
Norma Ronald plays Kay Lingard with cat-like amusement as she
watches Wilder keeping Corbett waiting while he signs a series of
letters.

Miss Lingard marks the distinction between a secretary and a
personal assistant. A combination wife and mother, she knows
where all Wilder's bodies are buried.

Although there were rumours in her second episode, *Don't Stick
Your Head Out* that Lingard's relationship with Wilder was slightly
too personal, the rumours were proved to be wide of the mark.
Lingard did, however, prove to be a most effective personal
assistant, anticipating Wilder's demands and acting as gate-keeper.
Despite being firm with interlopers, she could also be warm and
sympathetic. It's Lingard who points out to Arthur Sugden in *A
Condition of Sale* that his own secretary Margie is too ill to work

and sends her home. She also tries to soften the blow to the distressed Philip Hammond, waiting hopelessly for an audience with Wilder in *How Do You Vote*. But *A Condition of Sale* also shows Miss Lingard is coolly aware of what it takes to get on in the business world, and firmly resourceful in threatening situations. Although some episodes could relegate Miss Lingard to a virtual voice-over, announcing visitors over the tannoy, Norma Ronald was always effective.

Not surprisingly, when Sir John Wilder left the aircraft industry for Bligh Construction in *The Power Game*, Miss Lingard followed him. Once again, she showed herself Wilder's firm ally, backing him up in his fight back against a conspiracy in *Confound Their Politics* and later advising Wilder on his personal care in *Tax Return* when his wife leaves him. This episode also shows the personal sacrifices Lingard makes for Wilder when she delays a date to work late for him.

Norma Ronald was born in Northumberland in 1937. An actress since the age of 15, she met her first husband, David Butler at Joan Littlewood's Theatre Workshop.

In 1962 she established the role of gormless teenage secretary Mildred Murfin in the BBC radio comedy series, *The Men From The Ministry*. The series, which ran from 1962 to 1977 starred Richard Murdoch, Wilfred Hyde White and later Deryck Guyler as incompetent Whitehall civil servants.

In February 1965, following the end of *The Plane Makers,* Norma Ronald joined Frank Berry as host of *Night Spot*, a late-night variety series from Rediffusion set in a real night club. In her personal life Norma Ronald divorced in 1966, and the same year married Edward Judd (star of *The Day The Earth Caught Fire*) whose first wife, actress Gene Anderson had died in 1965.

Norma Ronald continued to work on radio, appearing in *Doctor in the House* (with Richard Briars as Simon Sparrow) in July and August 1968 . This may have been instrumental in Kay Lingard not appearing in the final series of *The Power Game*, which commenced production in August 1968.

However, the role of Miss Lingard did result in Gerry Anderson, a fan of *The Power Game*, casting Norma Ronald as Pam Kirby, secretary to Wymark's Jason Webb in the movie *Doppelganger*. She then continued into Anderson's TV series *UFO* as Miss Ealand.

In 1974, Norma Ronald appeared in the BBC Radio 2 series *Husband of the Year*. Organised in co-operation with local newspapers all over Britain, the series was a contest to find the most resourceful, tactful and loving husband of the year. Contestants were grilled by a panel of celebrities and also had to get themselves out of tricky situations in hypothetical scenarios performed by *"everybody's wife, Norma Ronald."*

The show transferred to ITV in 1975, where radio host Macdonald Hobley was replaced by Pete Murray. Norma once again appeared as the uber-Wife putting husbands to the test.

Preferring radio to on-screen performances Norma continued to appear in radio plays such as Ian Cullen's *Angel of the Deep* (1976) and re-united Peter Jeffrey in Wally K Daley's *What's Stigmata?* Jeffrey also starred as Acting Chief Constable Colonel Manton in a BBC Radio 4 adaptation of Kingsley Amis' *"The Riverside Villas Murder"* (26 June 1976). Norma Ronald starred as Mrs Trevelyan, the seductive neighbour of the teenage narrator. She also provided other vocal performances such as an adaptation of Spike Milligan's *Puckoon* for Columbia Records in 1980. Her last TV role was as the voice of the alien parent in *Chocky's Challenge* (1986). Sadly, Norma Ronald died in Clara Vale, Tyneside in 1993.

Wilder's World – For Serious Players Only

"You can almost feel their breath on the back of your neck already." John Wilder.

Most readers can happily skip the following chapter. Only those who are committed to following in the footsteps of Sir John Wilder need pay attention.

The lesson to take from this chapter is that while Sir John Wilder was operating in a very different world from that of 2022, his basic tactics still apply. In some ways, Sir John was ahead of his time.

As far as management education goes, Sir John Wilder's world ends in 1969. That means no Tom Peters on Excellence, or Chaos or Soft Stuff. No Kenichi Ohmae on strategy, no Michael Porter on competitive advantage, No Hofstede on culture. No Charles Handy analysing what organisations do, or Sir John Harvey-Jones applying the lessons learned in steering the now long-defunct Imperial Chemical Industries to world leadership. Definitely no *Wisdom of Psychopaths.*

At his core, Sir John Wilder is summed up by the union chief Bessiter as: *"a man who gets things done by a kind of selfish brute force."*

But there's a definite technique to applying that force.

Environmental Audit: Wilder's World

To use Sir John Wilder's weapons, you must understand that, while the world of the 1960's was very different, his tactics will never date.

In his first episode of *The Plane Makers*, Sir John Wilder has to arrange ahead-of-time to receive an overseas telephone call with insider information. Today he would receive that information on a burner phone. But the use he makes of that information would not change. Don't be deceived into thinking there is anything quaint about Wilder's World.

The Money Men

"Like all money men. He expects to find portents in statistics", says Bessiter (1), the union chief, of banker Sir Gordon Revidge, *"He's no different from a stone age soothsayer, breaking bones, throwing the bits up in the air and expecting the Gods to blow them down in prophetic patterns."*

The Plane Makers and *The Power Game* take place in the Britain of the 1960's, when both Conservative and Labour governments tried to control the economy *"to avoid a repetition of the Great Depression of 1929-1932,"* and the protectionism and devaluation that followed (2).

At the time, there was an undercurrent emerging from Chicago – encouraged by a belief that economics is a natural, rather than a moral science. It would not find full expression in Britain until 1970 when economist Milton Friedman popularised the idea that, *"the social responsibility of business is to increase its profits."* Over the next 50 years, the Chicago view of life as a competition between selfish individuals infiltrated economic thought until it became mainstream. As Jonathan Aldred put it, *"we've been encouraged to believe things about how we should behave – ideas about trust, justice, fairness have been transformed."* (3)

But in some ways, John Wilder anticipated the monetarist viewpoint. While it is unlikely that he would have believed it had an objective scientific basis, he clearly believed in life as a contest in which there could only be one winner.

Britain in the 1960's

Despite the 1950's humiliation of Suez, Britain itself still had a delusion of global influence. James Cameron-Grant MP has to remind a TV audience of Britain's declining power in the episode, *Other People Own Our Jungles Now*.

Britain had come out of the Second World War in debt, with the Government still forced to exert economic controls. Food rationing did not end until 1954, the same year that the ban on private housebuilding was removed.

Both Conservative and Labour Governments believed in the state modernising and controlling the economy. Free market critics on the right, *"(who) had severe reservations about the increasingly interventionist economic stances"* of both parties would have to wait 25 years for the influence of Hayek and Friedman to turn "reality" around. (4).

In the 1960's, the fashionable obsession was on the physical and non-merchandise trade deficit, as opposed to the 21st Century where monetarist thinking has led everyone to obsess over Government Budget Deficits.

In 1964, Conservative Keynesian Chancellor Reginald Maudling attempted to *"raise the productivity of the economy permanently"* when he cut taxes and increased spending in his "dash for growth" policy.

After the 1964 general election, the incoming Labour chancellor Jim Callaghan was faced with inheriting a prospective balance of payments deficit of £800 million. While the logical answer may have been to devalue the pound, it was politically unacceptable. National Insurance contributions, taxes and duties were increased, but in November 1967 the government was forced to devalue the pound.

Callaghan's rival, George Brown was appointed to a newly created Ministry, the Department of Economic Affairs, where he spent two years trying to convince employers and unions that a Prices and Incomes policy was needed to control inflation.

The Labour government continued with the National Economic Development Council ("Neddy") which was in many ways a model for the National Export Board seen in *The Power Game*. Set up by the MacMillan government, the NEDC survived into the Thatcher government because, *"though it never did any good, it did not do any actual harm."* (5).

When viewing *The Plane Makers* and *The Power Game* it is helpful to remember that an entirely different view of economic reality prevailed at the time.

By the 21st century, *"economic thought (would be) dominated by a single perspective...(neoclassical economics, that) ...paints markets as a naturally occurring, mechanical system, and the government as an external engineer who might want to make some tweaks or corrections should this system fail to deliver."* (6)

Deregulation of credit began in 1971. Freed from control, banks began offering credit to those firms which could pay the highest rate rather than those which passed subjective tests of quality. Risk passed to the borrower as interest rates rose. *"For the next thirty years, high real rates periodically bankrupted many fine individuals, firms, industries and economies."* (7).

The 1986 Big Bang deregulating London's financial markets eliminated traditional firms like Elbertson's with *"liveried doormen and...wood-panelled rooms"*. American firms swept into the City, hiring the brightest, rather than people from the right backgrounds, but also demanding feudal levels of devotion with 16-hour days and weekend working. (8).

The other major development was the emergence in the 1980's of activist shareholders who, in the most extreme cases, use borrowed money to acquire a target company and then sell-off the companies' assets to repay their debt. Lower key activists tend to acquire a smaller percentage of shares and then encourage other shareholders to call for higher returns (usually paid for by cost-cutting).

In a 21st Century version of *The Plane Makers*, it is probable that Wilder's *bete noir*, Sir Gordon Revidge would no longer be a merchant banker. Instead, he would be a hedge fund activist, pressuring Wilder to deliver more short-term wealth to shareholders. And by the final episode of *The Power Game*, perhaps Wilder himself would become a Mergers and Acquisitions activist.

Europe in the 1960's

In the 1960's, there were still two Europe's; The West, protected by NATO, and the East controlled by the Warsaw Pact. Between the two were solid walls and fences on the Eastern side, patrolled by armed guards to ensure that no-one escaped to the West. Germany itself was divided between East and West. And yet, the East and West still traded. The third series of *The Power Game* deals with some of these ambiguities. While an embargo list of "strategic items" that should not be sold to communist nations existed, this was gradually whittled down. In 1954 there were 350 items, but by 1960 there were only 24 (9).

Although we tend to think of the Soviets as all-controlling, there was a small club of non-aligned states such as Yugoslavia which played both sides off. As John Lewis Gaddis put it (10) *"There were limits to how much either Moscow or Washington could order smaller powers around, because they could always defect to the other side, or at least threaten to."*

It may seem ironic now that Britain made several attempts to join the European Economic Community or "Common Market" which then consisted of France, Belgium, Italy, Luxembourg, the Netherlands and the Federal Republic of Germany. Britain had applied to join in 1961 and 1967, but had been vetoed by President De Gaulle.

Meanwhile, Britain exploited its dominant, "have-your-cake-and-eat-it" role in the European Free Trade Association, which then included Austria, Denmark, Norway, Portugal, Sweden, and Switzerland.

Sir John Wilder generally profits by keeping Europe firmly in his sights. *In The Plane Makers* episode *The Flying Frigates* he sees off an attempt to remove him from Scott Furlong saying, *"I no longer need bank or state finance. I'm being financed continentally!"* In *The Power Game* episode *Confound Their Politics*, Wilder is made Special Plenipotentiary to the European Community *("one of the ripest plums on the tree")*. In *Nothing's Free*, Wilder returns with plans to put together an international construction project in Italy. And in *There's No Such Thing As A Dead Heat*, Wilder finally edges his enemies out in favour of a German partner.

The World of the 1960's

If you stepped back into 1963, you would probably catch your breath as you walked into the haze of coal and fuel oil smoke from domestic and industrial chimney's. Nearly everyone had a cigarette in their hand as they rode the upstairs deck of the bus, worked at their desk or had a lunchtime pint.

The world ran mainly on cash, and most calculations were

done in the head (or with some aid like a 'ready reckoner' or a slide rule). Computers were used only for the most complex calculations. Engineers working on M1 Motorway bridges designs used the Stantec Zebra computer at Bradford Institute of Technology. With no software as such, they *"devised their own programs, punched the paper tape input and retrieved the output on a teleprinter"* (11).

A 1960's manager would spend much more time doing things, rather than having meetings about doing things. Executives of the 1960's spent less than ten hours a week in meetings, compared to 23 hours a week in the 2020s! (12)

A 1960's manager would be developed by the company with the expectation of a job for life (Wilder tells Nigel Humphries in the Plane Makers episode, *The Old Boy Network*, that he'd been observing Humphries as a future executive. *"You're intelligent and you have the right background."*).

By the 1980's the trend for corporate downsizing began, with middle managers jobs being cut at twice the rate of non-managers (13). Today management prospects are only hired after they have taken care of their own education and training.

In the 1960's, Management Consultants were still a relatively small part of the landscape. As David Craig explains in *Rip-Off!* (2005), high-end, strategic consulting companies like McKinsey made their money from writing reports for CEO's that were never implemented. At the other end of the scale was operational performance improvement firms, *"who tend to work out 'on the shop floor' with supervisors and hourly-paid workers, driving through changes and...dramatic reductions in client personnel."* (14). The pioneer was Charles Bedaux, who masterminded a system where every task in a factory was timed and given a 'B value'. *"Then each worker's productivity – how many B units they completed for each hour they worked...could be accurately measured and compared to that of other workers."*

Bedaux-inspired consultants were vital during the second world war in helping industry get high production out of unskilled workers (such as housewives assembling Lancaster bombers). After the war, the performance improvement firms continued to flourish. *The Plane Makers* episode, *The Cat's Away* illustrates the often-justified fear which spread through the shop-floor when the 'time-and-motion' men appeared. But the early management consultants could not have dreamed of the explosion in consulting work which took place in the 1980's and 1990's.

It was still a deeply unequal world, with women generally earning much less than men, even if they did the same jobs. This was a position often supported by the trade unions since the general belief was that it was a man's role to support his family, and women were only working to earn a little extra cash. Although the contraceptive pill was available, it was usually only prescribed to married women. Nevertheless, there was an expectation that professional women should be 'nice' to men in order to get on (see *A Condition of Sale* and A *Bunch of Fives*).

Management Theory in the 1960's

The world of *The Plane Makers* and *The Power Game* rested solidly on the management theory of the 1950's and early 1960's. This generally reached back to the early part of the 20th Century.

 Frederick Winslow Taylor's *Principles of Scientific Management* (1909) argued that scientific methods would determine the most efficient working practices, with employees given work that matched their skills and motivation. Managers would coach and monitor employees to ensure maximum efficiency.

Henri Fayol's *Administration Industrielle et Générale* (1916) proposed 14 principles of management including division of work, clear communication, fair remuneration, minimising staff turnover and fostering team spirit.

Sociologist **Max Weber** identified bureaucracy as the most efficient form of organisation, proposing division of labour, employees hired according to skills, and an impersonal environment where promotion is based on achievement. Weber also argued that technical employees should be encouraged to view their craft as an end in itself (something that it echoed in Arthur Sugden's distinction between the different factories in the Scott-Furlong group. One factory makes parts. The other makes aircraft "we create!").

Professor Elton Mayo's *The Human Problems of an Industrialised Civilisation* (1933) developed the Human Relations Management Theory, which tempered the austerity of Taylor and Weber. Mayo's work showed that employees were motivated by more than just money. Teams could be highly motivated by a combination of inter-personal factors. It was the job of managers to identify and encourage those factors.

Douglas McGregor expanded on the Human Relations theory in *The Human Side of Enterprise* (1960) which contrasted authoritarian and participative managers (X and Y managers) and concluded that the participative approach was more productive.

Concepts which are now standards were certainly being developed in the 1950's and 1960's.

Sociologist and economic theorist **Vilfredo Pareto** published *Cours d'Economie Politique, or Course in Political Economy* (1897), in which he established what later became known as the Pareto Principle. 80% of consequences come from 20% of causes. While Pareto was originally talking about land ownership, the mathematical principle has been shown to apply across many business areas. Management consultant **Joseph M. Juran** began to apply the Pareto principle to quality management in the 1940's and published his approach in *Quality Control Handbook* (1951). Juran's approach did not find favour in the West, but was adopted in the 1950's in Japan. It was only in the 1970's and 1980's, when

Japanese industry eclipsed America and Britain, that the quality management approach was taken seriously.

Engineer and statistician **W Edwards Deming** was generally unknown in the West during the 1950's and 1960's. As part of the post-war occupation of Japan, he had taught statistical product quality administration (what is now known as statistical process control) to Japan's business leaders. Deming's methods were credited with improving productivity and quality leading to Japan's industrial rebirth. Again, it was only when Japanese industry began to compete that the West began to take Deming's ideas seriously. Deming's *Quality, Productivity and Competitive Position* (aka *Out of The Crisis*) was published in 1982, outlining his 14 Points for Management.

Management consultant **Peter Drucker** had published The *Concept of the Corporation* in 1940, based on his analysis of General Motors. In 1954, he published *The Practice of Management*, the first book to look at management as an art to be learned. *"The manager is the dynamic, life-giving element in every business."* Within this book, Drucker coined the term Management by Objectives; managers and employees agreeing challenging, but obtainable targets. Ironically, the Drucker Institute confirms that the Drucker never wrote the sentence most associated with him: *"What gets measured gets managed."* It is likely he would have disagreed with it. Drucker did say that productivity measurement, *"is the only yardstick that can actually gauge the competence of management and allow comparison between management of different units within the enterprise, and of different enterprises. For productivity includes all the efforts the enterprise contributes; it excludes everything it does not control."* (15) But the concept of a specific, targeted measurement is different from the scattershot generation of metrics which was becoming a reality in the 1950's and increased in the 1980's with the explosion of computer power. Drucker warned that the information should go to the manager himself, as, *"a means of self-control, not a tool of control from above."* (16)

Twelve O'Clock High – the only management tool of the 1960's

One of the finest films about leadership is *Twelve O'Clock High* (1949), starring Gregory Peck as the commander of a Second World War US Air Force bomber group. On release, the film was co-opted by the US military as a case study for officer training, and in the 1960's it was used by the Industrial Society (since 2002 The Work Foundation) to teach **John Adair's** principles of Action Centred Leadership.

In England, in 1942, a US Air Force bomber group is being used to test the theory of daylight strategic bombing over occupied Europe. The group suffers heavy casualties and fails to hit its targets. The medical officer (Paul Stewart) says the group has a higher-than-average rate of sickness. He is asked to certify the men fit for "Maximum Effort" but no-one at headquarters will define "Maximum Effort". Colonel Davenport (Gary Merrill) is relieved of command because his "overidentification with the men" means he can no longer discipline or motivate them.

Brigadier General Frank Savage (Gregory Peck) is put in command and takes a tough approach. When the group is not actively bombing, he puts them on training flights. At public debriefing sessions, errors and successes are identified. Savage assigns poor performers to a 'hard luck' crew with the name 'Leper Colony' painted on their bomber. He gradually instils pride in the group and identifies leaders who can take the group forward.

The group's success comes at a personal cost to Savage. Refusing to become close to his men, as Davenport had done, he remains isolated, absorbing the stress of each mission, seeing men die in combat and always remaining aware of scrutiny from headquarters. With the pride and performance of the group restored, Savage prepares to lead a bombing raid, but can't pull himself up into his plane. His body refuses to follow orders. He suffers a nervous breakdown and is only able to sleep when he hears the sound of the bombers returning successfully from their mission.

The film lends itself to management theories such as John Adair's Action Centred Leadership and Paul Hersey and Ken Blanchard's Situational Leadership. Both theories challenge the myth of 'born leaders' and examine the behaviour a leader must demonstrate in order to develop the performance of individuals within a team.

Although these theories were developed too late to have influenced John Wilder, it's noticeable that in the episode *No Man's Land* he uses the phrase from the movie, *"Overidentification with the men"*, to explain why he thinks Arthur Sugden is not the right man for the General Works Manager post.

Political Background to *The Plane Makers*

During World War Two, the national interest had dictated that the coalition Government support the mainly family-owned aircraft companies. Even if a project didn't result in a useable plane, the Government would still underwrite the costs. After the war, the new Labour Government, always wary of being seen as 'anti-business' didn't tackle the overcapacity, but announced it would commission no new fighters for ten years.

It was Conservative Defence Minister Duncan Sandys who in April 1957 published a White Paper saying that Britain's future defence lay in missiles rather than manned planes. In future the Government would only award contracts to groups of companies, not individual manufacturers.

Hawker Siddley Group bought the de Havilland Aircraft Company in 1960, later adding Folland and Blackburn. While de Havilland was front-runner in the race to produce a short haul airliner (the Trident) for British European Airways, Hawker launched its VTOL prototype in 1960 (one of the VTOL prototypes crashed at the 1963 Paris Air Show).

British Aircraft Corporation was formed in 1960 by Vickers and English Electric, with Bristol Aeroplane Company having a 20% stake. BAC took over Hunting Aviation later that year and expanded its design for a 30-seat jetliner into the 80 seat BAC 1-11 short-haul airliner which launched on 20 August 1963.

It is BAC and Hawker Siddeley Group which form the model for the Scott Furlong company, although ironically, Handley Page, which later assisted *The Plane Makers* with their research, resisted the pressure to merge.

The Plane Makers TV series took a politically neutral approach to Government. The Independent Television Authority required impartiality, but there were also practical reasons. The third series was made during but transmitted just after the 1964 General Election. The early episodes had to walk a tightrope without identifying if characters such as Sir Gerald Merle and James Cameron-Grant were part of Government or Opposition. In any event most of the politicians in *The Plane Makers* represent a type.

The 1960's establishment was still dominated by Oxbridge classics and humanities graduates with no technical expertise, although there were some cracks in the barriers during this period.

The Education (Administrative Provisions) Act 1907 had required all grant-aided secondary schools to offer 25 % of their places as free scholarships for students from public elementary schools. This enabled future Prime Minister Harold Wilson (among others) to attend Royds Hall Grammar School. The 1944 Education Act set up state funded Grammar Schools to teach the most intellectually able 25% of pupils. Future Prime Minister John Major attended Rutlish Grammar School. *"The Grammar School elite began with Wilson and ended with Major. Since then, we've been governed by privately educated Cabinets."* (17).

Although Sir John Wilder was educated at what Ken Bligh called a "minor" public school, he was careful to conceal that he took his degree at a *"red brick university"* (a civic university offering practical knowledge such as engineering or medicine).

In the *Plane Makers* episode *Loved He Not Honours More,* Wilder tells Don Henderson that both union chief Bessiter and Labour MP Sir Gerald Merle are "old Wykehamists", educated at Winchester College, the oldest public school in England. In reality, Hugh Gaitskell, former leader of the Labour Party had been educated at Winchester, as had Richard Crossman and Sir Kenneth Younger (Labour MP for Grimsby when Wymark lived there). This reflects the reality that a privately educated elite were represented across the political spectrum in the 1960's, just as today.

However, it's worth noting that that this is not a peculiarly British phenomenon. David W. Maurer, writing about confidence tricksters and their marks in 1940, noted that, *"Most marks come from the upper strata of society which, in America, means that they have made, inherited or married money. Because of this, they acquire status which in time they come to attribute to some inherent superiority..."* (18)

Motorways and construction.

"Motorways were then a thing of fascination and anticipated pleasure." (19)

Motorways were first envisaged in the late 1930's as part of national plan. War impeded progress, and although the Ministry of Transport appointed county council engineers to investigate new roads to motorway standards in 1947, there was no money to realise these plans.

It was not until the 1950's that the government felt confident enough to begin work on Britain's first motorway, the Preston By-Pass. Although this had been planned by Lancashire County Council in 1937, the legal powers to construct a road limited to certain classes of vehicle were only brought in with Special Roads Act 1949. The

Tarmac Group won the bid to construct the road in 1956, and the bypass was opened on 5th December 1958 by Harold MacMillan.

Although 60% of car owners voted Conservative in 1958, the Labour opposition was supportive, gambling that increasing affluence would widen the car ownership base. *"It saw cars as aspirational objects that would aid its own aspiration to electability."* (20)

The M1, Britain's first inter-urban motorway connecting London and Leeds, had been planned before the war, but again it was 1956 before the Ministry of Transport confirmed the first section (Luton to Dunchurch). Construction began in 1958 with two contractors (John Laing and Tarmac) taking separate sections, and it was opened in November 1959.

In *The Power Game* Ken Bligh tells Wilder a long schedule is the safest tender for road construction. *"The M1 took 19 months to complete and is costing 5 and a half million to put right."* (21)

Or as Neville Abraham put it, *"the longer a project takes, the more it may be delayed because of changes to avoid the design becoming obsolescent before it is built."* (22)

During the 1960's the Ministry of Transport authorised Country Council engineers and technicians to prepare tenders for several sections of motorway. Although the motorways featured in *The Power Game* are fictional, the road works are real. Fiction was hand-in-hand with fact.

Notes:

1 THE PLANE MAKERS, Loved He Not Honours More

2 KEEGAN, WILLIAM. Nine Crises

3 ALDRED, JONATHAN. License To be Bad

4 HENNESEY, PETER. Winds of Change, page 24.

5 MASON, KEITH. Front Seat, page 75.

6 EARLE, MORAN, WARD-PERKINS, The Econocracy, pp 92,82

7 PETTIFOR, ANN. The Production of Money.

8 MARKOVITS, The Meritocracy Trap page 295

9 HANSARD, 25 April 1961.

10 GADDIS, John Lewis. The Cold War, page 128

11 FRISTON, A.H (cited in). SIMS. F.A. The Motorway Achievement: Building the Network in the North East of England. Phillimore/Motorway Archive Trust 2009 page 100

12 PERLOW, HADLEY, EUN, Stop the Meeting Madness, Harvard Business Review, July-August 2017, Page 65

13 MARKOVITS, The Meritocracy Trap page 173

14 CRAIG, DAVID. Rip-Off! Page 53

15 DRUCKER, PETER. The Practice of Management pp 92-3.

16 DRUCKER, PETER. The Practice of Management pp 162.

17 BRAY, CHRISTOPHER. 1965. Page 150

18 MAURER, The Big Con, page 94

19 HENNESEY, PETER. Winds of Change, page 49

20 BRAY, CHRISTOPHER. 1965. Page 93

21 THE POWER GAME, Hagadan.

22 ABRAHAM, NEVILLE. Big Business and Government, page 100.

Ten Steps to the Wilder Way

The 2020's may herald a new dawn for the Wilder Way. Mergers and acquisitions have steadily cut the number of public companies over the past 20 years. The *Financial Times* reported in December 2021 that the year had seen the highest rise of mergers and acquisitions since records began 40 years ago. Much of this is fuelled by private equity groups exploiting the low debt money pumped into the economy during the Covid crisis. As companies fall, so do their executives. *No chief executive is safe, and the opportunity for a stealthy advance has never been better.*

So here are the ten steps that will help you walk the Wilder Way.

1. Make sure yours is the first plane off the runway. No-one remembers the also-rans. Don't spend so much time trying to get things perfect that someone else beats you to the market. In every aspect of your life, make sure you're out there first. Ries and Trout call it the Law of Leadership, *"It's better to be first than it is to be better."* (1)

2. Make others play with the cards you deal. In negotiation
or day-to-day business, always make sure you control the
options. If the playing field doesn't work for you, alter the
playing field. If you know someone is going to be obstructive
at a meeting, change the time and venue of the meeting and
make sure their copy of the memo gets lost.

**3. There's no substitute for preparation – unless it's
improvisation!** Overconfidence or laziness can blind us to
the need for preparation. But however much preparation you
do, there will come a time when you need to act on instinct.
Regarding the need for preparation, Chris Voss cautions,
*"When the pressure is on, you don't rise to the occasion. You
fall to your highest level of preparation."* (2). We can blind
ourselves to our need for preparation.

But when it comes to strategy and tactics, William
Poundstone makes a valid observation of playing the Rock,
Scissors, Paper game. Successful players combine strategy
with observation of their opponents' unconscious habits.
*"Like chessmasters, good rock, scissor, paper players
generally plan their openings and then quickly switch to
improvisation."* (3). When to switch from preparation to
improvisation? That's the million dollar question.

4. Let them know who's boss. Always keep a folder of five-
minute jobs (letters to be signed etc). Bring them out 30
seconds before your secretary shows a visitor into your office
and keep them waiting while you deal with the paper-work.
On no account make eye-contact or acknowledge their
presence (a well-polished cigarette case on your desk will
allow you to see their reflection). The whole purpose of the
exercise is to disrupt their thought processes.

5. Always See the Whites of Their Eyes. There is no substitute for a face-to-face meeting. A negotiation is a contest and you need every tool at your disposal to win. Chris Voss notes in Never Split the Difference, that most young business people use email (or WhatsApp) as a default, but *"Email doesn't allow for tone of voice effects, and it doesn't let you read the non-verbal"* (4). It also gives the other side far too much time to think! Sir John Wilder might have used Zoom instead of a long-distance telephone call to France, but no video conference will ever give you the opportunity to stride into another man's office, sit on the edge of his desk and thoroughly dominate proceedings.

6. Always have your parachute ready. Risk is the tinder for success. But don't make the mistake of thinking you're fireproof. Joseph T Hallinan says, *"Thinking positively can blind us to the pitfalls that lay camouflaged inside our ideas"* (5) and Zimbardo agrees, *"Most of us construct...egocentric biases that make us feel special...They boost our self-esteem and protect us against life's failures...but these biases mean we don't guard against risk."* (6). Revisit **Step 3** – always prepare for what you'll do when things go wrong! As Wilder says, when things fall apart, *"shuffle the pieces into the pattern that you want.."* (7)

7. Make Sure It's Your Face In The End Credits. The attention span of even the cleverest person is surprisingly short. Whether it's ending a meeting or finishing a project, it's the last person to speak or act that sticks in people's minds. If you have a spectacular success that unravels later, it's the success that people will remember (and you should be out of the way by the time it unravels!) Surround yourself with talent, but there can only be one leader and that is you!

8. Drive the knife deep and fast! Be ruthless in disposing of your enemies. If you don't destroy them utterly, they will always be lurking in the background ready to strike again. Especially if they're your wife's ex-admirers. As Machiavelli put it, *"Men must be either pampered or crushed, because they can get revenge for small injuries but not for grievous ones. So any injury a prince does a man should be of a kind that there is no fear of revenge."* (8).

9. Cynically cultivate useful people in a social context. Since the 1980's this has been called 'networking' but in Wilder's time it was called 'getting on'. There is no step too expensive or outrageous to get time alone with a government minister, whether it is arranging a demonstration flight of a plane or coincidentally checking into an exclusive health farm. Government Ministers are the 'big fish' but you should cast your net wide, and arrange social gatherings at least once a month. As Mark H. McCormack put it, *"All things being equal, people will buy from a friend. All things being not quite so equal, people will still buy from a friend."* (9).

10. Get the job done. Perfection and procrastination are for parsons. In business, it's finishing, and finishing first that counts.

Notes:

1 RIES,AL AND TROUT, JACK, The 22 Immutable Laws of Marketing (HarperCollins 1993) page 3.

2 VOSS,CHRIS. Never Split the Difference page 211

3 POUNDSTONE, WILLIAM. How To Predict The Unpredictable page 53

4 VOSS,CHRIS. Never Split The Difference page 236

5 HALLINAN, JOSEPH.T. Errornomics page 213

6 ZIMBARDO, PHILIP. The Lucifer Effect, page 261

7 THE POWER GAME. The Switch.

8 MACHIAVELLI, NICCOLO. The Prince, page 38

9 MCCORMACK, MARK. What They Don't Teach You At Harvard Business School, page 53

Appendix 1: Patrick Wymark – "He Would Light Up Like Guy Fawkes Night"

Patrick and Olwen Wymark

Patrick Wymark, *"was quite without 'side' or any inflated opinion of himself,"* said journalist Frank Whitmarsh in October 1970, "*He was an extremely good actor, in whom inborn talent had been developed by good training and plain hard work. As an actor he was too good to be squashed into the sardine tin of one part."*

Professor John Lawlor recalled that, *"His friends are to be found in every walk of life and to all of them he was passionately loyal. However long the interval, one took up at just the point where one had left off and his unerring memory for one's views was matched*

*only by his warm appreciation of anything he thought based on
common sense."*

Born Patrick Carl Cheeseman in Cleethorpes on July 11 1926,
Patrick Wymark was brought up in neighbouring Grimsby,
attending St Mary's Catholic School and the old Wintringham Boys
Grammar School in Eleanor Street, Grimsby.

A Talent for Drama

Former schoolmate William Cole said, *"young Cheeseman always
had plenty to say for himself and was very cheeky to his seniors,"*
but June Farley recalled that, *"He was a great all-rounder, very
popular. He mesmerised us playing Shylock at the age of 15."*

Amateur drama ran in the family. His parents, Maria and Tom and
older brother John were leading members of the local Caxton
Players, and Patrick appeared in a play called *Ante-Room* for the
1943 Grimsby and Cleethorpes Drama Festival. In the same year he
played snobbish Mr Collins in *I Have Five Daughters*, an adaptation
of *Pride and Prejudice* where a reviewer said Patrick was,
*"Outstanding...He alone of the men wore the costume of the period
as though it belonged to him, and his performance all through was
one of the highlights of the production."*

Learning the Wilder Walk

Despite attending St Cuthbert's, Ushaw, in Durham (*"A great place
for churning out priests"),* it became clear that he was not cut out for
the life of a priest (he later told the *Catholic Herald* that, *"celibacy
of the clergy caused terrible misery to good, good priests"*). Leaving
college he was called up into the Navy towards the end of the war.

Professor John Lawlor recalled that one beneficial legacy of
Patrick's time as a Midshipman in the Mediterranean was *"The
'Wilder Walk' (a frustrated pacing up and down with scowling
concentration) which was learned on the bridges of HM*

Minesweepers, "Trying to look as if I had the faintest idea what was going on'!"

On leaving the Navy, the 22-year-old Patrick was admitted to University College, London on an ex-serviceman's grant to study English Literature. Here he met Olwen Buck, the Oakland, California-born granddaughter (on her mother's side) of William Wymark Jacobs, author of *The Monkey's Paw*. He would later adopt her family name when he became a professional actor.

Amateur dramatics dominated his time at university and when his tutor said he should make up his mind if he wanted to be an academic or an actor, Patrick stormed across Waterloo Bridge to the Old Vic Theatre School and asked for an audition. The directors were concerned that his age and service experience might make him too headstrong to be trained. Olwen recalled that, *"We spent days together in Regent's Park where I helped him to learn his audition pieces. Eventually he went to the audition, and to the surprise of almost everybody except myself, he was immediately accepted."*

Patrick and Olwen married in Grimsby in July 1950, returning to London in September, where Olwen worked as a secretary to supplement his grant. Reviewing the student's graduation show in June 1951, *The Stage* praised Vanbrugh's comedy, *A Journey to London* with Jerome Willis as Uncle Richard, Prunella Scales as Betty, and *"Patrick Wymark (who) played Sir Francis with a good notion of country-squire vulgarity."*

Dicing with death in South Africa

Offered a term with the Old Vic Theatre Company as a student actor, Patrick made his one-line debut in October 1951 in *Othello.* Soon after, Olwen discovered she was pregnant with their first child, Jane and the management grudgingly increased his pay to £6 a week (about £200 a week in 2022). In April 1952 Patrick was given the role of the sergeant in *The Other Heart,* a new play starring Alan Badel as the poet Villon.

On 22 May 1952, Patrick Wymark sailed with other members of the Old Vic company on the SS Pretoria for a three-month tour of South Africa and Rhodesia. The tour would have a lasting, and almost fatal impact on Patrick Wymark. While in Salisbury, Rhodesia (Zimbabwe), *"I was driving along a main street when a car shot out from an intersection and ran into me. When I regained consciousness, I was in hospital. I had gone head first through the wind-screen and my lower lip was almost torn off. They put 25 stiches into the main wound, but for days I couldn't speak."*

Fearing that his career as an actor may be over, *"I asked the doctors if I could do any special exercises to help me regain full control over my voice. Nobody knew any special method, so I decided to simply go ahead and keep my lips moving as much as possible. It hurt like hell. But I just went on, reciting anything from Shakespeare to Toad of Toad Hall. Within three weeks I was back with the company."*

Back in Blighty

Patrick returned to England in September 1952, to play Friar John in the Old Vic production of *Romeo and Juliet*. From January 1953, he appeared as a heavy, elderly Salerio in *The Merchant of Venice*. Robert Urquhart (Henry Forbes in *The Plane Makers*) starred as Bassanio, Irene Worth as Portia and Paul Rogers as Shylock.

This was followed on February 24 1953 by three roles in *Julius Caesar*: the tribune Flavius, conspirator Trebonius and soldier Clitus. William Devlin (Sir Gerald Merle in *The Plane Makers*) played Brutus with Robin Bailey (Charles Grainger in *The Power Game*) as Anthony. After a spell as Third Priest in the Robert Donat *Murder In The Cathedral* (still available on Naxos CD), Patrick Wymark was given his longest sustained role as Charles, Duke of Suffolk in *Henry VIII*. Starring Paul Rogers as Henry and Jenette Sterke as Anne Bullen, the opening performance on May 6 1953 was attended by the Queen and Duke of Edinburgh – the first time in 200 years that a reigning monarch had attended a first night.

In 1954, Olwen's father, who was a professor at Stanford University, arranged for Patrick to be one of three guest directors at the San Diego National Shakespeare Festival. Among the scholarship students at the Old Globe (a reproduction of Shakespeare's Globe Theatre) was Dennis Hopper, playing Sebastian in *Twelfth Night*. Gretchen Gray, who played Olivia in the same production, recalled that Wymark grew increasingly frustrated trying persuade Hopper not to pronounce 'woman' as *"woe-man."* Patrick would say woman and Dennis would say woe-man. Finally, Patrick stomped on the stage: *"See this stage floor Dennis! What is it made of?" "Wood"*, replied Dennis. *"That's right! Wood! Now say woman!"*

While in America, Olwen discovered she was pregnant with daughter Rowan. Although Patrick was well-paid by the university, Olwen said, *"When you are used to the National Health Service, you forget just how expensive it can be to have a baby in America."*

Live on Television

Returning to England, Patrick had a spell of 10 weeks on the dole while waiting for an engagement as the Porter in the 1955 Shakespeare Memorial Theatre production of *Macbeth*. Patrick made his TV debut on 2nd October 1955, when BBC1 made an outside broadcast from Stratford of *The Merry Wives of Windsor*. Wymark played, *"the jovial Windsor innkeeper who devises and sets afoot the duel between Caius (Michael Denison) and Evans (William Devlin).*

More stage roles followed with *Hamlet*, *Measure For Measure* and *Toad of Toad Hall* in 1956. While appearing as Stephano in *The Tempest* at the Theatre Royal, Drury Lane, Wymark was also cast as Friar turned outlaw Will Lawless in the BBC's 1958 production of *The Black Arrow*. Producer Naomi Capon also cast another Old Vic School graduate, Alan Dobie as the grizzled retainer Bennett Hatch! In November 1958, Olwen also gave birth to son, Dominic.

After touring Moscow and Leningrad with the company led by Laurence Olivier and Vivien Leigh, Wymark joined the 59 Theatre Company in January 1959 for a six-month run at the Lyric Theatre, Hammersmith. Their first production was James Maxwell's translation of DANTON'S DEATH by Georg Büchner. Wymark starred as Danton, with James Maxwell, Fulton MacKay, Harold Lang as Robespierre and Patrick McGoohan as St Just . *"Danton is a sort of Hamlet inwardly disturbed by the part he's played in the revolution and now affecting not to take life seriously,"* The Times wrote, *"Mr Wymark well establishes the vein of honesty that runs through both the demagogue and the introspect."*

Further productions included *The Cheats of Scapin* with Lang, Mackay and Peter Sallis, and *Brand* starring Patrick McGoohan in the title role. The heavy dramatic season was followed in July 1959 by *One To Another*, a "Lyric Revue" starring Wymark and Beryl Reid, which later transferred to the Globe Theatre.

Both *Brand* and *Danton's Death* were broadcast on BBC 1, and Patrick Wymark also became a contributor to *Meeting Point* – a Sunday evening discussion programme for BBC Midlands. At some time during 1959, Patrick Wymark also appears to have made his film debut with a one-line appearance as half of a 'courting couple' in *The Devil's Bait* (Dir. Peter Graham Scott). More significantly, Wymark was cast by Peter Cotes as press baron Sir Charles Worgan in Arnold Bennett's *What The Public Wants* (BBC 1 October 4 1959). For the first time, TV audiences saw Wymark as a man of power.

Movies and Memorials

In 1960, Patrick Wymark made a brief appearance as Wylie, "a prosperous wide boy" in *The League of Gentlemen* while in *The Criminal* he was Sol, one of Stanley Baker's fellow prison inmates. He also played police minister Ortiz, in the *Danger Man* episode, *An Affair of State*, starring Patrick McGoohan.

In the same year, Wymark was offered a contract by Peter Hall, who had taken over the Shakespeare Memorial Theatre, changing the name to the Royal Shakespeare Company. Hall also set up a London base at the Aldwych Theatre and introduced the revolutionary idea of three-year contracts, offering actors a low but regular income. As an editorial in *The Stage* put it: *"They can work with a will and without financial worry."*

Although Wymark was often cast in comedic roles, Judi Dench observed that there was a mood of both laughing and crying in Wymark's clowns. *"He had a wonderfully merry face and a rotund figure but he was really melancholic, and that made him so good in those parts. You wouldn't have taken him for a melancholy or depressed man, though, and he was never depressing to others."*

Opening on 21st June 1960, the first production under Hall's management was *The Taming of the Shrew,* starring Peggy Ashcroft and Peter O'Toole. Wymark played Grumio, chief servant to Petrucio. On 15 December 1960, the Aldwych opened with John Webster's bloody tragedy, *The Duchess of Malfi,* in which Patrick Wymark played Daniel De Bosola, recently released from a sentence on the galleys for murder. De Bosola is given a position as Gentleman of the Horse in the household of the Duchess (Peggy Ashcroft) in order to spy on her for her brothers, the Duke (Eric Porter) and the Cardinal (Max Adrian). J. C Trewin wrote in the Birmingham Daily Post (Friday 16 December 1960) that *"Patrick Wymark puts a bold front on Bosola, a renaissance complexity that defies analysis."*

Devils and Drakes

Ian Richardson recalled that *"it's much more puritanical now than it was then. We used to go to a pub called The Black Swan - and they had a special dispensation to stay open late for the actors. I can remember Peter O'Toole and Patrick Wymark and Dinsdale Landen. We all tumbled into The Dirty Duck after the performance, and rolled out about an hour and a half later!"*

In 1961, Wymark appeared in John Whiting's *The Devils*, (made infamous by Ken Russell's film version) where he first played de Laubardement, before taking over the role of Father Barre from Max Adrian.

With theatres closed on Sundays, Patrick was also able to perform in live TV broadcasts. On Sunday 2 April 1961, he played detective Boucard in Jacques Gillies' *The Takers* (ATV 1961). Directed by Quentin Lawrence (who would later helm Wymark's first episode of *The Plane Makers*) the play pitted him against a gang hoping rob the world's fifth richest man. In the ABC/ITC film series *Sir Francis Drake* (ITC/ABC 1961) Wymark guest-starred in *The Garrison* – as Captain Williams, leader of the a besieged and betrayed British fort.

Wymark also starred as William Palmer, the 'Prince of Poisoners' in Rosemary Hill's adaptation of Robert Graves' *They Hanged My Saintly Billy*. (BBC 1, May 4 1962). He also made the first of several appearances as Oliver Cromwell on 3 August 1962, in *The Cruel Necessity*. For ITV he played pearl fisherman Manny Barnes in *The Sin Shifter* (16 September 1962) *"a raw boozy unpolished shell of a man"* and a detective in Giles Cooper's adaptation of Jean Cocteau's *The Typewriter* (20 November 1962).

Priests and Smugglers

Wymark's experience at St Cuthbert's bore fruit in two performances. In *The Paleto Confession* (Rediffusion 25 January 1963) he played a Catholic Priest who gives the confession to a wounded criminal and in *West 11* (Michael Winner 1963) he appeared as Father Hogan, the family priest and learner driver who suffers from, *"the sin of pride on me three-point turns"*.

On Sunday 6 January 1963, the BBC Home Service (as Radio 4 used to be called) broadcast *Schoolboy to Subaltern*, the first of three extracts from *My Early Life*, by Winston Spencer Churchill. The voice of Churchill would become another speciality for Wymark, with another set of readings in October 1963.

Wymark also appeared as Heemskirk in an adaptation of *Freya of the Seven Isles* (BBC 21 January 1963), a defecting Russian tuba player in *Our Man In Moscow* (BBC 1 March 1963), a resistance agent in *Moonstrike* (BBC 14 March 1963) and a member of the "new rich" whose conflict with the landed gentry provides a smokescreen for a Martian takeover in Angus Wilson's *The Invasion* (ITV 31 March 1963). For Argo records, Wymark also found time to play Falstaff in a recording of *The Merry Wives of Windsor*.

During the same year, Wymark played Joseph Ransley in the Walt Disney production of *Dr Syn Alias the Scarecrow*. Patrick McGoohan starred as Dr Syn, and Alan Dobie appeared as Revenue prosecutor Frank Fragg, who pressures Ransley into betraying the smugglers. Wymark also appeared as the General in charge of army forces at the climax *of Children of the Damned* (released 1964).

On 11 June 1963, Wymark appeared as Joe Brent, skipper of the Grimsby trawler Barnoldby in *The Seventh Wave* by Grimsby-based writer Elizabeth Dawson. Patrick Wymark, *"threw himself eagerly into playing the lead...largely because it was about Grimsby."*

That Certain Party

During the Summer, Patrick Wymark appeared at the Regent's Park Open Air Theatre, playing Bottom in *A Midsummer Night's Dream*. Olwen said, *"it meant taking an enormous drop in salary under often cold and wet conditions. But he enjoyed doing it."* While Rex Firkin was still searching for an actor to play John Wilder in *The Plane Makers*, he attended a party at which Patrick Wymark was, *"...very drunk – as I came to realise, a normal situation for him. The aggression and the excitement that he exuded when drunk was quite different to the gentle, nice man he was when sober. I thought that if we could manage to catch that aggression, the forceful manner that he had when tight, then we had something."*

During his first series of *The Plane Makers*, Wymark found time to fit in another radio play for the BBC Home Service on Tuesday 10

December 1963, starring in an adaptation of L.P.Hartley's *A Visitor From Down Under* for *Mystery Playhouse*. But the success of *The Plane Makers* quickly changed his life.

The Phantom Wilder

"There must be something compelling about Wilder," Patrick mused in April 1964, *"judging by the thousands of letters we've been getting from women. Men are drawn to him too. Perhaps they see the ruthless boss-figure they would like to be."*

But for Wymark, being reacted to like Wilder was, *"almost like science fiction, the way that Other One has grown out of thin air."*

So, Wymark was overjoyed to play the weak, drunken, possessive Alfred Colliver in Granada TV's *A Question About Hell* (27 April 1964). An update of *The Duchess of Malfi*, written by Kingsley Amis, the play co-starred Richard Johnson as his brother Norman, who conspires to spy on their widowed sister Angela (Caroline Mortimer).

On Friday 8 May 1964, Wymark starred in *The Detour* (Radio 3), a "comedy of menace" by Martin Walser which he would later remake for TV.

Wymark also recreated some of Winston Churchill's most memorable speeches for Jack Le Vien's documentary, *The Finest Hours*. Journalist Colin Frame was in the studio when Wymark auditioned, *"fresh from his triumphs in TV's 'Plane Makers' series. You had only to hear him snarling about, 'the Nazi war machine,' to hear the drama in his fine voice. Le Vien, who had not met him before, was bubbling with excitement."*

Released to cinemas in September 1964, the film was narrated by Orson Welles, who allegedly made a bid to record the Churchill speeches himself. Le Vien opted to stick with the Wymark version and also retained him for *The Other World of Winston Churchill*, a

'Hallmark Hall of Fame' documentary about Churchill's paintings, broadcast by NBC on 30 November 1964.

Prison Camps and Punishment

Between July and September 1964, Wymark played prison camp Major Jacomo in *The Secret of Blood Island* (1964). Reuniting Wymark with Quentin Lawrence, the film was released on a double bill with William Castle's *The Night Walker* in December 1964.

On 20th October 1964 Alan Dobie joined the third and final series of *The Plane Makers* as Wilder's nemesis David Corbett. And on 16 November 1964, Wymark starred in Rediffusion's two-and-a-half hour adaptation of *Crime and Punishment*. Stanley Miller's play introduced David Collings as murdering student Raskolnikov and Patrick Wymark as Porfiry, *"fascinating but enigmatic, a universal inquisitor, not the voice of an impersonal conscience"* (*The Times*). David Hope in *The Stage* compared Wymark's two distinct performances in as many days; *"Porfiry plays a waiting game, cat and mouse; like a judo expert he lets his victims' own actions lead him to his downfall. Wilder, in Porfiry's position would have had to mould the events himself."*

On 2nd December 1964 Wymark played Sigismondo Malatesta, a ruthless fifteenth-century mercenary in *Malatesta*, a BBC Wednesday Play adapted by Rosemary Hill from a story by Henry de Montherlant. Relaxing in the cultured surroundings of his palace in Rimini he learns that the Pope threatens his power and the evil side of his character reasserts itself. *"There were times when Wymark's performance seemed to be trying to burst out of the little box which imprisoned it (but) no conscientious account of the part could be small enough to fit in a television set."* (*The Times* 3 Dec 1964)

Top of the World

On 16 December 1964, Patrick Wymark received the Best TV Actor Award from the Guild of TV Producers and Directors at the

Dorchester Hotel. Once again, he attempted to step away from the doppelganger of Wilder, knowing that he had already filmed performances as Churchill in *Operation Crossbow* and the sleazy landlord in *Repulsion* would be released in May and June 1965.

January 1965 also saw production of *The Skull* (which would be released in November 1966). Wymark played Marco, the seedy antiques dealer who entraps Peter Cushing's obsessed collector.

For old time's sake Wymark also made a guest appearance in *Night Spot* (Rediffusion), a variety series hosted by magician Frank Berry and Norma Ronald (Miss Lingard in *The Plane Makers*).

On 6 March 1965 Wymark guest starred as villainous Jephro Rucastle in the *Sherlock Holmes* episode, *The Copper Beeches*. The BBC production starred Douglas Wilmer as Sherlock Holmes, Nigel Stock as Dr. Watson and Suzanne Neve as Miss Violet Hunter.

Once again, Patrick tried to depart from the Wilder image on 22 March 1965. In ATV's *Play of the Week: I Remember the Battle*, Wymark played William Peglar, a mediocre man who believes he had a touch of greatness in the war. Written by Douglas Livingstone, the play was directed by Dennis Vance.

Lock-In's at the Magdala

In his private life, journalist Neville Nisse reported that, *"Patrick Wymark is likeable and intelligent. What he enjoys most when he is not working is going down to his 'local' to meet his pals for a drink and a chat. "*

That local was The Magdala, in South Hill Park, Hampstead (the pub where Ruth Ellis shot David Blakeley). Despite being only 200 yards away, Olwen remarked that Wymark would usually take a taxi home, rather than walk. Director Ron Francis recalled, *"In those pre-breathalyser days, I would frequently give him a lift home after a lock-in. He was very keen on Beethoven and we'd often sit with a bottle of wine listening to recordings in his place."*

Wymark had ridden a motorbike during his days at Stratford and had traded up to a car. But Ron Francis recalled that, *"Pat wasn't one of nature's car drivers. He told me that, on his way home from Elstree, he was stopped by a police motorcyclist who felt that Pat had taken a corner badly. When the officer recognised him, he asked for an autograph and sent Pat on his way. Except that Pat had left the steering on a right-hand lock and as he drove off knocked the parked police bike over. Soon after that Pat employed a driver"*

Kings and Coppers

On Saturday 17 April 1965 Patrick Wymark attended a civic reception at Grimsby Town Hall to celebrate best TV actor award. His old schoolfriend Charles Eckberg recalled that Wymark had disappeared and *"had spent the afternoon looking up old friends and talking to them over a glass of beer in a working men's club."* With the Mayor and Burgesses of Grimsby waiting at the Town Hall, *"He arrived scarcely five minutes late - lolling in the back of a hire car asking, 'what's all the fuss about?'"*

On 22 April 1965, Wymark played a labourer in ATV's *Mainly Millicent*. Together with Millicent Martin, he discovers that singing in a manhole creates an echo chamber. A reviewer noted that the overlong sketch was funny, *"only because it was Mr Wymark in an unexpected role."*

From 7 June 1965 Wymark played King John in John Arden's *Left-Handed Liberty*, a play commissioned by the Corporation of the City of London to mark the 750th anniversary of the signing of Magna Carta. The title alludes to the fact that the monarch so quickly reneged on the freedoms we believe Magna Carta gave us.

On July 1965, Patrick began work as Inspector Holloway on the Amicus horror film, *The Psychopath* (released February 1966). Following completion, he began work on the Rediffusion series *Four of Hearts* (transmitted from 27 September 1965) - *"Four plays starring one versatile actor."*

And on 13 December 1965, Wymark returned as Sir John Wilder in the first series of *The Power Game.*

The Power Game goes Wilder

With the first series of *The Power Game* completed, Wymark stepped as far away as possible from the role of Wilder when he introduced *God's Trombone*, a religious variety show, on 4 May 1966.

On 17 May, he played the Old Russian Soldier in Louis MacNeice's *The Nosebag* for the BBC Home Service, and on 24 May 1966, he made his second appearance as Cromwell in the *Royalist and Roundhead* the first of Rediffusions TV's 13-part examination of the Civil War.

On 26 September 1966, *The Power Game* returned for a second series and on 27 October 1966, Wymark appeared on the BBC 2 quiz game *Call My Bluff.*

On 29 November 1966, Wymark, Jack Watling & Barbara Murray appeared in character in ITV's *A Royal Gala* in the presence of the Queen and the Duke of Edinburgh.

Patrick Wymark saw out a busy 1966 on Christmas Day, playing another comedy sketch in *Secombe, Friends and Relations* with Harry Secombe. He also made a personal appearance on 27 December 1966 at the Daily Mail Schoolboys and Girls Exhibition, with daughter Jane and sons Tristram and Dominic, riding bikes on a cycling proficiency display.

1967 The Judge, the Cherry Orchard and the Devil

On Sunday 29 January 1967, Wymark performed Launce's address to his dog Crab (from Two Gentlemen of Verona) for *Italy, My Italy* a charity Show in aid of the Italian Art and Archives Rescue Fund.

Patrick Wymark was now in the first wave of actors made into household names by television. A 1967 article on the celebrities most sought to open Summer Fetes noted that David Frost commanded a fee of £400 (about £7000 in 2022), and added that, *"Patrick Wymark and Patrick McNee are often asked for."* At the same time, he maintained a straightforward view of acting: *"It isn't a great spiritual pilgrimage. It's a job."*

Of his success, Wymark said, "*As income rises the cost of living seems to rise with it. I'm very fortunate, though, I can feed and clothe my children. I can bring them up well. I hope. But what more does one want than three good meals a day, and a comfortable bed?"*

From 14 February 1967, John Mortimer's stage play *The Judge* gave theatre audiences their first chance to see Patrick Wymark live since 1965's *Left-Handed Liberty*. Writing in *The Times*, Irving Wardle described Wymark's Judge as, *"a vicious, egotistical legislator, happiest when he is sniffing out crimes of lust and violence."*

1967 also saw the release of the Shirley MacLaine vehicle *Woman Times Seven (Sette Volte Donna)* .Wymark plays a Wilder-type businessman whose wife (MacLaine) learns that a rival plans to wear a copy of her dress to the first night of the Opera.

Wymark also joined Dennis Vance, Johnny Speight and Harry Secombe advising one of the unsuccessful groups bidding for the Yorkshire Television franchise. This may have given rise to the urban myth that Wymark was invited to sit on the board of companies following his success in the role of Sir John Wilder.

In *The Champions* episode *Operation Deep Freeze* (Filmed in 1967 but first broadcast ATV 30 October 1968) Wymark played General Gomez, leader of a small but aggressive South American state developing an atomic bomb in the Antarctic.

On Sunday 4th June 1967. Patrick Wymark returned to Grimsby to open the new church hall for St Stephens' Church, Roberts Street.

In July 1967, Wymark began a tour of Chekhov's *The Cherry Orchard*, ultimately transferring to the Queens Theatre, London in October 1967. Writing in *The Times*, John Peter said, *"This moving and versatile production....is based on two superlative performances by Lila Kedrova and Patrick Wymark, (as Ranyevskaya and Lopakhin.) Mme. Kedrova's portrayal here is a sustained masterpiece of bewildered but proud nobility. Mr. Wymark, too long absent from roles of such complexity, gives a virtuoso account of Lopakhin."*

While at the Edinburgh Festival, Wymark also played The Devil in six performances of *The Soldier's Tale* directed for Scottish Opera by Wendy Toye. The production, starring Nicky Henson, Una Stubbs and Gordon Jackson as the Narrator was televised by Scottish Television on Tuesday 4th September. After the Festival, Nicky Henson's next job was as puritan trooper Swallow in Michael Reeve's *Witchfinder General*. Coincidentally, although Patrick Wymark continued with the tour of *The Cherry Orchard*, he was able to use his Sunday off to film his cameo as Oliver Cromwell in the movie.

On 11 December 1967, Wymark starred as Bertie, a tycoon looking back on his life in Rediffusion's adaptation of Tyrone Guthrie's *Top of the Ladder*.

1968 Doppelgangers and Double Agents

On 20 January 1968, Patrick joined folk singer Julie Felix on *Once More with Felix* (BBC2) and during March 1968, he would play Air Vice-Marshal Trafford Leigh-Mallory in *The Battle of Britain* (released September 1969).

On Monday 4 March 1968, Wymark was *"Northern Guest of the Week"* on a special *"Northern"* edition of *Woman's Hour* (BBC Radio Four) which also featured Hallam Tennyson talking about his poet laureate grandfather, and *"Fisherman's Wife, Josephine Gibney of Cleethorpes."*

In March 1968, Wymark appeared in four *ATV Playhouse* productions: Strindberg's *The Father*, was followed on 12 March 1968 by John Mortimer's *The Judge*. On the same night Patrick and Olwen Wymark were guests of Prime Minister Harold Wilson at a Downing Street reception for Pierre Werner, the Prime Minister of Luxembourg. On 18 March, Wymark starred with Harold Lang and Valerie French in Martin Walser's *The Detour*, and on 25 March 1968, he played a crusading MP in *Public and Confidential* by Benn W Levy.

On 12 May 1968, Wymark played a hot-headed miner in *Howerd's Hour* . Written by Eric Sykes, ABC's Frankie Howerd comedy special was set in a Klondyke hotel run by Hattie Jacques.

In June 1968, Wymark spent two weeks in Colwyn Bay directing the Prince of Wales Theatre company in Blithe Spirit as a favour to manager Rex Browne.

During the spring, Wymark had filmed his role as Richard Burton and Clint Eastwood's commanding officer in *Where Eagles Dare* (released January 1969). During the summer, he played Jason Webb, a futuristic John Wilder, in *Doppelganger* (released October 1969). Producer Gerry Anderson was a big fan of *The Plane Makers* and remarked that Wymark, *"was a gentle, friendly man and a bloody good actor. But he was a terrible drinker."*

1969 Power Games and Princes

In August 1968, rehearsals began for the third series of *The Power Game*. Each episode had a two-week rehearsal schedule, but by now fellow cast members were beginning to notice that Wymark's concentration was impeded after lunch.

On 7 January 1969, the third series of *The Power Game* began, ending 1st April 1969 . On 7 May 1969, Thames TV screened *Frankie Howerd at the Poco a Poco*. Filmed at a club and casino, formerly the Empress Cinema, Stockport, Patrick Wymark and guitarist Hank Marvin were guests on the stage show.

From 1 May 1969 Patrick Wymark played Claudius in Tony Richardson's New York production of *Hamlet* starring Nicol Williamson with Francesca Annis as Ophelia.

Clive Barnes writing in the New York Times, said there was *"a paunchy dignity about Patrick Wymark's Claudius, and it was not his fault that the director was reluctant to make him a villain."*

Cromwell began filming in May 1969, with Michael Jayston, fresh from his success in the third series of *The Power Game* playing Cromwell's son-in-law Henry Ireton. Patrick Wymark plays Thomas Wentworth, Earl of Strafford (referred to as "Strafford" in the movie). Heavily made-up in a white-wig and beard, Wymark staggers around the court on sticks (Strafford suffered from gout), barking in a strong Yorkshire accent like some crippled pit bull. The film was released July 1970.

A health crisis

In October 1969, Patrick Wymark was due to appear in *Harvey* at the Devonshire Theatre, Eastbourne as a favour to producer Charles Vance. Just before opening night, he collapsed with a severe nosebleed and Charles Vance took the lead with a copy of the script in hand. The painful nosebleeds continued and two weeks later, Wymark had a four-hour operation. Olwen Wymark said, *"The surgeon told me at that time that these alarming nose-bleeds happened to many people without warning. Usually, they were people with high blood pressure. However, Patrick's blood pressure was normal."*

News reports emphasised his recovery in early November with concerns that his illness might hold up shooting on the Swedish-Russian film *Mannen Fran Andra Siden (The Man From The Other Side)*. Wymark was able to fulfil his role as industrialist Christian Holm on the movie which had begun filming in September 1969 and continued until February 1970. Unfortunately, the editing was contentious and *Mannen Fran Andra Siden* finally received its Swedish premiere in 1972.

1970 Nuns and Judges

In early 1970, Patrick Wymark made two appearances at the Gardner Centre for the Arts in Brighton. In February 1970, he played Torvald opposite Fenella Fielding as Nora in *A Doll's House*. In March 1970, Wymark starred in *The Nuns* by Eduardo Manet. He played the leader of a gang of con men posing as Nuns, who offer to help a wealthy aristocrat escape from a mob sacking the town.

In *Blood on Satan's Claw* Patrick Wymark plays a 17th Century judge confronting supernatural evil. Filmed as *The Devil's Touch*, and initially released as *Satan's Skin*, the film gives Wymark what would normally be a heroic role, but his performance is characteristically ambiguous and unpredictable. *"I enjoy costume drama,"* Wymark told journalist Neville Nisse in June 1970, *"and Cromwell and The Devil's Touch give me the chance to appease that urge"*. Sadly, Wymark would never see the final UK release in July 1971.

On 13 June 1970, Patrick Wymark made his last appearance on British TV in Jean Benedetti's *Lily*. The BBC 2 play dealt with the politically motivated trial of W.T. Stead (Iain Cuthbertson) who had exposed child prostitution in Victorian Britain. Wymark played Richard Webster, the hectoring and bullying Attorney-General who led the prosecution.

Sleuth in Australia

In July 1970, Patrick Wymark travelled to Australia to star in Anthony Schaffer's *Sleuth*. The London production starring Anthony Quayle and Keith Baxter had been an smash hit, transferring to Broadway in November 1970.

Eager to cash in on the 'slick, creepy thriller', the Harry M. Miller Company negotiated the Australian rights to *Sleuth*. Both *The Plane Makers* and *The Power Game* had been massive hits on Australian TV, so Patrick Wymark was cast as crime writer Andrew Wyke while John Fraser (who had also starred in *Repulsion*) played his wife's lover Milo Tindle. The production was directed by Harold Lang, a character actor and renowned acting teacher who had played Fraser's father in Bernard Kops *The Hamlet Of Stepney Green*. He was a personal friend of Wymark with whom he'd acted in *Danton's Death* and Lang had directed *The Technicians*, one of Olwen Wymark's first plays, in June 1969.

In his 2004 book *Close Up* Fraser states that Wymark's drinking made it difficult to rehearse (*'by noon he was slurring his words and forgetting his lines.'*) but after Wymark mishandled a live gun, Fraser threatened to call in the understudy if he thought he was drunk again. Whether because of Fraser's ultimatum, or through shock at the thought of nearly killing his co-star, Wymark would visit Fraser every evening, *"ostensibly a social visit, but in truth to let me see that he was sober."*

His Last Bow

Starting on 29 July 1970, the first run at the Theatre Royal, Sydney, was a great success. On Friday 16 October, Patrick Wymark made a final public appearance in Sydney at the *Miss Australia Quest* presentation ball. On Sunday 18th October, Wymark moved into a room on the 8th floor of the Sheraton Hotel in Melbourne, where the play was due to open at the Comedy Theatre. Wymark and Fraser began rehearsing for the opening on Thursday 22nd October.

Wymark and Fraser were scheduled to appear on Stuart Wagstaff's *In Melbourne Tonight* on Tuesday 20th October to publicise a *Hans Christian Anderson* TV special they had taped, and also promote their Melbourne opening.

Patty Mostyn, publicity director for the Harry M. Miller organisation, dropped Patrick Wymark off from rehearsals at 6pm. Wymark said he intended to relax before the TV appearance, but when the time came to drive to the studio he failed to respond to calls. As Wagstaff joked with American actor Richard Deacon *(The Dick Van Dyke Show)* about Wymark's tardiness, a pass key was used to enter Wymark's hotel room at 8.45. He was found dead of what later proved to be a heart attack aged 44. A shocked Stuart Wagstaff, announced the news at the end of his TV show.

Sadly, Harold Lang also succumbed to a heart attack while returning home, and died in a Cairo hospital on Monday 16 November 1970.

On 29 November 1970 *the Hans Christian Andersen* musical special was broadcast posthumously on the Nine Network.

Patrick Wymark was flown home and buried at Highgate Cemetery on 3rd November 1970 after a Requiem Mass at St Dominic's, Highgate. Two days later, on 5th November, a memorial service was held at Brompton Oratory.

On 21 October 1970, Barbara Murray told journalist Kenneth Eastaugh; *"He was larger than life and it seems ridiculous that he is dead. He was so alive, at times a bit of a knockabout clown, at others a great sentimentalist. But always an entertaining man."* She added that, *"He personified everything that one thinks of in actors. He adored playing Wilder. He would light up like Guy Fawkes night when it came to playing a rowdy bit."*

Left to support her family, Olwen Wymark developed her career as a writer, with the quirky play *Speak Now* (1971) in which married couples swap gender, and several episodes of Granada TV's *Crown Court*. For many years she was chair of the Theatre Committee of the Writers Guild of Great Britain, and following her death in 2013, is commemorated by the Guild's Olwen Wymark Theatrical Encouragement Awards.

Their daughter Jane appeared as Joyce Barnaby in *Midsomer Murders* and played Prime Minister Theresa May in David Hare's play *Ayn Rand Takes a Stand*. Tristram played doomed director Burke Dennings in the stage version of *The Exorcist* and General Thursday in the *Pennyworth* TV series. Rowan is now a happily retired teacher in New Mexico while Dominic is a production designer in Hollywood.

Appendix 2   Barbara Murray – Delicious Mischievousness

"An enticing presence, all misty eyes and pale beauty...her beauty seemed to strengthen in middle age, as did the regality that placed her firmly as a woman of a certain era, but there was a delicious mischievousness in her grand voice which ensured there was always more to the characters she played than just elegance and sophistication." *Simon Farquhar - May 2014 - The Independent*

Born in London on 27 September 1929, to variety artistes Freddie and Petronella, Barbara Murray was 17 when she won a 5-year contract with the Rank Organisation's *Company of Youth*, better known as the Rank Charm School. After small developmental roles in three or four films director Robert Hamer put Barbara forward for the role of Stanley Holloway's daughter in *Passport to Pimlico* (1949).

As well as a steady series of supporting roles in Rank movies such as *Boys in Brown* (1950) and *The Dark Man* (1951), she was also given stage experience with Newcastle Repertory Company and lent out, in March 1950, to the BBC Radio Home Service. She performed with Basil Radford and Naunton Wayne as the copyright-teasing Fanshawe and Fothergill in the six-part comedy thriller *That's My Baby*. On 25 December 1950, Barbara was again lent out for a live BBC television production of *A Christmas Carol*, starring 80-year-old actor-manager Bransby Williams as Scrooge.

In 1951, Barbara appeared in Rank's *Another Man's Poison*, starring Bette Davis and her husband Gary Merrill. She also played Woman Police Constable Lucy Loggart in *Street Corner* (1953). This ahead-of-its-time ensemble piece, written and directed by Muriel Box, dealt with women police constables, when they were still supposed to look after missing children and shoplifters.

In 1952, Barbara married actor John Justin, who she had met while working on the film *Hot Ice*. She turned down a renewed contract with Rank, in order to have more time with her husband. However, she had no intention of giving up her work to be a housewife and in 1954, shortly before the birth of her first daughter she starred as Joanna Winter in *No Other Verdict* at the Duchess Theatre.

On Sunday 2 October 1955, Barbara Murray played the Dark Lady in a BBC *Sunday Night Theatre* production of George Bernard Shaw's 1910 play *The Dark Lady of the Sonnets*. Written as part of the campaign to establish a "Shakespeare National Theatre", it shows Shakespeare (Alan MacNaughtan) lurking in Whitehall Palace for a late-night assignation with the Dark Lady. Through a misunderstanding, Shakespeare encounters Queen Elizabeth (Beatrix Lehmann) and he asks her to create a

national theatre, where he can write the plays he wants to write, rather than the plays the public want to see. The play was followed at 9pm by part two of a transmission from the Shakespeare Memorial Theatre of *The Merry Wives of Windsor*, **in which Patrick Wymark made his TV debut as the Host of the Garter Inn**

Barbara Murray returned to BBC TV on 21 October 1956, in *A Death in the Family*, written by Philip Mackie. Barbara played Stella, the ex-wife of film star Richard Eynesham, played by Stanley Baker. Barbara would act again with Baker in *Campbell's Kingdom*. The oil-prospecting drama starring Dirk Bogarde was financed by Rank on condition that producer Ralph Thomas first made the crowd-pleasing comedy *Doctor at Large* (starring Bogarde and Barbara)

From 3 December 1957 to 14 February 1959 Barbara starred with Ian Carmichael as a young couple hoping to adopt a baby in the West End comedy *The Tunnel of Love*.

On 1 June 1959 Barbara Murray found a change of pace as a film noir-ish femme fatale in the BBC serial *The Wife of Bath*, adapted by Margot Bennett from her 1952 novel. Set in a small seaside town it also starred John Justin as Hugh Everton, a damaged man in a menial job who now saw a chance to gain revenge on those who had wrecked his life and career. Barbara Murray played Lucy Bath, *"who glitters like a diamond and is almost as hard."*.

In November 1961, Barbara had an even greater change of pace when she accepted the lead in Thomas Clarke's five-part BBC TV serial *The Escape of R.D.7*. Produced and directed by James Omerod, the serial preceded *Doomwatch* by some years, dealing with the spread of a virus Barbara's character had developed to wipe out rats. Barbara also completed a role for ABC on 3 December 1961, in an *Armchair Theatre* adaptation of Robert Sheckley's 'The Seventh Victim'. Titled *Murder Club* the story is set in a future where consenting adults agree to take part in man-or-woman-hunts.

In 1962 Barbara Murray played Stella in Harold Pinter's *The Collection*, directed by Peter Hall for the Royal Shakespeare Company. John Ronane, the only holdover from Pinter's 1961 Rediffusion TV version, plays a young dress designer at the centre of intrigue between Stella, her jealous husband (Kenneth Haigh) and Ronane's flatmate played by Michael Hordern. The play ends with Stella silently refusing to confirm or deny her husband's accusations, giving him a look of friendly ambiguity Following the success of *The Collection*, Barbara travelled to Broadway for the premiere of Leslie Weiner's comedy *In the Counting House*, directed by Arthur Penn. Starring Sydney Chaplin, Howard Da Silva and Kay Medford, the play ran for only four performances, closing on December 15 1962. Barbara played an English secretary at a lingerie firm who Chaplin falls in love with. Since his Father-In-Law has a big stake in the firm, Chaplin's character knows leaving his wife would cause disaster. Though one reviewer found Barbara's performance intelligent and sympathetic, the play itself was dead in the water.

On 19 February 1963, Barbara appeared in the ITV *Play of the Week*; *The Cruel Deadline* playing reporter Celia Raeburn, who becomes emotionally involved with Ann Bulmer (Georgina Ward), the daughter of an MP caught up in a scandal (Ironically - or not - Georgina Ward was the daughter of a former Government minister). Barbara also appeared opposite Tony Hancock in *The Punch and Judy Man* (April 1963) and in two episodes of *The Saint*.

On March 5th 1963, Barbara opened at the Savoy Theatre in *Trap for A Lonely Man*. Written by French dramatist Robert Thomas, the play starred Michael Bryant as newly-wed Daniel Corbin, whose wife stormed out of their chalet in the French alps after an argument. Local policeman Andre Morell is unconcerned, saying she will come back when she cools down. As if to prove the policeman's words, a young priest Father Maxim (William Holmes) brings Florence Corbin (Barbara Murray) back to the chalet. But Daniel says the woman is not his wife. For Barbara Murray this was a strong part, building on the capacity for ambiguity she had demonstrated in *The Collection,* and *The Wife of Bath. Trap For A*

Lonely Man was later filmed as *One of My Wives Is Missing* starring Jack Klugman as Inspector Levine, James Franciscus as Daniel Corbin, Elizabeth Ashley as Elizabeth Corbin and Joel Fabiani as Father Kelleher.

During the play's run, Barbara was sent the script of *The Plane Makers* **episode** *Too Much To Lose.* She agreed to play John Wilder's wife after script editor Wilfred Greatorex offered to write the character into two more scripts (*A Question of Sources* and *Don't Stick Your Head Out.*) After that it was clear that, as she herself said, *" the chemistry worked".* Greatorex noted that, *"Men adore her...but women aren't jealous. Some of them become equally entranced by the way she plays the part. ".* However, it's notable that Barbara only appears in seven of the 29 episodes of the second series. She was critical of the female characters, saying the scripts were written, *"by men, for men, and the women weren't real. Weren't complete."*

In a 1969 interview, script editor Greatorex agreed that Barbara had a strong input into the way Pamela Wilder was written. *"Barbara suggested that we add a sense of humour and that a woman like Pamela would want to improve her existence instead of sticking in her shell. The result was marvellous. And she played the part with such subtlety, that it has been an eye opener for me about how to write a woman's part."*

In March 1964 Barbara's marriage to John Justin was dissolved. Although the grounds were cited as Justin's infidelity with two women (one named, the other un-named), *"the Judge exercised discretion over (Miss Murray's) admitted adultery."* She promptly married actor Bill Holmes, who gave up acting to become a teacher. Together they set up home in a top floor flat in Queens Gardens, Kensington with Barbara's three daughters. She told reporters that theirs was a marriage of equals. She taught him how to cook so that they could share the meals. *"At first he wasn't interested, but now he enjoys cooking."* When she was exhausted after working on a TV series, he looked after her, but, *"when it is getting towards the end of school term and he is worn out, I look after him."*.

Very much a myth-buster, Barbara met reporters in casual clothes that *"Pamela Wilder would never wear."*. Telling them she was *'pear shaped'*, she said she was not interested in high fashion but was *"designing clothes for herself and other 'pears'. They're slick clothes but...very practical."*. She also said that, *"Even before the £50 travel allowance she spent her holidays on the English Coast instead of the Cote d'Azur."* She also said she hated parties and the London scene. *"All I want from marriage is to be loved, to have fun at home."*

The third series of *The Plane Makers* began in October 1964 with Pamela Wilder played by Ann Firbank. Producer Rex Firkin said in his autobiography that this was because he neglected to book Barbara until she was already committed to the BBC's *The Indian Tales of Rudyard Kipling* (July -Dec 1964), where she played Mrs Hauksbee. Whatever the reason, Firkin made sure that Barbara was signed up for the first and second series of The *Power Game.*

In February 1967, Barbara took over the role of the blind Susy in the stage thriller *Wait Until Dark . The Stage* noted that whereas Honor Blackman had portrayed the blind Susy with a self-assertiveness that left little doubt she would triumph against the manipulative Harry Roat (Peter Sallis), *"Miss Murray, on the other hand, is presenting a softer, warmer characterisation....the battle for self-reliance, even before the invasion of her home, is hardly won."*

In 1968, she appeared in a supporting role in the thriller *A Dandy In Aspic*, and also played Caesonia, wife of Caligula (Ralph Bates) in the 2 November 1968 episode of Philip Mackie's *The Caesars*. After this, a return to the Wilder household was like a walk in the park and the third series of *The Power Game* began transmission in January 1969.

On 20 December 1969, Barbara took over the lead opposite Paul Daneman from Nyree Dawn Porter in London Weekend's comedy *Never a Cross Word* (*"stepping into the role of scatter-brained Deirdre Baldock is Power Game girl Barbara Murray"* as the TV Times put it).

In late 1970, Barbara played Ammonia, in the film version of the Frankie Howerd comedy, *Up Pompeii*. She then took on the role of Victoria from Zena Walker opposite Alfred Marks in the second series of Yorkshire TV's Victorian comedy, *Albert and Victoria* (1971). Sadly, Barbara herself was replaced after two episodes by Frances Bennett after suffering a miscarriage during rehearsals. Barbara told Stewart Knowles that she didn't really want to work while pregnant but, *"I only discovered I was going to have a baby a couple of days before we started Albert and Victoria and I didn't want to let everybody down."*.

Anxious to get back to work, she guest starred in the 11 October 1971 episode of *The Rivals of Sherlock Holmes*. Playing Lady Wiltshire in *the Duchess of Wiltshire's Diamonds*, she was one of the few non-detectives to appear in the title credits. The episode starred Roy Dotrice as the mysterious "Klimo"/aka Simon Carne. She and Dotrice would be reunited in the film *Tales From The Crypt* (released 1972).

At the end of 1971, Barbara Murray made the front cover of the Christmas TV Times for her starring role in Terence Feely's play *Who Killed Santa Claus?* She played TV star Barbara Love. Just before her Christmas party she is threatened by a voice on the then-novel medium of a telephone answering machine and then receives a miniature coffin. As the guests for her party arrive, the question is which one has a reason to kill her. Broadcast on Boxing Day 1971, the Anglia TV play had overtones of Brian Clemens *Thriller* (for which Feely often wrote) and is still a favourite among amateur dramatic societies.

In April 1972, Barbara took over the role of Kay Sherwin from Sue Lloyd in Yorkshire TV's *His and Hers*. As the TV Times put it, *"Barbara Murray, one of the three wives of Alfred Marks in **Albert and Victoria**, is the second wife of Ronald Lewis in the return of this series about a stay-at-home husband and his executive wife/"*

Barbara Murray continued with stage and TV roles starring in the 1974 BBC series *The Pallisers*, and ITV's theatrical saga *The Bretts* (1987-1989). She also made guest appearances in *Robin's Nest* (1979-1980) as Tony Britton's ex-wife, Eric Sykes' 1977 Yorkshire TV adaptation of *Charley's Aunt* as Donna Lucia, and *Doctor Who* in the equally farcical *Black Orchid* (1982

Barbara Murray retired to Spain in 2000.

Quotes come from Peter Genower "Lady Wilder - Queen of Ten Million Hearts" TV Times March 15 1969 and Stephen Vizinczey, "Barbara Murray, Gorgeous, Tender, Tough" and Eileen Anderson *The Journal 14 April 1969 "Lady Wilder, the Charmer Every Woman Would Like To Be."*

Appendix 3   Wilfred Greatorex.

Born in Liverpool in 1922 and educated at Blackburn Grammar School, Greatorex served in the RAF during the war before becoming a journalist. As assistant editor of John Bull, the Odhams news and fiction magazine, Greatorex was used to nurturing writers. His first TV play for the BBC, *After the Crash* (1961), was a dramatised documentary looking at the work of the Ministry of Aviation's Accident Investigation Branch. He followed this in 1962 with *The Net*, a dramatised documentary series about the Immigration Service, which he spent six weeks researching at London Airport. In the same year he contributed episodes of ATV's Probation Officer.

Greatorex's contribution to the *Plane Makers, Front Page Story* and *The Power Game* is documented throughout this book. In 1965, he told Michael Gowers, *"Too many script editors are just script clerks. I see editing in the fullest sense of the word, picking storylines, determining the level of the story telling, working closely with writers on ideas. If a writer has something to say, I am never too busy to see him." (Liverpool Echo 20 February 1965).*

During the break between the second and third series of *The Power Game,* Greatorex contributed episodes to ATV's *Man In A Suitcase* (1967) and also adapted John Cleary's novel *The High Commissioner* as *Nobody Runs Forever* (1968) in which Australian detective Rod Taylor is sent to London to arrest diplomat Christopher Plummer. In June 1969, Greatorex also worked with producer Gerry Anderson (a big fan of The *Power Game*) on an abortive science fiction thriller called *Youth Is Wasted on The Young.* *

In 1958, Greatorex had written a textbook on the Arnhem invasion with Major-General R.E. Urquhart, and in 1968 he was hired to bring his drama-documentary touch to the screenplay *of The Battle of Britain* (1969).

Following the final series *of The Power Game*, Greatorex created three series in succession. *Hine* (1971) starred Barry Ingham as a freelance arms dealer, tweaking the nose of the establishment. *The Man From Haven* (1972) starred Ian Holm as a blackmailer, tormenting the owners of Swiss bank accounts. *The Inheritors* (1974), for Harlech Television, starred Robert Urquhart as a Welsh landowner being pursued for death duties by tax official Richard Hurndall. Despite a poor reception from critics, the six-part serial still attracted over 12 million viewers.

In 1975, Greatorex moved to the BBC, contributing episodes to *Oil Strike North* and serving as script consultant for the same producer, Gerard Glaister on the first series of *Secret Army* (1975)

In 1977 Greatorex was allegedly inspired by a VAT inspection to create the dystopian Edward Woodward thriller *1990*. Produced by Prudence Fitzgerald, **1990** ran for two seasons before the Public Control Department of Robert Lang was finally overthrown. Greatorex returned to ITV in 1982 with a personal project called *Airline*. The series starred Roy Marsden as a recently demobbed RAF pilot who starts his own air freight business with a RAF-surplus Dakota. Originally planned to run for at least three series, the series was cancelled after Greatorex fell out with Yorkshire TV during pre-production of the second series. From then on, Greatorex concentrated on writing novels.

For more on Youth is Wasted on the Young, see Beyond the Borders of Fear (Scatola publishing 2021) by Harry Dobermann – shameless plug.

Appendix 4   Edmund Ward

Only six months after the production of his first TV play (*Recruiting Poster*, August 1962), Edmund Ward was chosen to write *Don't Worry About Me*, the opening episode of the first series of *The Plane Makers*. Even though producer Rex Firkin was not happy with the progress of the first series, he still chose Ward to write the first episode of the revamped *Plane Makers* – the one that introduced John Wilder. It was Ward who wrote the opening and closing episodes of the last series of *The Plane Makers* and the first two series of *The Power Game*. It was probably only because Ward had joined Yorkshire TV to launch his own series *The Main Chance*, that Ward did not write for the third series.

Born in Nottingham in 1928, Edmund Ward was educated at the Henry Mellish Grammar School and London School of Printing, but was forced by his father to train as a book keeper at Boots, the Chemists head office before departing for Sweden in 1950. Ward earned his money in the construction industry, and later became a construction trade journalist, a background he would later exploit in *The Hanged Man* (1976). His first novel, in 1957, was *Summer in Retreat* followed by *The Gravy Train* in 1958.

After Patrick Wymark expressed the need for a breather from the character of John Wilder, Ward contributed to Greatorex and Firkin's newspaper series *Front Page Story* (1965). Reviewing The Quiet Load in The Stage, Marjorie Norris wrote that, *"I don't believe all newspapermen have the verbal felicity he gave to this lot, but it is the mark of an Edmund Ward script that the throwaway lines are the ones that hit you hardest."*

In 1967, Ward wrote four episodes of the ATV series *Man In A Suitcase* and also adapted Nicolas Freeling's *Van Der Valk* novel *Death in Amsterdam* as *Amsterdam Affair* (1968).

In 1968, Ward joined one of the new ITV contractors, Yorkshire TV, where he teamed up with John Batt to launch the legal series *The Main Chance*. Barrister Malcolm John Batt, used the pen name of John Malcolm. As a student, Batt had composed *Non-Stop* which was used as the theme music for ITN Evening News from 1955 until the 1980's. Unsurprisingly, Batt also composed the insistent theme tune for The Main Chance. In his professional life, Batt was part of the defence team which overturned the conviction of Sally Clark for the murder of her baby sons in 2001.

Premiering on 18 June 1969, *The Main Chance* starred John Stride as brilliant young lawyer David Main. Having established a successful practice in London, he returns to his native Leeds to buy into the staid and respectable practice of Henry Castleton (John Wentworth) and his daughter Margaret (Margaret Ashcroft). Henry describes him as, *"Shrewd and energetic. But his manners leave a lot to be desired."*

Writing in the TV Times in December 1970, Anthony Davis wrote that the second series, *"established Main as a character to rival the late Patrick Wymark as John Wilder. Like Wilder, Main was seen as ruthless, clever and domineering. And it is worth noting that some of his best scenes were written by Edmund Ward, who also wrote many of Wilder's best."*

Ward also drew on his own past in the construction industry press with the episode, *The Professional* (2 July 1969). This introduced Charles Ian Grady (Anthony Bate), *" a professional 'wrecker' , an agitator, a man with his own motives, probably political, for fomenting industrial strife."* Ward was obviously fascinated by the ambiguous character, played with persuasive eloquence by Anthony Bate, and would write three-part series called *Grady* in 1970.

During this period, Ward also scripted the horror movie *Goodbye Gemini* (1970), starring Judy Geeson.

In 1972, Ward launched a six-part series, *The Challengers*, starring Colin Blakely and Michael Gambon as opposing Members of Parliament in an industrial town with two constituencies.

In 1975, Ward created *The Hanged Man* starring Colin Blakely as construction boss Lew Burnett who survives three attempts to kill him and *decides "The only way I can stay alive is to stay dead. Find out who wants to kill me. And why!"* Two supporting characters from this series were spun-off by Ward into *Turtle's Progress* (1979-1980).

After leaving Yorkshire TV, Edmund Ward contributed to series such as *1990, The Professionals* and *Bergerac*. Ward also scripted *A Prayer For The Dying* (1987), albeit the version before star Mickey Rourke and director Mike Hodges disowned the studio recut.

Appendix 5 Raymond Bowers

According to his Wikipedia entry, Raymond Bowers was an Australian, writing for the amateur theatre while working as a journalist in Perth. In 1954, aged 34, he journeyed to London and in 1955 sold *In Writing* to the BBC. Broadcast in the Sunday Night Theatre slot on 1 January 1956, it starred Bernard Lee and Terence Morgan. Bowers followed up with a six-part serial called *Opportunity Murder* in April 1956. His stage play, *It's The Geography That Counts*, was the last production at the St James's Theatre in London before its demolition. The play marked John Gregson's first stage performance for six years. Adapted for Australian radio as The Man in Question (1958), Bowers subsequently sold it to the BBC as *Listen James* (23 July 1961) starring John Carson.

Bowers also served as script supervisor to *ATV's The Adventures of Robin Hood,* and wrote episodes of *Deadline Midnight* and *Harpers West One.*

Bowers, who lived with his son Michael and daughter Roberta in Earls Court, was brought in to *The Plane Makers* to write *The Thing About Auntie*, the episode which introduced William Devlin as Sir Gerald Merle MP. The episode contained many of the verbal flourishes which made Bowers' scripts popular with actors, and he returned with the episodes *Loved He Not Honours More* and *A Matter of Priorities*. Bowers told a journalist in 1966 that, *"What is sayable by modern actors is something the writer himself must feel."*

Bowers became a significant contributor to the third series of *The Plane Makers* and its successor *The Power Game*. At the same time, Bowers contributed to a wide range of spy series such as *Danger Man, The Rat Catchers* and *Man In A Suitcase.* In later years, he contributed to *Hadleigh, Upstairs, Downstairs* (*The Swedish Tiger*), and *Crossroads*.

Appendix 6   Peter Draper

Writer of many of the most entertaining *Power Game* scripts, Peter Draper was born in Porthcawl, Wales on 28 April 1929. Joining the Bristol Old Vic company as an actor and stage manager, he determined to become a writer. After working in an advertising agency, he joined two partners in 1950 to start the Milton Head Pottery Company in Brixham, Devon.

Draper was 31 when he sold a play about Dame Edith Cavell to H.M. Tennent's, the Agency which was producing all non-series drama for Associated Television. Starring Dame Flora Robson and Donald Pleasance, *And Humanity* was broadcast on 5th March 1958.

Tennent's contracted more ATV drama from Draper including *The Paraguayan Harp* (13 Feb 1959 and *Sunday Out Of Season* (13 March 1959) in which Maggie Smith plays a student trying to forget a love affair who meets intelligent young local Alec McCowen in a damp, windy, Welsh seaside town. (ATV would transmit a remake on 7 February 1965, starring Ian McKellen as Victor and Lynn Redgrave as Elaine.)

On 6 May 1960 *The Big Night* starred Robert Stephens as Frank Rush, a married man who wonders if romance is passing him by. He talks his friend Tom Pugsley (Barry Foster) into a night around the pubs where he meets actress Madeleine Grail (Judith Stott). Invited back to her flat, Frank discovers that her character and background is different to what he expected. Stephens praised Draper as having the knack for, *"expressing odd, contradictory thoughts, and the foolish behaviour of men of all ages."*

In 1961, Eyre and Spottiswood published Peter Draper's novel *A Season In Love* . Set in the late 1950's, it is narrated by Sam Wilson who returns to London after working in South African but is immediately disillusioned. His local pub has been demolished and his friend Bruno has gone off to Paris. Sam also discovers that Bruno has left his long-time lover Sophy for a French student living in London. When Sam meets Claudine, he detects a hint that she may be "available" and determines to seduce her so that he can restore Bruno's relationship with Sophy. But instead, he finds himself falling in love with her.

The novel explores many of the themes that would recur in Draper's teleplays. At one point Wilson visits the former site of the Festival of Britain which had *"begun to take on the appearance of something in decay. The plaster-work of some of the gaudy set pieces left over from the Festival was beginning to show some cracks,"* But nonetheless an elderly couple remark that they wish they could have come to the Festival and walk *"almost reverently as though they were passing through the courtyard of a Venetian palace."* Draper evokes a run-down, war-battered London, where men of a certain class live in *"cheap Bayswater hotels".*

In 1963, Draper contributed his first script to *The Plane Makers* with *A Good Night's Work* (27 May 1963) starring Alec McCowen as John Rodway. Draper would write two more scripts for the second series of *The Plane Makers –Any More For The Skylark* (28 October 1963), and *Don't Stick Your Head Out* (14 October 1963) the episode which introduced Ingrid Hafner as the mistress of John Wilder and first explored the moral tightrope of Wilder's marriage.

Draper would address those issues further in *The Funambulists* (21 October 1963) directed by John Moxey. *The Play of the Week* starred Francis Matthews as Michael, who has had several affairs but suspects his wife Susannah (Judi Dench) is being unfaithful. He hires detective James Stack (Peter Barkworth) to follow her, but is surprised when Stack goes further than expected. Draper told the *TV Times* that *"Stack is one of those innocent people who get hurt by the deceptions of clever people."* He likened them to tightrope walkers or *"funambulists"* who *"play around with moral attitudes"* but may fall off the rope.

During the same period, Draper wrote *The System* for Michael Winner. Released in October 1964 (and retitled *The Girl Getters* in America) it starred Oliver Reed as beach photographer Tinker, the leader of a gang in a West Country seaside resort who compete to "make" the young female tourists. *"For three months the place is thick with them. (In winter) after six o'clock there's nothing moving in the streets at all. Everyone's home watching telly. And the girls are the same girls you knew last year...so we make it while we can...the best girls, a different one every week if you want. "* Much like the lead character from *A Season in Love*, Reed finds his heart being broken by strong-willed model Jane Merrow.

Filmed at Brixham, Paignton and Torquay, the film (and Draper's) lasting legacy appears to be the West Country term "grockles" used to describe tourists. Opinions are divided as to whether Draper invented the name, or simply picked up a very localised slang, but the term has persisted to this day.

In 1965, Draper contributed two episodes of *Front Page Story*, Wilfred Greatorex and Rex Firkin's follow-up to *The Plane Makers*, which took the same approach to *The Globe* (the fictional counterpart of the *Daily Herald/Sun* which Sir Gerald Merle had been a director of in *The Plane Makers*). One of Draper's episodes, *"The X-Men"*, featured Rupert Davis as Felix Rakstro, an acquaintance of reporter Denny Tarrant (Derek Godfrey) being investigated by the fraud squad.

In late 1965, Peter Draper contributed seven episodes to *The Power Game*, many of them exposing the tangled love lives of Wilder, his wife Pamela Wilder (Barbara Murray) and their lovers. Not surprisingly, Penguin Books found this an opportune moment to release a paperback of *A Season In Love*.

Peter Draper continued to write TV plays such as the *Half Hour Story* on 13 September 1967. Titled *"Bug"* it starred Bob Monkhouse as radio ham Q.P.Jakes who suspects his wife of being unfaithful and attempts to hire detective R.J. Smellie (Bill Owen). But the detective takes offence at the electronic recording devices which Jakes has been using to track his wife.

Draper also re-united with Oliver Reed and Michael Winner for *I'll Never Forget What's 'Is Name* (1967). Reed plays Andrew Quint, an executive who takes an axe to his desk at Orson Welles' advertising agency, intending to give up the rat race and work on a small literary magazine run by old university friend Norman Rodway.

Filmed in "Swinging London" the film shares some quirks with *Blow Up* and *If*; Frank Finlay appears in a surreal flashback as a Headmaster telling young Andrew that, *"Games are the essence of life and the value of team games is that they teach us to live together…the man who is not interested in sport is not interested in living with other people."*

In a twist worthy of *The Prisoner*, Quint eventually discovers that the literary magazine and the entire building has been bought up by Welles who is installed in a luxury apartment on the top floor.

In 1969 Draper contributed three more scripts to the third and final series of *The Power Game*. In *The Goose Chase*, Draper creates the memorable character of Professor Mobbs who is attempting to recruit Wilder's assistant Lincoln Dowling (Michael Jayston) to MI6.

Peter Draper contributed to Wilfred Greatorex's 1971 series about arms dealer Hine and in 1972 made his way over to the BBC writing the now wiped, *Death Cancels All Debts* for the BBC 2 horror *series Dead of Night*. A Great British Writer (Sebastian Shaw) now sunk in alcoholism and encroaching dementia is haunted by a presence which manifests itself as snatches of *"Fur Elise"* played on a piano. The play, which could well reward a 21st Century remake , asks if the presence hold the key to a literary mystery? How much does a ghost owe to our memories? What might happen if the memories are confused.

In the same year Peter Draper contributed a play called *A Persistent Coffin* to the BBC 1 anthology series *The Man Outside.* This was spun off into a six-part BBC2 comedy series *The Perils of Pendragon* broadcast in 1974. Set in the Welsh village of Pendragon, it starred Kenneth Griffith as Isaac, a shop-keeper deeply suspicious of the sins of the flesh. John Clive played his mercenary Welsh nationalist nephew Rosko.

The familiar dark humour *("One day my boy, you are going to find yourself particularly famous around these parts as the victim of a particularly nasty unsolved murder, ")* may have gone too far when references to contemporary politics made one of the six episodes too sensitive to broadcast near the 1974 general election. Screened opposite ITV's more popular *Kung Fu* and *Billy Liar* the series remains little known with all tapes subsequently wiped by the BBC.

Undeterred, Peter Draper was invited to write scripts for series such as the original *Poldark* (1975). Peter Draper's final TV script was The Damask Collection an episode of *Jemima Shore Investigates* (1983) starring Patricia Hodge. He died in Exeter in 2004.

Bibliography

ABRAHAM, NEVILLE. Big Business and Government: The New Disorder (1974). Macmillan.

ADAMS, CHARLES.F. Common Sense in Advertising (1965) McGraw-Hill

ALDRED, JONATHAN. License to be Bad (2019) Allen Lane

BRAY,CHRISTOPHER. 1965:The Year Modern Britain Was Born (2014) Simon & Schuster

BROWN, ARCHIE. The Myth of the Strong Leader (2014) Vintage

BURKE, JOHN. The Power Game (1966) Pan

CRAIG, DAVID. Rip-Off! (2005) The Original Book Company

DAVIES, DAN. Lying For Money (2018) Profile Books

DAVIES,AERON. Reckless Opportunists (2018) Manchester University Press

DAVIS, CLIFFORD. How I made Lew Grade a Millionaire (1981) Mirror Books Ltd.

DAVIS,DAN.Lying For Money (2018) Profile Books

DENCH, JUDI. Scenes From My Life (2005) Orion

DRAPER,PETER. A Season in Love (1966) Penguin

DRUCKER, PETER. The Practice of Management (1968) Pan

DUTTON, K & MCNAB,A. The Good Psychopath's Guide to Success (2014) Penguin

EARLE,J.MORAN,C.WARD-PERKINS,Z.The Econocracy (2017) Penguin

ELLIOT, JOHN.Mogul, the Making of a Myth (1970) Barrie and Jenkins

FIRKIN, REX, MARSON, RICHARD (Ed.) High Drama (2012) Kaleidoscope Publishing

GADDIS, JOHN LEWIS. The Cold War (2007) Penguin

GRAEBER, DAVID. Bullshit Jobs (2018) Penguin.

HALLINAN, JOSEPH T. Errornomics (2009) Ebury Press

HAMILTON, JOHN. Beasts In The Cellar (2005) FAB Press.

HAMILTON-PATERSON, JAMES. Empire of the Clouds (2010) Faber and Faber

HANDY, CHARLES. Understanding Organizations (1985) Penguin

HENNESSY, PETER. Winds of Change (2019) Allen Lane

HODGE, MARGARET.Called To Account (2016) Little,Brown

HOFSTEDE,G & HOFSTEDE G.J. Cultures and Organizations (2005) McGraw-Hill

HUNT,HUGH. Old Vic Prefaces (1954) Routledge & Kegan Paul

KAY, JOHN. Obliquity (2010) Profile Books

KEEGAN, WILLIAM. Nine Crises (2019) Biteback Publishing

LITTNER, CLAUDE. Single-Minded (2016) Piatkus.

MACHIAVELLI (TRANSLATED. GEORGE BULL). The Prince (1975) Penguin

MASON, KEITH. Front Seat (1981) Mason

MAURER, DAVID.W. The Big Con (1940,2000) Arrow Books.

MCCORMACK, MARK.H. What They Don't Teach You At Harvard Business School (1986) Fontana

OWEN,JO. How To Lead (2015) Pearson

PETTIFOR, ANN. The Production of Money (2017). Verso

POUNDSTONE, WILLIAM. How To Predict The Unpredictable (2015) Oneworld.

POWELL, JONATHAN. The New Machiavelli (2010) The Bodley Head.

RICHARDS, STEVE. The Prime Ministers (2020) Atlantic Books

RIES, AL and TROUT, JACK. The 22 Immutable Laws of Marketing (1993). Harper Collins.

SIK, GEORGE. I Think I'll Manage (1997) Headline

SIMS, F.A. The Motorway Achievement (2009) Phillimore and Co.

SITWELL, WILLIAM. Eggs and Anarchy (2016) Simon and Schuster

SNOW, C.P. Science and Government (1960, 2013) Harvard University Press

VOSS, C & RAZ, T. Never Split The Difference (2016) Penguin

WYMARK, OLWEN. The Gymnasium and other plays (1971) Calder Boyars

ZIMBARDO, PHILIP. The Lucifer Effect (2007) Random House

Acknowledgements.

Once again, I acknowledge the memoirs of Rex Firkin, edited by Richard Marson, which give insight into the beginnings of The Plane Makers and The Power Game.

Thanks to Peter Mead of Scatola Books for agreeing to go forward with the project.

Many thanks to Victoria Bennett of the BFI Library Special Collections for arranging access to material from the Wilfred Greatorex Collection.

Personal thanks to Steve Hardy for putting me in touch with director Ron Francis for his memories of Patrick Wymark, online thanks to David Brunt for a Thing About Auntie and third person thanks to Billy Smart for uncovering the BBC2 Power Game sketch. Thanks also to Marcus Heslop and Philly for The Devil's Bait. Martin Marshall, Ian Fryer, Richard Bignell and Stephen La Riviere also uncovered 'wonderful things."

More thanks to Alwyn Rogers and Kylie Walker for proof-reading the text and making many intelligent suggestions. Sadly, any remaining errors are due to my persistent last-minute tinkering.

Thanks again to George Sik for reviewing the Wilder's World section. Again, any remaining errors are my own.

Thanks and admiration to Andrew-Mark Thompson for the cover design and Richard Farrell for the powertoons.

Last but not least, unending thanks to my wife Teresa for sustaining me and putting up with my mental absences.